Tried and teste

What people across the UK are s
Law Express Question&Ansv

'Covers all the main areas in a clear and concise way, and provides some excellent advice on how to tackle exam problems and write essays.'
Gwilym Owen, Lecturer in Law, Bangor University

'Students should in this book find a useful and valuable revision guide. The Q&A format is an appropriate and effective means of enhancing students' preparation for law assessments and for improving academic performance. . .'
Dr George K. Ndi, PGR Leader, University of Huddersfield Law School

'A useful, practical and informative revision guide, which makes good use of various pedagogical features to enhance accessibility to students.'
Adam Pendlebury, Senior Lecturer in Law, Edge Hill University

'This series covers well the important techniques for identifying legal issues and applying case-law to factual scenarios.'
David Selfe, Director, School of Law, Liverpool John Moores University

'Revising with this series is like having a tutor there. . .'
Mariette Jones, Senior Lecturer in Law, Middlesex University

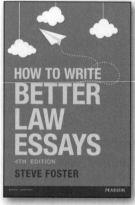
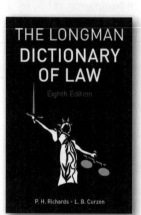
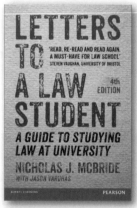

Question&Answer

CONSTITUTIONAL AND ADMINISTRATIVE LAW

4th edition

Vicky Thirlaway
Senior Lecturer in Criminal and Public Law,
Sheffield Hallam University

Pearson

Harlow, England • London • New York • Boston • San Francisco • Toronto • Sydney
Dubai • Singapore • Hong Kong • Tokyo • Seoul • Taipei • New Delhi
Cape Town • São Paulo • Mexico City • Madrid • Amsterdam • Munich • Paris • Milan

Pearson Education Limited
Kao Two
Kao Park
Harlow CM17 9NA
United Kingdom
Tel: +44 (0)1279 623623
Web: **www.pearson.com/uk**

First edition published 2012 (print)
Second edition published 2014 (print)
Third edition published 2016 (print and electronic)
Fourth edition published 2018 (print and electronic)

ISBN: 978-1-292-14898-4 (print)
    978-1-292-14914-1 (PDF)
    978-1-292-14922-6 (ePub)

British Library Cataloguing-in-Publication Data
A catalogue record for the print edition is available from the British Library

Library of Congress Cataloging-in-Publication Data
A catalog record for the print edition is available from the Library of Congress

10 9 8 7 6 5 4 3 2 1
22 21 20 19 18

Print edition typeset in 10/13pt Helvetica Neue LT W1G by SPi Global
Printed by Ashford Colour Press Ltd, Gosport

NOTE THAT ANY PAGE CROSS REFERENCES REFER TO THE PRINT EDITION

Contents

Acknowledgements

I would like to thank my students at Sheffield Hallam University for their encouragement, patience and enthusiasm, and for making me want to go to work in the morning.

Vicky Thirlaway

Publisher's acknowledgements

The publisher would like to thank the following for their kind permission to reproduce the following:

The material in this guide is up-to-date and accurate as the law stood in February 2017, although some minor updating has been possible at later stages in production.

Text Credits

16: The European Convention on Human Rights and Fundamental Freedoms, © European Union, 1995–2017. **17:** Scott v Scott [1913] AC 417, Incorporated Council of Law Reporting. **23:** Delegated Powers and Regulatory Reform Committee 2015. Contains public sector information licensed under the Open Government Licence (OGL) v3.0. http://www.nationalarchives.gov.uk/doc/open-government-licence. **25:** Equal access to justice in the big society, The Sir Henry Hodge Memorial Lecture, p. 3, available at http://www.supremecourt.uk/docs/speech_110627.pdf. Contains public sector information licensed under the Open Government Licence (OGL) v3.0. http://www.nationalarchives.gov.uk/doc/open-government-licence. **33:** Viscount Cranbourne: Hansard text for 22 February 2000: http://www.parliament.the-stationery-office.co.uk/pa/ld199900/ldhansrd/vo000222/text/00222-08.htm. Contains public sector information licensed under the Open Government Licence (OGL) v3.0. http://www.nationalarchives.gov.uk/doc/open-government-licence. **59:** R(Shindler) v Chancellor of the Duchy of Lancaster [2016] 3 WLR 1196 (Lord Dyson MR para 58, Incorporated Council of Law Reporting. **61:** JH Rayner (Mincing Lane) Ltd & Others v Department of Trade and Industry [1990] 2 AC 418, Incorporated Council of Law Reporting.

61: European Communities Act 1972. Section 2 of the Act, © European Union, 1995–2017. **62:** R (Miller) v Secretary of State for Exiting the European Union [2017] 2 WLR 583, Incorporated Council of Law Reporting. **62:** Thoburn v Sunderland City Council [2002] EWHC 195. Contains public sector information licensed under the Open Government Licence (OGL) v3.0. http://www.nationalarchives.gov.uk/doc/open-government-licence. **65:** R v Lambert [2001] UKHL 37. Contains public sector information licensed under the Open Government Licence (OGL) v3.0. http://www.nationalarchives.gov.uk/doc/open-government-licence. **67:** R (Jackson) v Attorney General [2006] 1 AC 262 at para 160, Incorporated Council of Law Reporting. **80:** Bill of Rights 1688. Contains public sector information licensed under the Open Government Licence (OGL) v3.0. http://www.nationalarchives.gov.uk/doc/open-government-licence. **83:** Response to government consultation on the Green Paper, 2012, Cm 8318, Para. 2. Contains public sector information licensed under the Open Government Licence (OGL) v3.0. http://www.nationalarchives.gov.uk/doc/open-government-licence. **86:** 1999 Committee. Contains public sector information licensed under the Open Government Licence (OGL) v3.0. http://www.nationalarchives.gov.uk/doc/open-government-licence. **94:** R v Parliamentary Commissioner for Standards ex parte Al-Fayed [1998] 1 WLR 669, Incorporated Council of Law Reporting. **96:** Foreword to the Draft House of Lords Reform Bill, May 2011, p. 5, available at http://www.official-documents.gov.uk/document/cm80/8077/8077.pdf. Contains public sector information licensed under the Open Government Licence (OGL) v3.0. http://www.nationalarchives.gov.uk/doc/open-government-licence. **129:** Secretary of State for the Home Department v AF (No.3) [2009] UKHL 28. Contains public sector information licensed under the Open Government Licence (OGL) v3.0. http://www.nationalarchives.gov.uk/doc/open-government-licence. **143:** Section 12, The (fictitious) Local Authority (Patient Care) Act 1987. Contains public sector information licensed under the Open Government Licence (OGL) v3.0. http://www.nationalarchives.gov.uk/doc/open-government-licence. **145:** R v Secretary of State for the Home Department ex parte Brind [1991] 1 AC 696, Incorporated Council of Law Reporting. **149:** IRC v National Federation of Self-Employed and Small Businesses Ltd [1982] AC 617, Incorporated Council of Law Reporting. **174:** R v Secretary of State for the Home Department ex parte Amin [2006] UKHL 51. Contains public sector information licensed under the Open Government Licence (OGL) v3.0. http://www.nationalarchives.gov.uk/doc/open-government-licence. **200:** Plunkett [2013] EWCA Crim 261. Contains public sector information licensed under the Open Government Licence (OGL) v3.0. http://www.nationalarchives.gov.uk/doc/open-government-licence. **232:** White Paper (1997) Your Right to Know (Cm. 3818). London: HMSO. Contains public sector information licensed under the Open Government Licence (OGL) v3.0. http://www.nationalarchives.gov.uk/doc/open-government-licence. **237:** R(Evans) v Attorney General [2016] UKSC 21 per Lord Neuberger para 115. Contains public sector information licensed under the Open Government Licence (OGL) v3.0. http://www.nationalarchives.gov.uk/doc/open-government-licence. **239:** M v Home Office [1994] 1 AC 377, Incorporated Council of Law Reporting. **240:** Duport Steels Ltd v Sirs [1980] 1 WLR 142, Incorporated Council of Law Reporting.

Guided tour

How to use features in the book 📖 and on the companion website 🖱

What to do for every question – Identify the key things you should look for and do in any question and answer on the subject, ensuring you give every one of your answers a great chance from the start.

How this topic might come up in exams – Understand how to tackle any question on this topic by using the handy tips and advice relevant to both essay and problem questions. In text, symbols clearly identify each question type as they occur.

Before you begin – Visual guides to help you confidently identify the main points covered in any question asked. You can also download them from the companion website to pin on your wall or add to your revision notes.

Answer plans and Diagram plans – A clear and concise plan is the key to a good answer, and these answer plans and diagram plans support the structuring of your answers.

Answer with accompanying guidance – Make the most out of every question by using the guidance; recognise what makes a good answer and why. The length of the answers reflect what you could realistically achieve in an exam and show you how to gain marks quickly when under pressure.

Make your answer stand out – Impress your examiners with these sources of further thinking and debate.

Don't be tempted to – Spot common pitfalls and avoid losing marks.

Try it yourself – Compare your responses with that of the answer guidance on the companion website.

Visit **www.pearsoned.co.uk/lawexpressqa** for a wealth of
additional resources to support your revision, including:

All diagrams from the book to download and print. Pin
them to your wall or add them to your own revision notes.

Additional Essay and Problem questions with **Diagram
plans** give you more opportunity to help you to practise and
hone your exam skills.

You be the marker Evaluate sample exam answers and
understand how and why an examiner awards marks.

Table of cases and statutes

Cases

TABLE OF CASES AND STATUTES

Cumming v *Chief Constable of the Northumbria Police*
[2003] EWCA Civ 1844

Digital Rights Ireland Ltd v *Minister for
Communications, Marine and Natural Resources*
(C-293/12) EU:C:2014:238; [2015] Q.B. 127
(ECJ (Grand Chamber)), 213
Douglas v *Hello!* (No. 3) [2006] QB 125 221
DPP v *Jordan* [1977] AC 699
DPP v *Whyte* [1972] AC 489
DSD and NVB v *Commissioner of Police for the
Metropolis* [2014] EWHC 436 (QB), 129
Duport Steels Ltd v *Sirs* [1980] 1 WLR 142, 240

Entick v *Carrington* [1765] 19 St Tr 1029; 2 Wils 275
4, 13, 16, 105

Flockhart v *Robinson* [1950] 2 KB 498 184
Fox, Campbell and Hartley v *United Kingdom* [1990]
13 EHRR 157

GCHQ case see Council of Civil Service Unions v
Minister for the Civil Service [1985] AC 374, 4, 5,
54, 139, 157–60
Ghaidan v *Godin-Mendoza* [2004] UKHL 30 66, 115,
116, 134
Gillan and Quinton v *UK* [2009] ECHR 28 67, 120, 191
Guzzardi v *Italy* [1980] 3 EHRR 333 138

Handyside v *UK* [1976] 1 EHRR 737 113, 119, 122, 133
Hannon and Dufour v *NGN Ltd* [2014] EWHC 1580 (Ch),
227
Harris v *Donges (Minister of the Interior)* [1952] 1 TLR
124 70
Hatton v *UK* [2003] 37 EHRR 28 119
Hirst and Agu v *Chief Constable of West Yorkshire*
[1987] 85 Cr App R 143 187
Home Office v *Tariq* [2011] UKSC 35 19
Huntingdon Life Sciences Ltd v *Curtin* [1997] *The
Times,* 11 December 181

IRC v *National Federation of Self-Employed and Small
Businesses* [1982] AC 617 149, 169
IRC v *Rossminster* [1980] AC 952 13

Jackson v *Attorney General* [2005] UKHL 56, [2006] 1
AC 262 70, 71

JH Rayner (Mincing Lane) Ltd & Others v *Department
of Trade and Industry* [1990] 2 AC 418, 39, 61
John Terry (previously referred to as LNS) v *Persons
Unknown* [2010] EWHC 119 (QB) 222
Junor's Case (HC 38 1956–57)

Kay v *Commissioner of Police of the Metropolis* [2008]
UKHL 69 185
Kaye v *Robertson* [1991] FSR 62 223–7
Kenlin v *Gardiner* [1967] 2 WLR 129 203

Lewis v *Chief Constable of the South Wales
Constabulary* [1991] 1 All ER 206 203
Lister v *Forth Dry Dock Engineering* [1990] 1 AC 546
Lord Coe v *Mirror Group Newspapers* [2004] QBD,
unreported 225

M v *Home Office* [1994] 1 AC 377 13, 239
Makudi v *Triesman* [2014] EWCA Civ 179, 81
McCarthys Ltd v *Smith* [1979] ICR, 785
Mellat v *HM Treasury (No 2)* [2013] UKSC 39, [2014]
AC 700, 196
Mengesha v *Commissioner of Police for the Metropolis*
[2013] EWHC 1695 (Admin)
Madzimbamuto v *Lardner-Burke* [1969] AC 645
Malone v *UK* [1984] 7 EHRR 14, 212
Mercury Communications Ltd v *Director General of
Telecommunications* [1996] 1 All ER 575
Mosley v *United Kingdom* [2012] EMLR 1 222, 226
Murray (John) v *UK* [1996] 22 EHRR 29

Novartis Pharmaceuticals UK Ltd v *Stop Huntingdon
Animal Cruelty* [2010] HRLR 8 181, 186

Observer and Guardian v *United Kingdom* [1992] 14
EHRR 153 221
O'Hara v *UK* [2002] 34 EHRR 32
O'Reilly v *Mackman* [1982] 1 WLR 550
Oxford University v *Broughton* [2008] EWHC 75 (QB)
181

Pepper v *Hart* [1993] AC 593, 82
Percy v *DPP* [2001] EWHC 1125 242
Pickstone v *Freemans* [1988] AC 66
PJS v *News Group Newspapers Ltd* [2016] UKSC 26, 221
Police v *Reid* [1987] Crim LR 702 186
Prebble v *Television New Zealand* [1995] 15 LS 204 81

Statutes

■ Statutory Instruments

■ International Conventions and Treaties

What you need to do for every question in Constitutional and Administrative Law

HOW TO USE THIS BOOK

Books in the *Question and Answer* series focus on the *why* of a good answer alongside the *what*, thereby helping you to build your question answering skills and technique.

This guide should not be used as a substitute for learning the material thoroughly, your lecture notes or your textbook. It *will* help you to make the most out of what you have already learned when answering an exam or coursework question. Remember that the answers given here are not the *only* correct way of answering the question but serve to show you some good examples of how you *could* approach the question set.

Make sure that you refer regularly to your course syllabus, check which issues are covered (as well as to what extent they are covered) and whether they are usually examined with other topics. Remember that what is required in a good answer could change significantly with only a slight change in the wording of a question. Therefore, do not try to memorise the answers given here; instead use the answers and the other features to understand what goes into a good answer and why.

The study of the British constitution poses challenges for students, as there is seldom one 'correct' answer to a question. Essay questions demand that you will be able to analyse various competing theories about the nature of the constitution, and formulate a reasoned argument. In order to be persuasive, a legal argument must be supported by evidence and, therefore, you must ensure that you are able to point to examples of the operation of the constitution drawn from historical and current events, academic argument and judicial decisions. Where you are expressing a view or opinion of your own, remember that you still need supporting evidence to show the examiner why you have reached that conclusion. You need to be specific. Comments such as 'many have argued that . . .' will not attract high marks. It is far more authoritative to say something like 'Dicey argued that . . .', as this shows your examiner that there is a source for your opinion.

Make sure that you use the terminology correctly and consistently; it is important not to say 'government' if you mean 'Parliament', for example.

Constitutional and administrative law is changing at a rapid pace. Since the last edition of this book, major developments have occurred in several areas; reforms to the procedural requirements for judicial review, new legislation for the devolved regions, and of course the impact of the decision to leave the European Union. To do well in this subject, you need to keep abreast of developments by paying attention to the press, the law reports and journals.

A common mistake made by students is to see the examination as a memory test. Whilst you certainly do need to remember a lot of law, take care not to make the mistake of thinking you are only required to show how much law you remember. Many students submit answers (particularly to problem scenarios) that are too descriptive. Far higher marks are given to those students who have the confidence to select the legal provisions most relevant to the facts given in the question. You should concentrate on applying the law to the facts you have been given and using this to draw conclusions about the likely outcome for the party or parties you are asked to advise. Similarly, essays require you to show the ability to use the law that you have learnt in order to formulate an answer to the specific question, and marks will not be given for including irrelevant information.

Sources of the constitution

How this topic may come up in exams

Generally, examiners ask essay questions that require you to engage with the debate about the sources of the constitution and the ideas (doctrines) said to underpin it. Students sometimes struggle with this topic, as it requires some knowledge of history and of political theory. It can be difficult to find authorities to support arguments, and you will need to ensure that you can remember some key points made by theorists and academics. There will be considerable overlap between this part of the syllabus and the role of Parliament, especially when considering the doctrine of the separation of powers. Although parliamentary supremacy could be included in this chapter, it is dealt with separately in Chapter 3.

■ Before you begin

It's a good idea to consider the following key themes of sources of the constitution before tackling a question on this topic.

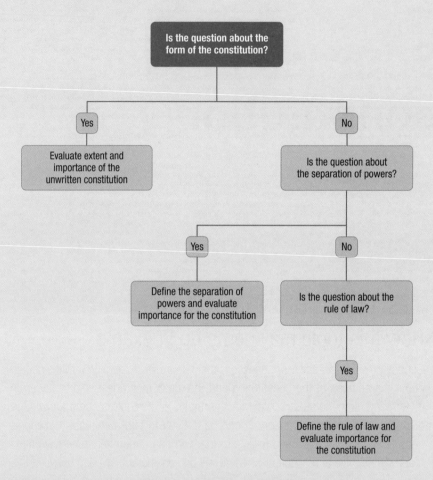

A printable version of this diagram is available from **www.pearsoned.co.uk/lawexpressqa**

 Question 1

The proliferation of statutes dealing with aspects of constitutional arrangements means that the description of the United Kingdom constitution as 'unwritten' is now wholly inaccurate. Discuss.

Answer plan

→ Explain the distinction between written and unwritten constitutions.

→ Discuss whether or not the constitution could have been described as wholly unwritten.

→ Identify some key statutes for discussion.

→ Consider whether unwritten sources remain relevant.

→ Argue that a written constitution demands a higher form of law.

Diagram plan

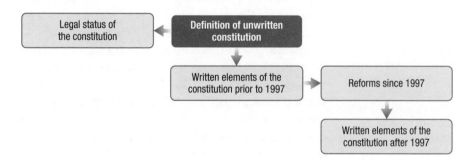

A printable version of this diagram plan is available from **www.pearsoned.co.uk/lawexpressqa**

Answer

[1] This definition is quite basic, but shows that you do recognise that the term 'constitution' should be defined by its role, rather than the form it takes.

A constitution is described as a set of rules and practices that determine how power is divided within a state.[1] The UK constitution is sometimes described as 'unwritten', as there is no single written document codifying the relevant laws. This is unusual; the United Kingdom is one of only three nations without a written constitution. However, in the decades since 1997, there has been a sustained programme of constitutional reform under Labour, Coalition and Conservative governments. Arguably, the result has been a shift towards codification.

1 SOURCES OF THE CONSTITUTION

[2] The focus of the argument will be that the distinction between 'written' and 'unwritten' constitutions is not so much about the format but about the notion of a superior form of law.

[3] Discussion of change to the constitution demands that you are able to outline the historical development of the United Kingdom's arrangements. However, it is important to keep this brief, so that the balance of your answer can concentrate on the main focus of the question, which is the impact of change.

[4] It is worth demonstrating an awareness of the kinds of cases that can be classified as constitutional, but take care not to spend too long describing these, as the question specifically refers to legislation.

[5] It is crucial to identify some key statutory provisions, but there is no need to provide a complete list.

However, many aspects remain uncodified and, to understand the constitution, it is still necessary to refer to numerous sources, some of which can properly be described as 'unwritten'. The term 'written constitution' also denotes a source of law superior to 'ordinary' law. In the United Kingdom, despite an increasing number of codified rules, the constitution has no special status.[2]

The UK constitution does not come from a single revolutionary point in history. Rather, the system of governance has evolved in piecemeal fashion, over time.[3] It would be wrong, however, to suggest that it could ever have been accurately described as entirely unwritten. An analysis of the historical development of the constitution demonstrates the existence of documentary sources, such as legislation and case law, alongside conventions and prerogative powers. Statutes that could be mentioned include the Bill of Rights 1689, which redefined the relationship between the monarch and the legislature; the various Acts extending the franchise; the Parliament Acts of 1911 and 1949, which shifted the balance of power between the Commons and the Lords; and the European Communities Act 1972, which made provision for community law to take effect in the domestic courts. Key judgments affected the role of the executive. In *Entick v Carrington* (1765) 19 St Tr 1029, the exercise of arbitrary government power was curtailed, and in *Council of Civil Service Unions v Minister for the Civil Service* [1985] AC 374 (the *GCHQ case*), the right of the judiciary to scrutinise the use of executive power was asserted.[4] It is correct to say, however, that the operation of the state depended in large part on tradition and practice, and the exercise of the historical powers of the prerogative.

It is undeniable that the period between 1997 and the present day has seen immense constitutional change.[5] The Blair administration steered through legislation to alter the composition of the House of Lords, to devolve executive power to Northern Ireland, Scotland and Wales, to ensure that the European Convention on Human Rights can be enforced in the domestic courts, and to increase access to information regarding the state. Perhaps the most systematic alteration to constitutional structures came in the form of the Constitutional Reform Act 2005. The Act was designed to strengthen the separation of powers and the rule of law through a number of measures, including reform of the office of Lord Chancellor, and the separation of the Law Lords from the legislative assembly. The Coalition government was responsible for the Fixed-term Parliaments Act 2011, which abolished the prerogative power to dissolve Parliament.

Despite an increase in written sources of constitutional power, unwritten sources also remain, although the relevance of such sources is, perhaps, debatable. Prerogative powers, normally exercised by the executive in the name of the Crown, can be abolished by the creation of statute (see, for example, *A-G v De Keyser's Royal Hotel Ltd* [1920] AC 508[6]). It could be argued that the prerogative no longer occupies a position of constitutional importance; the supervisory role of the judiciary now seems to be entrenched in the wake of the landmark ruling of the *GCHQ case*. In addition, it appears unlikely that any government could use the full extent of powers available without fear of political consequence. For example, in 2003, the decision to declare war on Iraq was reached following a vote in the House of Commons. Strictly speaking, this was unnecessary, as declaration of war is a prerogative power. Giving evidence to the Liaison Committee, the then Prime Minister stated that it was 'inconceivable' that the power would be exercised without reference to Parliament. However, since that time, three Private Members' Bills calling for the abolition of the prerogative have been tabled and have failed to gather executive support. It is fair to say that, in 2007, the government stated a commitment to reform of the prerogative, but, save for the minor changes introduced by the Constitutional Reform and Governance Act 2010, no sustained or substantive change has materialised.

Unwritten conventions remain part of the constitution.[7] Dicey (1885)[8] defined conventions as 'understandings, habits and practices' that are considered to be binding, but have no legal force. Jennings (1959a) considered that conventions are crucial to the operation of the constitution and must be followed, arguing that their unwritten nature allows for flexibility and change in accordance with developing societal and political norms. Those who suggest that codification is desirable point to the lack of consequence when a convention is ignored. Loveland (2012), for example, points to the Matrix Churchill affair of the 1990s, when, in the absence of legally enforceable controls, the convention of ministerial 'responsibility' seemed to shift towards a less onerous concept of 'accountability'.

A commitment to codification of the prerogative has not been made, but there has at least been widespread acknowledgement of the need

[6] Here, you are using the case simply to provide support for the proposition of law you have made. There is no need to give more detail; you have already set out the *ratio* of the case.

[7] It is important to consider the continued importance of unwritten elements of the constitution, to support the developing argument that the shift towards codification is far from complete.

[8] Reference to Dicey will be important in most essays about the nature of the constitution, as his work is still seen as the source of many of our ways of describing or explaining the system. If you are able to refer to other theorists as well (as in the remainder of the paragraph), this will increase your mark, as it shows that you have read around the topic.

[9] This is a good point to make, as it is evidence that some aspects of the unwritten constitution appear to enjoy continued support.

[10] This is the crux of the argument that was set out in the introduction.

[11] This is a solid conclusion, which sets out a clear point of view; showing confidence with the subject matter.

to consider the issue. However, there has been little commitment to the codification of conventions. Indeed, the Coalition government's failed House of Lords Reform Bill expressly confirmed that many of the operational conventions should remain.[9]

The significance of these issues is not simply the question of whether constitutional arrangements are written or unwritten. They are, rather, symptomatic of the fact that there is no deference to constitutional principles that will take precedence over all other forms of law.[10] There is no method of forcing compliance with constitutional arrangements governed by convention, and still some reluctance by the courts to curtail the prerogative.

It cannot be said, then, that the proliferation of legislation reforming aspects of the constitution has resulted in a written constitution. It may be the case that there are a greater number of written sources of the constitution. Certainly, the Constitutional Reform Act 2005 was significant, as it expressly referred to the doctrines of the separation of powers, and to the rule of law. Constitutional lawyers have long argued that these doctrines are part of our constitution, but the Act placed this on a statutory –and hence written– basis. As has been shown, however, informal, unwritten sources of power remain and these are subject to limited control. Nations described as possessing a written constitution are distinguishable not simply by the existence of a document, but rather by the acknowledgement that the constitution represents a superior form of legal power. This cannot be said to be the case in the United Kingdom, which does not afford the constitution such an elevated position.[11]

✓ Make your answer stand out

- By making reference to K.C. Wheare's (1966) classifications of constitutions as 'supreme' or 'subordinate' in *Modern Constitutions* (2nd edn), Oxford: Oxford University Press.

- By developing the argument regarding 'superior law' by outlining the difference between the powers of the Supreme Court in the United Kingdom and the Supreme Court of the United States, which has the power to declare legislation 'unconstitutional'.

- By suggesting that 'superior law' is impossible in the light of the doctrine of parliamentary supremacy. This will show the examiner that you are able to make connections between different topics in the syllabus.

Don't be tempted to . . .

■ Try to explain the workings of the constitution in great detail. There is no need to outline the various functions of the executive, legislature and judiciary here.

■ Include a detailed list of all constitutional changes since 1997, as the question requires analysis of the impact of changes rather than a descriptive account.

Question 2

'For the first time, we have a clear separation of powers between the legislature, the judiciary and the executive in the United Kingdom.' (Lord Phillips of Worth Matravers)

With reference to the Constitutional Reform Act 2005, consider the extent to which there is a clear separation of powers in the UK constitution.

Diagram plan

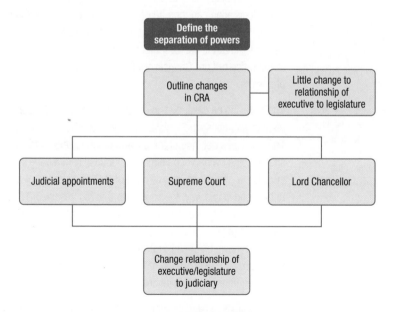

A printable version of this diagram plan is available from **www.pearsoned.co.uk/lawexpressqa**

Answer plan

→ Explain the meaning of 'separation of powers'.

→ Describe the extent to which a separation of powers existed prior to the 2005 Act.

→ Outline the key provisions of the Act.

→ Consider how far there is a true separation of powers.

→ Consider whether or not a true separation of powers is possible.

Answer

[1] Reference to Montesquieu is essential, as it shows an awareness of the origins of the doctrine.

The doctrine of the separation of powers was first espoused by the political theorist Montesquieu in the eighteenth century.[1] The doctrine has been considered to be an important element of the constitution since that time. The Constitutional Reform Act 2005 (CRA) introduced changes intended to reinforce the importance of the doctrine of the separation of powers. In order to assess the impact of these changes it is necessary first to establish the pre-existing position. The success of the legislation can then be considered. It will be suggested that a complete separation of powers is neither desirable nor possible. It will be argued that the establishment of the Supreme Court and reforms to the office of Lord Chancellor did reinforce a functional separation of powers.[2]

[2] The introduction should outline the main argument to be adopted in the remainder of the essay; this will reassure the examiner that there will be a coherent structure to the argument.

[3] It is important to be able to explain succinctly what is meant by the term 'separation of powers' without spending too long outlining the development of the doctrine.

The state can be described as consisting of three bodies that perform distinct functions: the legislature; the executive; and the judiciary. The traditional doctrine of the separation of powers states that there should be no overlap of personnel or functions among the institutions in order to prevent abuses of power.[3] If the separation of powers is understood in this way, then it is clear that Montesquieu (1989) must have been outlining an idealised position, for there has always been an overlap of personnel in the institutions of the United Kingdom. This does not inevitably mean that the doctrine should be dismissed, as there can still be separation of function, and a system of checks and balances among the institutions.

[4] It is not possible to deal with every aspect of the interaction between the powers in detail, so a more confident answer will highlight a few areas for discussion.

The examples of overlap prior to the CRA are numerous, but, for the purpose of this discussion, three will be considered.[4] First, the Law Lords sat in the House of Lords as part of the legislature. Second, the unique position of the Lord Chancellor, who, as head of the judiciary, Speaker of the House of Lords, and a Cabinet Minister, occupied a position at the heart of all three institutions of the state. Last, and linked to the Lord Chancellor's office, was the system of senior judicial appointments that were made on his recommendation. This system had long been the subject of criticism and, certainly, the fact of executive involvement in determining the composition of the judiciary posed a challenge to claims of the existence of a separation of powers. If one role of the judiciary is to restrain executive abuse of power, then even the hypothetical possibility of executive influence can be seen to threaten the integrity of the system.[5]

[5] It will be suggested later that the CRA focused primarily on judicial independence, so it is worth stating why this is seen as critical.

In 2003, the government unexpectedly announced plans to abolish the role of Lord Chancellor. The CRA did not go as far as abolition, but instead severely curtailed the role (ss. 2–22).[6] The Lord Chancellor now retains a role as government minister but no longer sits as a judge or acts as Speaker of the House of Lords. In addition, the Law Lords now sit as the Supreme Court, which, in a visible symbol of separation, is located outside the Houses of Parliament. A new system for judicial appointments was introduced, to limit the possibility of accusations of executive influence (s. 61). Indeed, the Act specifically charges the Lord Chancellor, and all ministers, with a responsibility to uphold the independence of the judiciary, and not to seek to influence any decisions made in court proceedings (s. 3).

[6] The CRA introduced many changes, so it is necessary to be able to focus on those relevant to the question, and to be able to explain the effect on the office of Lord Chancellor and the House of Lords.

The pronouncement made by Lord Phillips suggests that, prior to the establishment of the Supreme Court, not only was there a lack of separation, but, more particularly, that this was evidenced by the inclusion of senior judiciary in the legislature. It is, of course, true that the Law Lords were entitled to sit in the House of Lords, and to participate in debate. By convention, however, they declined to participate in proceedings concerning legislation that they might, in future, have to adjudicate upon. The physical change of location and the alteration of title could be understood as a piece of symbolism, representative of the desire to promote transparency in our constitutional arrangements.[7] Alternatively, the creation of a separate institution, coupled with the obligations imposed on judges by the Human Rights Act 1998, could be viewed as a part of a pattern of an increasingly vocal and opinionated judiciary.

[7] Marks will be afforded for the ability to form a reasoned view about the impact of legislative change rather than simply stating the law.

The alterations to the office of Lord Chancellor were part of a systematic attempt to effect real constitutional change. At the beginning of Labour's programme of constitutional reform, Lord Irvine defended

[8] This reference shows that you are familiar with the way in which policy has shifted over time – from defence of the office towards reform.

[9] Inclusion of Bagehot here will be rewarded, as it shows ability to explore the topic a little more, by demonstrating awareness of the fact that it is arguable whether a separation of powers is desirable.

[10] The answer has tended towards suggesting that change has been largely cosmetic. Inclusion of this quote shows familiarity with the case, but, more importantly, points towards an understanding that it is important that fairness is transparent in the organisation of the state.

[11] The question focuses on the CRA 2005, but mention of the later statute demonstrates up-to-date knowledge.

[12] In the interests of balance, it is useful to be able to point to evidence that contradicts the view given by Lord Phillips of Worth Matravers.

[13] It is important not to be too descriptive when using case law. Sometimes, as here, there is no need to include any of the facts. The reference to a specific point made in the judgment shows familiarity with, and understanding of, the case.

the role,[8] arguing that the unique function of the office was to allow communication between the organs of state so that each could understand the objectives of the other. The office was a clear example of what had been described by Bagehot in the nineteenth century as the almost 'complete fusion' between the institutions, which he considered to be the 'efficient secret' of the constitution.[9] Nonetheless, the numerous responsibilities of the Lord Chancellor in all areas of government led to the possibility of tensions between the various roles. Lord Woolf highlighted the need for statutory protection for judicial independence, rather than convention and reliance on mutual respect, and linked this to the preservation of the rule of law. The restriction of the Lord Chancellor's role, and the removal of his powers of judicial appointment, then, can be viewed as an acknowledgement of the truth of the famous maxim that 'justice must not only be done, it must be seen to be done' (*R v Sussex Justices ex parte McCarthy* [1923] All ER 233).[10] The possibility of executive influence over the composition of the judiciary has, then, been diminished. This has been reinforced by regulatory changes introduced by the Crime and Courts Act 2013, which included the removal of involvement of the Lord Chancellor in the appointment of judges below the High Court (Sch. 13, Pt 4).[11]

The CRA focused on judicial independence. It did not address other aspects of the constitution that threaten the separation of powers, such as the fact that government ministers sit as part of the legislature, or the quasi-judicial function exercised by Parliament in the regulation of its own affairs.[12] It could be suggested that the judiciary had proved to be able to maintain independence despite judges' position in the Lords, under the supervision of the Lord Chancellor. There are many instances in which the Lords have been willing to confront both the legislature and the executive (consider the rebuke Lord Hoffmann delivered in *A v Secretary of State for the Home Department* [2004] UKHL 56).[13] Although the CRA may be more concerned with form than substantive change, it is important to ensure that independence is protected and thus it must be seen as a positive step. The CRA did impact on one aspect of the separation of powers, but, without addressing the relationship between other institutions of state, it can only be viewed as a step towards a robust functional separation.

Make your answer stand out

- By incorporating primary sources in the theoretical discussion. You could refer to additional cases in which the importance of a separation of powers has been sanctioned; see, for example, the comments of Lord Diplock in *Duport Steels Ltd* v *Sirs* [1980] 1 WLR 142.
- You could argue that a view of the impact of the Act may depend on the definition of the separation of powers that is adopted. The answer has already indicated that Montesquieu and Bagehot saw the separation of powers differently, and development of this point would show the examiner that you have the ability to utilise theoretical perspectives to assess primary sources of law.
- If space allowed, reference could be made to other academic perspectives. Specifically, you could consider Marshall, who makes the point that there is no clear or consistent definition of the principle: Marshall, G. (1971) *Constitutional Theory*. Oxford: Clarendon Press.

! Don't be tempted to . . .

- Become distracted by outlining the personnel and/or functions of the institutions. There is a temptation to show 'how much you know' about the operation of the constitution, and students often begin this kind of answer by describing how the different institutions operate. This approach will not gather marks and it is more important to focus on analysing the impact of the Act mentioned in the question.
- Similarly, it is not enough to outline the provisions of the CRA here. An answer that sets out the key changes and then draws conclusions about the effect of the Act will appear quite weak. This question really does require you to show that you understand some of the academic and judicial comment on the issues covered by the Act. The conclusions that you draw will then be supported by evidence.

Question 3

'In the mouth of a British Constitutional Lawyer, the term "rule of law" seems to mean primarily a corpus of basic principles and values, which together lend some stability and coherence to the legal order.' Allan, T.R.S. (2001) *Constitutional Justice: A Liberal Theory of the Rule of Law*. Oxford: Oxford University Press.

Discuss the relevance of the concept of the 'rule of law' to the United Kingdom constitution.

Diagram plan

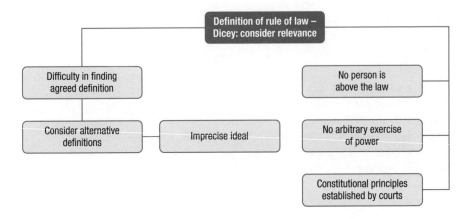

A printable version of this diagram plan is available from **www.pearsoned.co.uk/lawexpressqa**

Answer plan

→ Try to define the 'rule of law'.

→ Acknowledge the variety of definitions.

→ Consider the current position, with examples.

→ Argue that the rule of law is relevant as an ideal.

→ Argue that the rule of law needs clearer definition and protection.

Answer

[1] You should be able to summarise Dicey's three 'rules' accurately and succinctly.

[2] This question demands that you acknowledge the difficulty in defining the rule of law, but all questions dealing with the doctrine require demonstration of understanding of the Diceyan position.

The 'rule of law' is a term often invoked by politicians, judges and academics, but the definition is far from certain. The lack of a clearly discernible meaning is problematic, as it has been said to underpin the organisation of the state. The Constitutional Reform Act 2005 formally recognises the importance of the rule of law (s. 1).

Dicey saw the rule of law as embodying three concepts: no person should be punished except for a distinct breach of the law; no person is above the law; and constitutional principles are established in the common courts.[1] To assess the relevance of the rule of law in the modern constitution, these are a useful starting point for analysis, but it must be remembered that there are alternative definitions that could be considered.[2]

Entick v *Carrington* is a key constitutional case, as it is one of the first times that the judiciary articulated the principle of legality. Therefore, it is important to recognise the importance of the case in a discussion about the rule of law.

4 This is a really useful authority to cite, especially alongside *Entick*. The two cases are, in a sense, two sides of the same coin. While you should not set out the facts in any detail, you should provide enough information to demonstrate how the case shows that a law does not need to be fair.

5 Dicey is sometimes dismissed by students as being outdated, which is a valid view, but there is a need to point to evidence of this.

6 Here, the answer shows an ability to relate legal theory to the way in which the constitution operates in practice. This shows that you really understand the significance of the point that Dicey was making by the first rule.

7 Again, the case of *Entick* v *Carrington* is central to this aspect of the topic, so you need to show the examiner that you are aware of this.

8 It is always important to demonstrate knowledge of two sides of a debate, but crucial to be able to find some examples to support each side of the argument.

Dicey's first rule can be interpreted as expressing a need for protection from the arbitrary exercise of power. **Entick v Carrington** (1765) 2 Wils 275 articulated this principle of legality by holding that, in the absence of statutory or common-law authority, entry to a citizen's home was unlawful.[3] It is worth noting that the requirement for legality as part of the rule of law does not necessarily mean that the judiciary will be concerned with the fairness of a particular provision. **IRC v Rossminster** [1980] AC 952 required the courts to consider powers of search and seizure that were, in the view of Lord Scarman, a 'breathtaking' interference with privacy and property.[4] As the lawful authority existed, the principle of legality was satisfied. Dicey was critical of the use of discretionary authority, and would undoubtedly be disturbed by the range of discretionary powers now afforded to the executive – for example, in the administration of the welfare state. It is important to remember that he wrote at a time when the functions of government were few. This cannot be said to be the case in the complex society we now inhabit, where the job of administration would be impossible were it not for the exercise of discretion.[5] A modern explanation of this part of the principle of the rule of law would, perhaps, require not the absence of discretionary powers but rather a robust system to regulate the exercise of discretion.[6] Therefore, judicial review of executive action can be seen as central to the rule of law. Attempts to exclude the court's power of review have been rejected by the judiciary; in **R (Cart) v Upper Tribunal; R (U and XC) v Special Immigration Appeals Commission** [2009] EWHC 3052 (Admin), it was held that judicial review was available, and, further, is a 'principle engine of the rule of law'.

The notion that 'no man is above the law' seems straightforward. Dicey cited **Entick v Carrington** as support for this proposition, declaring it to be one of many instances where government officials were called to account.[7] **M v Home Office** [1994] 1 AC 377 is an example of a government minister being held in contempt of court after ignoring a court order. This would seem to suggest the truth of Dicey's statement. There are, though, examples of classes of persons who are not subject to the law in the same way, such as those enjoying diplomatic immunity or MPs protected from defamation in Parliament.[8]

Part IV of the Anti-Terrorism, Crime and Security Act 2001 attempted to create a law to which only one class of persons – foreign nationals – would

[9] Many commentators refer to this as an important constitutional case, and it is a useful one to be aware of for this topic area.

be subject. The court's opposition (***A v Secretary of State for the Home Department*** [2004] UKHL 56[9]) can be used to support the argument that the judiciary plays an important role in preserving the rule of law. Arguably, this aspect of the principle also implies that there must be equal access to the courts. In certain circumstances, it has been held that Article 6 of the European Convention on Human Rights requires that the state should fund legal representation in order to ensure that litigants in proceedings are equal (***Steel and Morris v UK*** (2005) 41 EHRR 22).

[10] The final proposition can be difficult to explain, so you will be rewarded if you can provide a clear explanation.

The final element of Dicey's conception of the rule of law[10] expresses his belief that the common law was capable of protecting individual rights, obviating the need for a written constitution. The Human Rights Act 1998 incorporates the rights under the European Convention on Human Rights into domestic law, and, therefore, arguably, the role of the courts is diminished.

[11] It is not going to be possible to consider the range of complex debate regarding the meaning of the rule of law, but ensure that you are familiar with the broad differences between those who see it as linked to morality, and those who view it as a structural issue.

There have been many other explanations of the rule of law.[11] Craig (1997) argues that there are two main schools of thought. One approach is the formal conception of the rule of law, which is concerned with the process of law making, and simply demands that laws are made according to an open clear process, and that obligations imposed by the law are prospective and clear. The rule of law, on this definition, is not concerned with the content of those laws. A substantive conception of the rule of law suggests that the law embodies rights, and that distinctions can be drawn between good and bad laws. Raz (1979) notes that there are numerous definitions of the rule of law, but rejects efforts to imbue the doctrine with a moral ideology. He argues that some features are required, including the requirement for clear, prospective laws, an independent judiciary, and review powers being available to the courts. Even when this simplified definition is adopted, there are still some problems in asserting that the modern constitution unambiguously relies on the rule of law.[12] Examples of retrospective legislation are rare, but can be found. The War Damage Act 1965 is often cited, but, more recently, the High Court issued a declaration of incompatibility concerning the Jobseekers (Back to Work Schemes) Act 2013, which had been passed to confer retrospective validity on regulations previously held to be unlawful (***R (Reilly) (No. 2)***

[12] Here, you reassure the examiner that you are using the material to address the question.

[13] This is a good case to cite, as it shows familiarity with more recent developments. There is no need to set out detail about the case, however, as the only reason to include it here is to demonstrate that retrospective law is occasionally enacted even now.

v _Secretary of State for Work and Pensions_ [2014] EWHC 2182 (Admin)[13]. Attempts to limit the availability of, and funding for, judicial review (Legal Aid, Sentencing and Punishment of Offenders Act 2013) have attracted comment on the basis that this may have an impact on the rule of law (see, for example, Liberty's contribution to the report stages of the Criminal Justice and Courts Bill 2014, available at https://www.liberty-human-rights.org.uk). Nevertheless, if a formal definition is considered, it is easier to argue that the rule of law is part of the constitution.

[14] The conclusion may appear quite short, but the final argument was set out in the preceding paragraph. It is crucial, though, to provide a direct answer to the question.

The rule of law is not a precise legal doctrine, and there are aspects of Dicey's description of its operation that seem less relevant in a modern context. If the key elements, as suggested by Raz, are accepted as broadly accurate, then it seems clear that the concept remains both relevant and central.[14]

 Make your answer stand out

- By showing a knowledge of a broader range of academic theorists in this area. The answer references Raz and Craig, but there are many people you could mention. Some useful sources are: Allan, T.R.S. (2001) _Constitutional Justice: A Liberal Theory of the Rule of Law._ Oxford: Oxford University Press; Craig, P. (1997) Formal and substantive conceptions of the rule of law: an analytical framework. _Public Law_, 467; Jowell, J. and Oliver, D. (eds) (2000) _The Changing Constitution_ (4th edn). Oxford: Oxford University Press; Raz, J. (1979) _The Authority of Law._ Oxford: Oxford University Press.

- By considering the relationship between the doctrine of the rule of law and other principles said to underpin the constitution. This answer refers to the role of the judiciary; it could be argued that a functional separation of powers is necessary to uphold the rule of law. The examiner will be impressed by an answer that demonstrates understanding of how different topics considered on the syllabus overlap.

- By engaging in a more discursive consideration of retrospective legislation. You could, for example, argue that the ruling in the _Reilly_ case demonstrates that the rule of law is functioning effectively, as the independent judiciary appropriately rejected the offending legislation.

! Don't be tempted to . . .

■ Treat the question as an invitation to outline Dicey's theory and ignore other definitions of the rule of law. This is an area of the syllabus that students tend to find very difficult, mainly because we would like there to be one 'correct' definition of the rule of law. If you are able to show that you understand that there are competing definitions, you will be rewarded.

■ Ignore primary sources. Although this is a very academic area of the syllabus, there are key cases that can, and should, be incorporated into your answer because they illustrate how the judiciary approaches the rule of law. Weaker answers are often limited to mention of *Entick v Carrington*. Marks will be given to the answer that can refer to more recent cases, such as *A* v *Secretary of State for the Home Department* [2004] UKHL 56 and *R (Reilly) (No. 2)* v *Secretary of State for Work and Pensions* [2014] EWHC 2182 (Admin).

Question 4

'In the determination of his civil rights and liabilities or of any criminal charge against him, everyone is entitled to a fair and public hearing . . . . . .' (Article 6, European Convention on Human Rights and Fundamental Freedoms)

To what extent are closed material proceedings compatible with the rule of law?

Answer plan

➡ Explain the rule of law as defined by Dicey and consider where the requirement for open justice sits.

➡ Demonstrate the general judicial acceptance of the principle.

➡ Outline the changes made by the Justice and Security Act 2013.

➡ Consider the judicial approach to closed material proceedings (CMPs).

Diagram plan

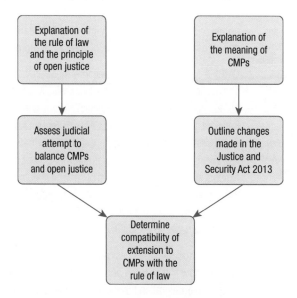

```
┌─────────────────────┐          ┌─────────────────────┐
│   Explanation of    │          │   Explanation of    │
│   the rule of law   │          │   the meaning of    │
│  and the principle  │          │        CMPs         │
│   of open justice   │          │                     │
└──────────┬──────────┘          └──────────┬──────────┘
           │                                │
           ▼                                ▼
┌─────────────────────┐          ┌─────────────────────┐
│   Assess judicial   │          │   Outline changes   │
│    attempt to       │          │     made in the     │
│   balance CMPs      │          │     Justice and     │
│   and open justice  │          │  Security Act 2013  │
└──────────┬──────────┘          └──────────┬──────────┘
           │                                │
           └──────────────┐  ┌──────────────┘
                          ▼  ▼
                 ┌─────────────────────┐
                 │     Determine       │
                 │   compatibility of  │
                 │    extension to     │
                 │    CMPs with the    │
                 │     rule of law     │
                 └─────────────────────┘
```

A printable version of this diagram plan is available from **www.pearsoned.co.uk/lawexpressqa**

Answer

[1] As this question specifically requires you to discuss CMPs, you should not spend too long considering the definitions of the rule of law. Dispense with the definition as swiftly as you can in order to focus on the central issue.

[2] The introduction should be used to show your understanding of the links between the various concepts set out in the question. You do need to set out the importance of open justice.

[3] The question refers to Article 6, which should be seen as an invitation to make the connection between the right to a fair trial and the rule of law.

Although the precise requirements of the rule of law are the subject of academic debate, the centrality of the principle to the constitution is generally agreed.[1] Dicey described the rule of law as having three components: equality before the law; an absence of arbitrary justice; and judicial protection of rights. Despite the fact that these maxims do not expressly refer to open justice, many argue that public hearings are required to maintain the rule of law by ensuring protection from the arbitrary abuse of power.[2] In *Scott v Scott* [1913] AC 417, Lord Shaw declared that allowing an expansion of judicial discretion to order hearings in camera would be to 'shift the foundations of freedom from the rock to the sand'. More recently, Lord Neuberger (2011a) declared that court hearings conducted in public are a central part of the commitment to the rule of law. Thus, it can be seen that, in seeking to protect the right to a public hearing, Article 6 of the Convention enshrines an aspect of the rule of law.[3] However, departures from the principle of open justice are not unknown. Anonymity orders can be made in both civil and criminal hearings where justice requires this. It is routine for proceedings in both family and youth courts to be closed to the public. Closed material proceedings (CMPs), though, go beyond these exclusions by allowing for hearings to occur in the absence of a party to the case or their legal representative.[4]

[4] It is surprising how many students attempt to answer this question without explaining what is meant by a CMP. Make sure that you define all the key legal terms in any question.

CMPs are not new, but have become more prevalent in recent years. The Justice and Security Act 2013 was initially proposed in the wake of collapsed litigation concerning British citizens detained at Guantanamo Bay. The government requested CMPs to deal with parts of the evidence that it wished to adduce in defence of claims made that MI5 and MI6 had been complicit in torture, arguing that disclosure would damage national security.[5] In the absence of specific statutory authority to do so, the Supreme Court held it had no power to order CMPs in the civil action and therefore disclosure would have to be made. The government then settled the cases to avoid the potentially damaging disclosure.

[5] Here, more detail is provided about the facts of the case than is usually required. It is included to make clear the government's rationale for seeking to change the law.

The Act introduced the possibility of CMPs across the civil justice system (previously they were permissible only in specific tribunals, such as special immigration tribunals or the Investigatory Powers Tribunal). The higher courts can now make an order for CMPs in any civil case, either of the court's own volition or (as is more likely) on application by the Secretary of State (s. 6).[6]

[6] As you have explained the effect of CMPs earlier in your answer, the detail provided here can be brief, but do make sure that you highlight the precise section that you are referring to.

Section 12 of the Act requires the Secretary of State to produce an annual report detailing the number of cases in which CMPs have been used. A written ministerial statement was produced in July 2014, stating that five applications had been made and two granted (available at http://www.parliament.uk/documents/commons-vote-office/July-2014/22%20July%202014?27-JUSTICE-ClosedMaterialProcedure.pdf). The Bingham Centre has been critical of this, arguing that the report gives insufficient information about the cases, making it impossible to monitor why applications are made, granted, refused or revoked. This is a 'matter of democratic accountability, especially because the cases where CMPs have been or almost certainly will be sought often engage the behaviour of governments and the adequacy of oversight mechanisms' (McNamara and Lock, 2014).[7]

[7] This is a useful quote because it links back to the question, as the rule of law is so frequently aligned with democratic ideals.

The use of CMPs in control order cases has generated a considerable amount of judicial attention since 2005, as both domestic courts and Strasbourg struggled to determine whether such hearings could be compatible with Article 6. The right to cross-examine witnesses

[8] This shows awareness of the distinction drawn in the ECHR between civil and criminal proceedings.

[9] You must show that you understand the role of a special advocate.

[10] These are key authorities on the issue of CMPs and must be included. There is no need to give further detail about the facts.

[11] This is an important point and demonstrates an understanding of how the law is developing.

[12] Although you do not need to explain the facts of this case, it is really important that you cite at least one case to support your claim.

[13] This is a good point to make, as it demonstrates awareness of both sides of the arguments regarding the collapse of the Guantanamo cases.

[14] The answer has dealt with a wide range of issues: make sure that you take care to link back to the question's focus on the rule of law.

is protected only in respect of criminal proceedings (Art. 6(3)), but questions remain as to whether CMPs can meet the standard of fairness required to comply with Article 6(1).[8] The government has relied upon the special advocate procedure, in which a court-appointed advocate deals with those parts of the evidence which are closed and the defendant continues to be represented by their own advocate in respect of the 'open' proceedings.[9]

In *A v UK* [2009] ECHR 301, the ECtHR held that enough information about the closed material must be disclosed to allow the defendant to give instructions to the special advocate: a ruling accepted and confirmed by the Supreme Court (*Secretary of State for the Home Department v AF* (No 3) [2010] AC 269).[10] While these rulings show strong support for open justice, later decisions diluted their impact by emphasising that the amount of disclosure required by Article 6 may depend upon the nature of the proceedings and the likely impact upon the defendant.[11] It appears that an enhanced amount of disclosure is necessary where liberty is at stake, but where the incursion upon the defendant's rights is not as grave, the use of the special advocate may be less problematic (for example, the case of *Home Office v Tariq* [2011] UKSC 35 dealing with covert surveillance).[12] Special advocates have expressed misgivings regarding the procedure on more than one occasion (Chamberlain, 2009a).

The balance between procedural fairness and national security is undoubtedly difficult. If it were to be the case that proceedings had to be dropped to avoid court-ordered disclosure of damaging and sensitive evidence, then it could be argued that the rule of law would be undermined, as a class of persons may be able to evade its reach.[13] In considering the Binyam Mohammed case (*R (Mohammed) v Secretary of State for Foreign and Commonwealth Affairs* [2010] EWCA Civ 65), however, Otty (2012) argues that settlement occurred not because of the refusal of the courts to endorse CMPs, but because the state could not have won the case.

CMPs can now be ordered during any civil proceedings in respect of 'sensitive' information, a term defined at section 6(11) as material that could, if disclosed, be damaging to national security. It could be argued that potential injustice is avoided as, after all, even if the defendant's advocate does not see all the evidence, the judge will be able to provide the constitutional protection from executive abuse that Dicey warned against.[14] Lord Kerr, however, warned against

[15] This is a useful paragraph, as an alternative point of view is noted, but the inclusion of Lord Kerr's view is a persuasive argument against the position.

this assumption in *Al Rawi and others* v *Security Services and others* [2011] UKSC 34, calling the argument 'a fallacy'. He reiterated the common-law principle, now enshrined in Article 6, that evidence must be capable of withstanding challenge if it is to be relied upon.[15]

It is clear from the authorities that CMPs are not, by definition, incompatible with the rule of law, provided that the 'gist' of the evidence is disclosed. The spread of such proceedings in the absence of enhanced safeguards to govern disclosure, however, threatens the important principle of open justice that is so central to the doctrine.

 Make your answer stand out

- By discussing the implications of the decision by the Supreme Court in *Bank Mellat v HM Treasury* [2013] UKSC 38, asserting a general power to order closed material proceedings, but setting out a series of guidelines emphasising that the state is required to prove strict necessity in each case.

- By considering the relationship between the rule of law and the separation of powers. The reference to comments made by Lord Kerr could be the starting point for this part of the discussion. This seems to suggest that the ability of the judicial system to hold the executive to account is not solely the responsibility of the judges, but is, to a certain extent, a result of the litigation process.

- By considering the controversy regarding the first criminal trial to be dealt with behind closed doors in 2014, and of the possibility of trials without jury. This would give a broader discussion of the issues concerning open justice, but do note that the question requires you to focus on CMPs.

! Don't be tempted to . . .

- Write a general answer discussing the rule of law and the right to a fair trial. Few marks will be awarded here for arguing that the rule of law demands an impartial tribunal and equal treatment for all citizens. The question makes it clear that your answer should concentrate on CMPs and open justice.

- Make general statements about CMPs without reference to any decided cases. Here, you will need to show some knowledge of the case law both in the domestic courts and in Strasbourg.

- Ignore the need to provide a balanced argument. A number of answers fail to examine the points made by those who support the extension of CMPs. In order to be persuasive, an answer must consider opposing views and explain why the reader should reject them.

Question 5

'At the heart of the development of our constitutional arrangements, Parliament is there to protect us from authoritarianism, from despotism, from an over mighty monarch, but also from an over mighty executive.' (Lord Judge, *Ceding Power to the Executive*, University of King's College, London, 12 April 2016)

Discuss the extent to which Parliament is able to control the use of executive powers.

Answer plan

➜ Set out the constitutional function of Parliament and refer to the separation of powers.

➜ Identify statutory power conferred to ministers as the key focus for discussion.

➜ Explain the background, and the response, to the Strathclyde review.

➜ Assess the extent to which the use of 'Henry VIII clauses' impacts on parliamentary supremacy.

➜ Conclude that parliamentary control is inadequate.

Diagram plan

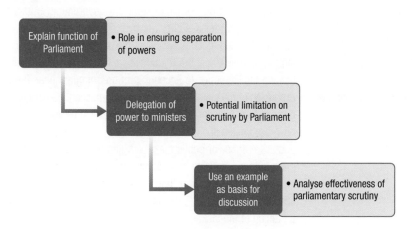

A printable version of this diagram plan is available from **www.pearsoned.co.uk/lawexpressqa**

Answer

[1] Where a question includes a quotation, it is always helpful to refer to the source. First, it can assist you in identifying the topic area that the examiner would like you to focus on, and, secondly it demonstrates that you have read and understood the context in which the remarks were made.

In a speech given to University of King's College,[1] Lord Judge warned against the proliferation of statutes that confer powers on government ministers, and against what appeared to be a government attempt to reduce the role of the House of Lords in the scrutiny of such powers. Following the rejection of a statutory instrument concerning cuts to tax credits in the upper chamber, members of the government suggested that the unelected chamber were frustrating the will of the elected House of Commons, and Lord Strathclyde was asked to undertake a review of the role of the Lords in respect of secondary legislation.[2] It will, however, be argued that the dispute in fact arose from an attempt by many in the Lords to exercise the proper constitutional function of scrutiny of the executive; a function that is increasingly difficult in the face of the rapid growth of delegated powers.

[2] There are a number of ways in which the question could be tackled, so it is helpful to set out the approach that you are going to take in the introduction.

The doctrine of a separation of powers was described by Montesquieu as a central feature of the United Kingdom constitution and perceived as a protection from tyranny. The separate functions of the executive, legislature and judiciary are commonly seen as a necessary means of achieving not simply efficient government, but[3] also of ensuring against misuse of power by preventing any one part of the state holding too much power. The role of Parliament, then, may be legislative in essence, but the additional function of scrutinising and holding the executive to account is of great importance. The rapid expansion of the state, however, creates significant barriers to effective scrutiny. As Elliot and Thomas note (2014, p. 99), government now 'assumes responsibility for a bewildering variety and seemingly endless number of public tasks' ranging from the maintenance of infrastructure, policing, education, health and the welfare state. It is therefore unsurprising that ministers are given power to make secondary legislation; Parliament would not have time to complete a fraction of the task if primary legislation was required.

[3] The question does not explicitly refer to the doctrine of separation of powers, but the concept underpins the statement made by Lord Judge and you should, therefore, briefly explain why it is relevant.

Delegated legislation now forms the vast majority of legislation in the United Kingdom, with a minimum of 3,000 statutory instruments every year. The bulk of these are passed by 'negative resolution', meaning that if Parliament makes no objection within 40 days, then the instrument passes into law. However, the sheer volume of material, and the ever-increasing power given to the executive, makes effective scrutiny 'difficult or impossible' (Greenberg, 2016). Lord Judge noted that, since 1950,[4] a total of 170,000 statutory instruments had been laid before Parliament, and only 17 had been rejected by either the Commons or the Lords. He also reminds us that neither House has the power to amend secondary legislation.

[4] The use of some figures in this paragraph is helpful because it clearly demonstrates the reason that the task of scrutiny is so daunting.

Many statutory instruments are unobjectionable; dealing with technical detail or uncontroversial decisions. Erskine May describes secondary legislation as 'essentially procedural or subsidiary'. A growing concern, however, has been a perceived tendency for government to use delegated powers for a broader range of policy objectives (see, for example, Fox and Blackwell (2014)),[5] and to pass primary legislation that contains little legislative detail. The Children Act 2016, for example, was subject to criticism during the committee stages on the basis that 'whilst it may contain a legislative framework, it contains virtually nothing of substance beyond the vague "mission statement" in clause 1(1)' (Delegated Powers and Regulatory Reform Committee, 2015).[6]

[5] Vague statements such as 'many people think' or 'some have argued' are frowned upon; you need to show that you can pinpoint some sources.

[6] You have to use some concrete examples from legislation, and there are numerous examples you could choose. The Children Act 2016 is helpful because it allows you to include the reference to the Select Committee report.

[7] In October 2015, the House of Lords rejected a statutory instrument made under section 22 of the Tax Credits Act 2002, which, if passed, would have resulted in cuts amounting to some £4.5 billion. The decision was controversial, with government ministers stating that in, doing so, the Lords had disregarded the will of the elected Commons and disregarded the convention that it would not block money Bills. As a result of the decision, Lord Strathclyde was asked to review that powers of the upper House in respect of secondary legislation. His report, published in December, gave several options for limiting the power of the Lords. Critics, however, have pointed out that the presentation of the conflict as being between the elected and the unelected parts of Parliament was misleading.[8] A proposal with such a large financial implication could hardly be described as technical, procedural or subsidiary. Giving evidence to the House of Lords Select Committee on Secondary Legislation, Lord Norton noted that the 'mischief' lay with the use of secondary legislation for improper purposes, and that the focus should now be on ensuring that secondary legislation should not be employed as a means of avoiding scrutiny (Select Committee Report 2016, para 69).

[7] The reasons for the controversy regarding the proposed cut to tax credits are complex, and it is important not to be diverted into a lengthy explanation of the disputed convention. You need to be as brief as possible.

[8] Again, a source is needed in this paragraph, which is why the quotation from Lord Norton follows.

Greenberg argues that the changing shape of legislation cedes too much power to the executive by increasing the discretion and control of ministers after enactment (Greenberg 2015, p. 96). This can be through sweeping powers to make delegated legislation, increased discretionary powers, or through the use of so-called 'Henry VIII clauses'. From a constitutional perspective, the bulk of delegated legislation is, at least, subject to regulation by judicial review. Where an Act contains a clause permitting a minister to alter, repeal or create primary legislation, then that possibility of oversight is removed. Lord Judge has been sharply critical of the growing use of such clauses, suggesting that they should be 'consigned to the dustbin of history' in his 2010 speech at the Lord Mayor's dinner.[9] The House of Lords Constitution Committee described them as a 'constitutional oddity' and warned that they should be used only in narrow circumstances and with adequate parliamentary supervision (Report on the Public Bodies Bill 2010). In the same speech, Lord Judge counted 120 such clauses in a single parliamentary session: this form of legislation is far more common than would be expected of an 'oddity'.

[9] Reference to the earlier speech is helpful here, as it shows the breadth of your reading.

Greenberg's analysis (2015) suggests that broad powers to make post-enactment amendments, and the proliferation of clauses delegating power to ministers, may be the result of a decline in the standards of parliamentary drafting coupled with the expansion of government and the demand that creates for legislation and regulation. Nevertheless, the end result is clear: an increasingly large degree of power in the hands of the executive and a diminishing amount of parliamentary oversight.[10] In this context, then, the role of the Lords in the examination of Bills, and delegated legislation, is critical.

[10] Here you are able to bring together the various issues that have been raised.

Parliamentary control of executive power underpins the constitution by providing assurance that the over-concentration of power is avoided. Post-legislative control by the judiciary is not sufficient, and may not even be possible when dealing with the use of 'Henry VIII clauses'. It seems clear that the sheer volume of legislation means that the degree of scrutiny that can occur is limited, and any suggestion of further limitation by restricting the role of the Lords is troubling.

Make your answer stand out

- By discussing the concerns that are emerging regarding the role of Parliament following the decision to leave the European Union. Prior to the referendum, some commentators suggested that the process might require broad "enabling" legislation delegating power to Ministers (see, for example, Obiter J's blog-post on 11 June 2016, available at http://obiterj.blogspot.co.uk/2016/06/uk-and-eu-11-more-on-what-if-it-is). At the time of writing, this appears to be the likely outcome of the government's proposed Great Repeal Bill.

- By providing more detail of the scope of some 'Henry VIII' powers: for example, you could outline some of the provisions of the Finance Act 2008, which was one of the examples highlighted by Lord Judge in his 2010 speech.

- Expanding the scope of your answer to consider the role that executive dominance of the Commons plays in constraining robust scrutiny: although the current administration has a narrow majority, the possibility of an 'elective dictatorship', as described by Lord Hailsham, further reinforces the importance of the upper House.

 Don't be tempted to . . .

- Provide too much description of the background to the tax credits instrument and its rejection in the Lords. The key issue is the government response.

- Spend too much time explaining the structure of the constitution and the meaning of the separation of powers in general terms. Discussion of the doctrine must be focused on the issue of the relationship between Parliament and the executive.

Question 6

'[It] is not enough simply to have a system of law. You have to have access to it when you need it.' (Baroness Hale (2011) Equal access to justice in the big society, The Sir Henry Hodge Memorial Lecture, p. 3, available at http://www.supremecourt.uk/docs/speech_110627.pdf)

With reference to recent constitutional developments, discuss the extent to which the rule of law requires there to be access to justice.

Answer plan

→ Give a definition of the 'rule of law'.

→ Connect the notion of access to justice to the rule of law.

→ Discuss the various ways of understanding 'accessibility' in this context: complexity; funding; or ability to bring a case.

→ Argue that restrictions are justifiable but must be approached with caution.

Diagram plan

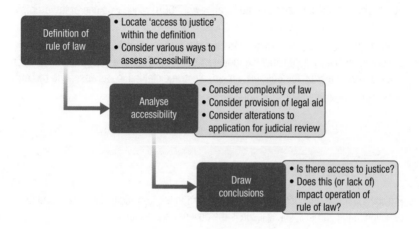

A printable version of this diagram plan is available from **www.pearsoned.co.uk/lawexpressqa**

Answer

Despite the frequency with which the rule of law is invoked, there is limited consensus about what the principle requires, or whether it is particularly evident in the United Kingdom constitution. There does, however, appear to be a general acceptance across the political and theoretical spectrum that accessibility of the law is crucial. There may, however, be different ways to assess this. First, accessibility could be understood as the ease with which laws can be located, and how easy they are for the lay person to understand. Secondly, it is possible to consider the issue by asking whether or not citizens are able to bring the legal issues that concern them for determination in a court. Lastly, it should be considered whether, and to what extent, the state should shoulder the cost of legal advice and representation.

It is arguable that the combination of complex legislation and cuts to legal aid for representation have threatened the operation of the rule of law by limiting access to justice.[1]

Dicey stated that the rule of law has three components. The first is that there should be no punishment without law (the legality principle). The second is that all persons are subject to the law and should be treated equally by the law. Finally, he argued that constitutional principles should be established by the decisions of the courts. It is the second principle that is most relevant here, as Craig has pointed out: 'This formulation is concerned primarily with equal access to the courts, not with the nature of the rules individuals find when they get there'[2] (Craig, 2007). Others, notably Fuller, argue that the rule of law is substantive, and requires that the legal system embodies concepts of natural justice. Raz rejects the idea that the rule of law is associated with any particular moral or political philosophy, making the point that the rule of law is concerned with formal process rather than substantive content. Common ground, however, is that there should be access to the courts, so that it can be seen that access to justice is accepted as being integral to the rule of law.[3]

If justice is to be accessible to all, then citizens must be able to find and understand legal provisions. This proposition would appear to be fairly non-contentious. Most theoretical analyses of the rule of law accept that a primary function of the principle is to allow citizens to understand their rights and responsibilities, and plan their lives accordingly. The practical reality is rather different. The modern legal system is required to deal with a society larger and more complex than Dicey could possibly have envisaged. Consequently, the volume of legislation produced is great. Lord Neuberger is one of several members of the judiciary who have been critical of what he described as a 'welter of ill-conceived legislation – poor in quality and voluminous in quantity'. During the period 1997–2007, statutes created a staggering 3,600 new criminal offences: a crime a day. In 2013, 3,292 statutory instruments were approved. It is difficult to see how it is possible to be certain of legal obligations, rights and remedies when the majority of these provisions receive little publicity. Legal professionals sometimes struggle to keep up, as highlighted by Lord Bingham who cited the case of **R v Chambers** [2008] EWCA Crim 2467[4] (2011, pp. 41–42). The case travelled through the courts until the day before the Court of Appeal gave judgment before any party (lawyers

---

[1] This question is quite complex, as it requires you to define and discuss the meaning of 'access to justice' and then to relate this to the definition of the rule of law. There are a number of different ways in which the answer could be structured. It is useful to give an overview of the approach you will take in your introduction.

[2] It is useful to demonstrate here which aspect of the rule of law will be the primary focus, as this will mean that you do not have to spend unnecessary time dealing with the less relevant aspects of the doctrine.

[3] This paragraph shows familiarity with a range of theorists, but does not become diverted into a lengthy analysis of the differences. The purpose here is to establish the importance of access to justice to the rule of law.

[4] The use of factual information and citation of a particular case shows evidence of wider reading, and helps to make the point far more persuasive. As the question explicitly requires you to consider recent developments, it is important to make sure that you can provide fairly up-to-date examples for each substantive point.

or judges) realised that regulations relevant to the case had been changed in 2001. Ignorance of the law, then, is certainly understandable even if it cannot provide a defence.

The question of the relationship between legal aid and access to justice is politically contentious, and successive governments have attempted to curb expenditure on legal aid. The first significant statutory reduction came with the Access to Justice Act 1999, which removed most monetary claims from the scope of civil legal aid, beginning the proliferation of conditional fee arrangements (CFAs), which are commonly referred to as 'no win, no fee' agreements. Critics of the policy argued that, far from restricting access to the courts, CFAs led to an increase in unmeritorious, and even fraudulent, claims due to the low risks for claimants (see, for example, the *Telegraph* article: Hawkes, Whiplash drives false insurance claims to 1 billion[5]). The Legal Aid, Sentencing and Punishment of Offenders Act 2013 introduced further alteration to the availability of civil legal aid, taking most family, immigration, employment and prison law matters out of the scheme. In addition, section 58 altered the nature of conditional fee arrangements by mandating the deduction of success fees from awards made to claimants.

[5] Students are wary of using media reports in their work, and it is true that such references must be used with caution as they are no substitute for legal or academic authority. This is an example of a permissible use of a newspaper article: it is simply providing evidence of a factual basis for asserting that there has been criticism.

The changes to legal aid have been justified on the basis of the need to reduce the cost to the taxpayer, and to tackle the perceived greed of both claimants and the legal profession.

It should be noted that the availability of legal aid has no bearing on the ability of any person to issue proceedings andthat therefore, in theory, access to the court remains. A person unable to obtain legal representation is free to represent themselves. Critics of restrictions to legal aid point out that this may be realistic. Potential litigants may have a number of vulnerabilities (such as educational level, mental health issues, language barriers or fear) preventing the successful preparation and presentation of a case[6] (Kaufman and Owen, 2013). Genn (2013) notes that the impact assessment produced by government acknowledged that the changes would have a disproportionate effect on women, the disabled and ethnic minorities. This must raise questions concerning the requirement for all citizens to be treated equally by the law.

[6] If you did not provide an academic or statistical reference here, the comment would be easier to disregard as merely a point of view: you must always consider how to incorporate evidence to support your opinion.

Access to justice is necessary to protect the rule of law. It is clear that state aid in civil proceedings is not, in and of itself, the only way to provide access to the courts. When the effect of the removal of legal aid is considered in conjunction with complex and voluminous legislation, however, it can be seen that the individual faces significant challenges in accessing justice. There must be a balance between limiting costs, curtailing vexatious or greedy litigants and maintaining the rule of law.

 Make your answer stand out

- By making the connection between the rule of law and the separation of powers. An independent judiciary operating to consider claims against the executive can be said to demonstrate the role of the separation of powers in protecting the rule of law. Too often, students fail to make links between the different topic areas in the syllabus.
- By staying up to date with developments. There is a growing body of case law and academic comment regarding cuts to legal aid and their legality.
- By making reference to relevant recent case law. *R (Whitson and others)* v *Secretary of State for Justice* [2014] EWHC 3044 (Admin) is a recent example of the courts' approach to executive attempts to restrict the availability of costs in certain types of civil cases.

! Don't be tempted to . . .

- Write generalised statements of opinion without reference to any evidence. This type of question is sometimes attempted by students who are not able to draw upon the work of academics or examples of relevant case law or statutes. This can lead to weak answers that lack specificity.
- Spend too much time explaining the meaning of each part of Dicey's explanation of the rule of law. The temptation, when faced with a question like this, is to treat it as an invitation to simply describe the doctrine: you should attempt this question only if you are confident that you can explain how access to the courts interacts with the rule of law.

Try it yourself

Now take a look at the question below and attempt to answer it. You can check your response against the answer guidance available on the companion website (**www.pearsoned.co.uk/lawexpressqa**).

> Emphasis on the constitutional importance of the rule of law gives undue importance to the judiciary. Discuss.

www.pearsoned.co.uk/lawexpressqa

 Go online to access more revision support, including additional essay and problem questions with diagram plans, and You be the marker questions, to and download all diagrams from the book.

The unwritten sources of constitutional power: prerogative powers and constitutional conventions

2

How this topic may come up in exams

Essay questions are more common in this area. Problems may require you to recognise situations in which particular conventions could apply. There is little case law concerning conventions, and therefore you will need to have a number of illustrative examples to draw on. It is important to be able to discuss a range of academic opinions. You should be able to discuss the relationship between prerogative powers and constitutional conventions and the issues raised following the referendum vote to leave the European Union. This area of the syllabus overlaps with consideration of the separation of powers.

■ Before you begin

It's a good idea to consider the following key themes of the unwritten sources of constitutional power before tackling a question on this topic: prerogative powers and constitutional conventions.

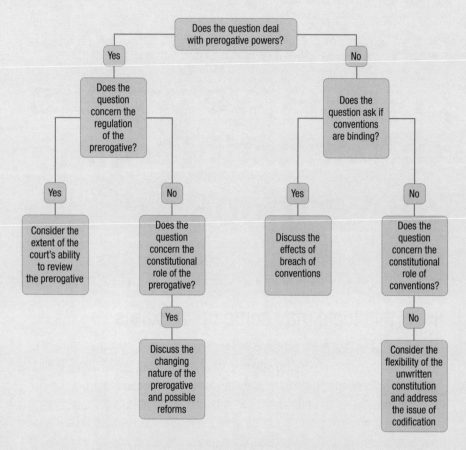

A printable version of this diagram is available from **www.pearsoned.co.uk/lawexpressqa**

 Question 1

'Is it not true that we have found that constitutional conventions that are universally accepted can, arguably, have greater force and staying power than legislation? But surely those conventions, by definition, can apply only if they are universally accepted.' (Viscount Cranbourne: *Hansard* text for 22 February 2000: http://www.parliament.the-stationery-office. co.uk/pa/ld199900/ldhansrd/vo000222/text/00222-08.htm.)

To what extent do constitutional conventions remain an important part of the constitution of the United Kingdom?

Answer plan

→ Outline the definitions of conventions given by Dicey and Jennings.

→ Consider particular conventions and the consequences of their breach.

→ Analyse how particular conventions could be said to lose their force.

→ Consider whether or not some conventions could be codified.

→ Draw some conclusions about the extent to which conventions are binding.

Diagram plan

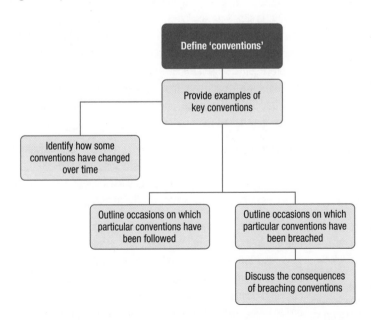

A printable version of this diagram plan is available from **www.pearsoned.co.uk/lawexpressqa**

Answer

The constitution of the United Kingdom is generally described as 'unwritten'. While it is true to say that it is not codified within a single document, much of the constitution can be found in formal, written sources. Conventions are an informal unwritten source of the constitution.[1] The origins and enforceability of conventions are uncertain and, while some may appear to have great force, others will fall away over time. Some would argue that the possibility of evolution and change gives the unwritten constitution the benefit of flexibility and responsiveness. Alternatively, it could be suggested that it is inappropriate for rules governing important areas of conduct in public office to be so poorly defined and without legal sanction.[2]

Dicey defined conventions as habits, understanding and practices that are not enforceable by the courts.[3] Constitutional conventions are perhaps more than simply 'habits', however; as Waldron (1990) points out, they are accepted as rules by those who are bound by them despite the lack of legal enforceability (p. 62). Loveland (2012) suggests that the function of a convention is to 'fill in the gaps' in the constitution (p. 271). It can be hard to determine when a form of conduct is simply an accepted practice, and when it should be considered to be a convention that forms part of the constitution. Jennings (1959a) argued that a convention requires precedent, acceptance of the precedent by the individuals concerned, and a reason for the rule (p. 134).[4] It is clear, then, that a constitutional convention emerges from tradition and practice, and can indeed carry great weight, as a breach may have severe consequences.

Conventions regulate some of the key relationships between individuals working in the various organs of the state and can therefore be said to be of considerable constitutional importance,[5] and yet a cursory examination highlights how the rules are far from fixed.

By convention, the government of the day should be supported by a majority in the House of Commons, and should resign if it is unable to do so.[6] While, for many years, it was assumed that this meant that defeat on any major policy issue would lead to resignation, as Loveland points out, this was consistently ignored from the 1970s onwards; so the rule now appears to be that resignation need follow only the loss of an explicit motion of no confidence.

[1] In order to deal with the issue of conventions, you do need to explain that the constitution is 'unwritten', but you should be as brief as possible.

[2] This question requires an examination of the pros and cons of conventions, so it is helpful to set out the main arguments in the introduction.

[3] Any discussion of conventions must include Dicey's definition as a starting point.

[4] It is a good idea to mention Jennings here as, in addition to Dicey, he is one of the most important theorists who have written about this subject.

[5] You need to be able to explain the function of conventions because the question is asking for an evaluation of their place in the constitution.

[6] A good answer will need to be able to examine how a number of conventions have developed over time. There are many conventions that you could focus on, but, whichever you choose, make sure that you can give some concrete examples to support the argument.

The conduct of ministers in office is largely governed by convention. There are different aspects to this: individual and collective responsibility. The convention of collective responsibility requires all Cabinet Ministers to support government policy once it has been determined, irrespective of their personal views.[7] Numerous examples can be found that demonstrate compliance with the convention, including the resignation of Michael Heseltine over the Westland affair, and, more recently, the resignation of Robin Cook, who was unable to support the Iraq war. Collective responsibility can also be used to illustrate the lack of clarity that surrounds the definition and application of conventions. The rule was suspended by the Labour government in the 1970s, allowing ministers to air their views regarding membership of the European Community, to encourage a public debate. The suspension was temporary, voluntary and limited to a single issue. This perhaps demonstrates the utility of conventions, which allow flexibility in government. It may be acceptable to envisage a rule that can, with agreement from all parties, be lifted. The convention was flouted, seemingly without agreement, by Clare Short, who, like Robin Cook, was opposed to the Iraq war. She spoke out publicly against the war but remained in Cabinet for another two months, which demonstrates that the operation, or otherwise, of the convention appears to depend upon the discretion and preference of the Prime Minister of the day rather than any legal principle.[8]

The convention of individual responsibility holds a minister accountable for conduct while in office, but the requirements of the rule have shifted over time. It no longer appears to be the case that personal 'scandal' will inevitably result in resignation. In the 1990s, newspaper accounts of an affair led to the resignation of Cecil Parkinson, whereas John Prescott remained in office following similar revelations. Perhaps this is indicative of the constitution responding to reflect the shift in attitude of the public at large.[9] However, as numerous commentators have pointed out, the rule has rarely been fixed, and sexual scandal generally leads to resignation only if there are other implications.[10] Parkinson was a member of a government that stressed moral values, but had fathered an illegitimate child; it could be argued that it was this hypocrisy that led to the view that he was unfit for office.[11]

It appears that a minister is still accountable for failings within their department, but this convention is also subject to a variety of interpretations. Hence, although the Prime Minister refused to accept it,

[7] Collective responsibility is a good convention to focus on, as there are so many examples that help illustrate instances where convention is followed, and instances where it appears to have been ignored.

[8] This is a good point to make, as it helps to develop an argument that conventions are governed by political pressure rather than legal principle.

[9] Here, you acknowledge the argument that flexibility of the unwritten constitution is its greatest strength. As this is one of the key points that is made in favour of conventions, it should certainly be mentioned.

[10] The answer is referring again to the argument that political issues are the main issue that determines how a convention will operate in any given circumstance. This is going to be a key part of the conclusions, so it is helpful to keep showing how the examples you choose support this opinion.

[11] You do need to be familiar with the facts of the examples that you choose, so that they can be used to support your argument. Remember, though, that you are using the facts to make a point, so keep it as brief as you can.

William Whitelaw felt compelled to offer his resignation following the discovery of an intruder in Buckingham Palace. Thereafter, ministers appeared to draw a distinction between matters of policy and matters of administration. James Prior refused to resign following a prison escape, on the ground that it did not result from any decisions that he had made.

[12] Rather than simply stating that conventions are important, the answer points to evidence of this by outlining how both government and the judiciary have acknowledged their role.

[13] A good answer will be familiar with a range of academic opinion, and be able to analyse a number of differing academic views.

[14] This is a key point and one that is supported by the examples explored earlier on in the answer.

The precise obligation imposed by a particular convention can be hard to define, and may alter over time and in differing circumstances. The relevance of conventions to the constitution is clear. The Cabinet Office has published guidance on the operation of ministerial responsibility, and the appointment of government. Conventions may not be enforceable in the courts,[12] but they are recognised as an aid to interpretation (see, for example *A-G v Blake (Jonathan Cape, third party)* [1998]). Jaconelli suggested that, while there may be no legal consequence, loss of office occurs so regularly as a result of a breach of convention that it can be considered to be a sanction (Jaconelli (2005)). However, Loveland highlights that it is common for a minister to resign, only to be reinstated a short while later (Cecil Parkinson, David Blunkett and Peter Mandelson, to name but a few). Dewan and Dowding (2005)[13] suggest that ministerial resignation is triggered less by convention than by political expediency, and occurs when it is required to improve public perceptions of government.[14]

It appears that conventions can fall out of use if public or political opinion allows. While this demonstrates the ability of the constitution to adapt to changing times, it is perhaps a concern that these 'vital pillars' (Loveland (2012), p. 261) of the constitution have no legal basis.

✓ Make your answer stand out

■ By exploring the argument that conventions should be codified in more detail. You could note that the Constitutional Reform and Governance Act 2010 has placed the Ponsonby convention on a statutory footing, and consider whether this signifies a move towards codification. An authoritative discussion regarding the benefits and perils of codification can be found in de Smith, S. and Brazier, R. (2008) *Constitutional and Administrative Law* (8th edn). London: Penguin.

■ By noting occasions when conventions have been supported during the process of constitutional reform. You could point to the Sewel convention, which was established during the process of devolving powers to Scotland, or the introduction to the draft House of Lords Reform Bill 2012, in which the Coalition endorsed the preservation of conventions in the second chamber.

■ By considering the relationship between conventions and the prerogative, and emphasising the role that they play in regulating the use of discretionary power. You could comment upon consideration of the prerogative regarding the deployment of armed forces and ask whether or not it is possible to see a new convention that Parliament should be consulted, as this occurred in 2003 and 2013.

! Don't be tempted to . . .

■ List all the conventions that you can remember. It is far better to concentrate on two or three examples, and to spend time exploring how they operate in some detail. Remember that marks are awarded for the ability to analyse the question, rather than simply remember the law.

■ Ignore the need to be able to provide examples to support your argument. This topic can pose difficulties because there is a lack of case law authorities (due to the nature of conventions) and therefore your revision will need to include remembering illustrations from recent political history.

Question 2

The controversy following the referendum vote to leave the European Union highlights the uncertainty that arises from the uncodified constitution.

Discuss.

Answer plan

→ Briefly explain the meaning of 'uncodified'.

→ Outline the background to the *Miller* case.

→ Outline the key issues concerning prerogative powers, the Sewel convention and the European Communities Act 1972.

→ Consider the extent to which codification could have avoided uncertainty.

Diagram plan

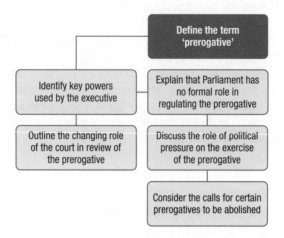

A printable version of this diagram plan is available from **www.pearsoned.co.uk/lawexpressqa**

Answer

[1] Weaker answers would spend too much time describing the constitution. It is important to show an understanding of codification, but to keep this as brief as possible.

The United Kingdom is one of the few states that does not have a codified constitution. This means that there is no single legal source to prescribe and regulate the powers of the institutions of state. Instead, the constitution has evolved over time and is drawn from statute, common law, residual prerogative powers and conventions regulating conduct. It is often argued that the constitution is underpinned by organising principles requiring a separation of powers and adherence to the rule of law, and an acknowledgement of the legislative supremacy of Parliament.[1] The vote to leave the European Union has resulted in litigation questioning the relationship of the legislature and the executive, and arguably demonstrated that the 'unwritten' constitution (prerogative powers and constitutional conventions) creates a lack of certainty.

The European Union Referendum Act 2015 (EURA) allowed the then Prime Minister, David Cameron, to fulfil a manifesto commitment to allow the public to decide whether or not the United Kingdom should remain in the European Union. The electorate voted, by a fairly narrow margin, to leave. That decision has created considerable controversy and resulted in a Supreme Court case to determine whether or not the

² Here, the answer clearly
signals the key points that are
going to be discussed.

² Here, the answer clearly
signals the key points that are
going to be discussed.

³ Given the portrayal of the
case in some media outlets,
it is useful to reassure the
examiner that you understand
this point.

⁴ Whenever you use a phrase
like 'some commentators',
it is important to provide
references to demonstrate
that the statement is based
on evidence.

⁵ Here, the answer has clearly
shown an understanding
of the issues raised by the
prerogative, and there is
no need to provide further
definitions of the prerogative
or general commentary
regarding the status of such
powers in the constitution.

⁶ The facts of the case are
not required here, as it is
simply being used to support
the assertion that the limit
on the prerogative has been
established.

process of withdrawal could be initiated by the executive without the
consent of Parliament. Arguably, the issues that were addressed in
R (Miller) v Secretary of State for Exiting the European Union
[2017] arose from the lack of certainty about the extent of executive and legislative power resulting from the absence of a codified
constitution.²

The case has received a great deal of media attention, but it is important to clarify that the Supreme Court was not being asked to address
the merits of the decision to leave the European Union and there was
no attempt by any of the claimants to overturn the result of the ref-
erendum.³ It has been suggested by some commentators that, given
that EURA was silent on the process that would follow a vote to leave,
the result should be treated as merely advisory (see, for example,
Renwick (2016)).⁴ However, there has been an acknowledgement by
all political parties that the result must be honoured. The legal dispute
concerned the correct process for initiating the withdrawal process.
Article 50 of the Lisbon Treaty 2007 provides that a member state
can give irrevocable notice to withdraw, instigating a two-year period
to negotiate the terms of exit.

The Prime Minister announced the government's intention to trigger
Article 50 by March 2017, using the Crown prerogative to regulate
foreign affairs. The claimants in *Miller* argued that the use of the prerogative in these circumstances would be unlawful, as parliamentary
authorisation was required. All parties to the litigation accepted that
the Crown prerogative allows ministers to enter and withdraw from
treaties.⁵ However, it has long been established that the Crown cannot
use the prerogative to alter the common law to affect the rights of
citizens (**JH Rayner (Mincing Lane) Ltd & others v Department
of Trade and Industry** [1990]).⁶ The central issue, therefore, was
whether or not giving notice of withdrawal would have that effect. To
determine this required consideration of the effect of the European
Communities Act 1972 (ECA) and in particular section 2 of the statute,
which allowed for European law made under the treaties 'from time
to time' to take effect without further domestic legislative enactment.

Lord Neuberger, in the leading judgment, stated that the effect of
section 2 was constitutionally unique, and meant that the European
Union institutions were a separate and overriding source of law.
Commentators have highlighted the seeming inconsistency with the

[7] This is a useful comment to include because it addresses the issue of 'uncertainty' required by the question.

earlier Supreme Court decision in **R (HS2 Action Alliance Ltd) v Secretary of State for Transport** [2014] (see, for example, Edwards (2017)).[7] The dissenting judgment given by Lord Reed rejected the approach and accordingly the suggestion that an Act of Parliament is required. Elliot (2017) has suggested that the majority's reluctance to contemplate that the legislature had intended to authorise ministers to exercise the power to withdraw was, at least in part, influenced by the constitutional significance of the decision.

[8] This aspect of the case is often overlooked, but the issues relating to constitutional conventions are relevant to a question focused on the uncodified constitution.

The second strand of the litigation concerned the role of the devolved institutions in the withdrawal process, and in particular whether or not the consent of the regions is required.[8] The devolution settlements have all expressly preserved the supremacy of the Westminster Parliament. The Sewel convention, however, states that the consent of the regions will normally be sought prior to legislation that will have an impact on them. In the wake of the Scottish independence referendum, the Scotland Act 2016 and the Wales Act 2017 placed the convention into statute. Constitutional conventions were defined by Dicey as habits, understandings or practices that are not legally enforceable. The Supreme Court was unanimous in finding that simply including the convention in the statute did nothing to alter the legal effect: a recognition of the expectation that consultation will normally occur does not amount to a legal requirement that the convention must be followed. There are questions concerning the regions, though that have yet to be addressed. The devolution settlements prohibit the regional assemblies from legislating in contravention of EU law and there will, therefore, need to be a reconsideration of the competencies.[9]

[9] It is important to include this point as part of the argument that the uncertainty created by the 'Brexit' process is likely to continue beyond the *Miller* case.

[10] These 'sound bites' from the judgment are worth including here because they relate directly to the question.

In describing the constitutional background to the case, the court acknowledged that the United Kingdom lacks 'a single coherent code of fundamental law' and instead has evolved in a manner that is 'pragmatic' rather than principled (*Miller* at para 40).[10] It did, however, describe that evolutionary process as one that has been marked by a gradual reduction in the prerogative powers of the Crown in favour of acknowledging the supremacy of Parliament. Viewed from this perspective, then, the reluctance to hold that a minister can make a decision with such significant consequences is unsurprising. The fact that the judges were not able to reach a unanimous decision on the central question is perhaps an indication that the uncodified constitution does indeed create uncertainty, and certainly allows for differing interpretations of the extent of prerogative powers and of parliamentary intentions at the time of passing the ECA. It is also clear that the constitutional uncertainty surrounding the devolved regions is likely to continue during the 'Brexit' process. The benefit of flexibility that the uncodified constitution is said to provide may now be outweighed by the uncertainty that it creates.

✓ Make your answer stand out

■ By ensuring that you stay up to date on this important and rapidly developing area of constitutional law. At the time of writing, there have been media reports that further court actions might be pending and, of course, the process of negotiating terms is likely to prove contentious.

■ By considering the constitutional significance of the case in relation to the issue of parliamentary supremacy. It is worth exploring why the majority considered the Commons vote to be essential, despite the fact that it was clear that the decision to leave the EU was unlikely to be opposed. Arguably, the decision has a significance extending beyond the Brexit process and is part of increasing judicial willingness to challenge executive power.

■ By referring to additional academic comment. When dealing with current legal issues it is important to be able to source reputable and reliable material. Blogs by the UK Constitutional Law Association, the UCL Constitution Unit and Professor Mark Elliott are all good resources.

! Don't be tempted to . . .

■ Treat the question as inviting a general discussion of the merits of the uncodified constitution. You should not attempt this question unless you are comfortable with the legal issues raised by the *Miller* case. Even though it is not explicitly referenced in the question, it would be impossible to provide an answer that ignored the litigation.

■ Provide too much description of the sources of the constitution that were an issue in *Miller*. You do not need to give lengthy definitions of either the prerogative or constitutional conventions, or provide examples of their operation beyond this case.

■ Consider the political impact or likely effect of the decision to vote to leave the EU. You must make sure that you are focused on the constitutional issues that the referendum has raised.

❓ Question 3

The (fictional) government is planning to develop greenfield sites across the north of England in order to manage a housing crisis and stimulate growth in the economy. The matter is included in the Queen's Speech. The Cabinet is torn by a very public row about the plans. In a radio interview, the Minister for the Environment, Gulfraz Khan, declares that the plans are 'ludicrous' and states that his colleagues are making a grave mistake.

He is placed under considerable pressure from colleagues to resign, but he refuses to do so.

A few days later, a scandal erupts when an interview is published with a young woman who claims that she had an affair with Mr Khan while she was a student on a work placement in his constituency office. The media call for his resignation, but he refuses.

The plans for development go ahead, but, within weeks, it is clear that the cost will be several million pounds more than originally thought. The plans drawn up by the Department for Housing contain serious anomalies. During Question Time, the opposition calls for the resignation of the Minister for Housing. He refuses.

A political storm follows over the next few weeks, and numerous MPs demand a vote of no confidence. The vote takes place and the government loses by three votes. The Prime Minister declares that there will be no election.

Discuss.

Answer plan

➜ Outline the role of conventions in the constitution.

➜ Discuss the effect of a breach of the convention of collective Cabinet responsibility.

➜ Consider the differing approaches to ministerial responsibility that may apply in relation to personal, and political, scandal.

➜ Explore the ramifications of failing to comply with the convention regarding a vote of no confidence.

Diagram plan

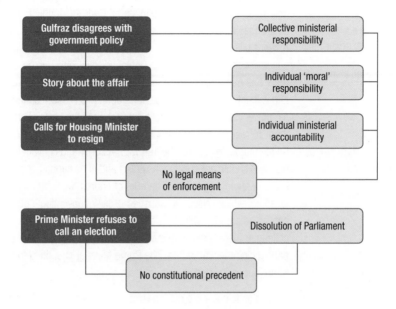

A printable version of this diagram plan is available from **www.pearsoned.co.uk/lawexpressqa**

[1] Before addressing the facts of the scenario, the answer should identify conventions as the subject matter. A brief explanation of constitutional conventions is necessary: Dicey and Jennings are a useful starting point.

[2] You should make reference to the facts of the scenario in your introduction; this reassures the examiner that you are going to be focused on addressing the problem rather than a generalised discussion about conventions. However, don't fall into the trap of writing out all the facts in place of an introduction.

Answer

The United Kingdom is often said to have an unwritten constitution, and there is no single documentary source setting out the roles and responsibilities of the different organs of government. Much of the constitution is now codified, but some of the business of state is regulated by the operation of unwritten conventions. Dicey defined conventions as understandings, habits and practices that are not enforceable by the courts. Jennings (1959a) identified that a key characteristic of a convention is that individuals feel themselves to be bound by it.[1] Arguably, the unwritten nature of this element of the constitution leads to difficulty in identifying the precise requirements of a convention. Further, conventions may change over time. The events that occur in relation to the development plans are governed by various constitutional conventions.[2] The requirements of each will be considered, and the ramifications of breaching the conventions will be assessed.

The relationship between Cabinet Ministers is not prescribed by law, but instead is regulated by conventions. These have, to a degree, now been formalised in the Ministerial Code of Conduct published by the Cabinet Office. By convention, the Cabinet exercises collective responsibility and presents a unified approach to policy. Any differences of opinion can be aired in Cabinet discussions, but, once agreement has been reached, all ministers will publicly support the policy and will not speak or vote against it.[3] Jennings (1959b) stated that, if a minister cannot express public support, then the convention obliges them to resign. In 2003, Robin Cook resigned from the Cabinet as he felt unable to support the Iraq war. According to convention, then, Mr Khan should not criticise the policy and, if he cannot support it, he should resign his position. There is, of course, no legal requirement to do so, which raises the question of how conventional obligations can be enforced.[4] While Mr Cook did resign his position, his Cabinet colleague Clare Short remained in post for two months after publicly denouncing the war in Iraq. The Prime Minister is entitled to dismiss Khan, but cannot legally require his resignation.[5]

In addition to collective responsibility, by convention, a minister takes individual responsibility for the conduct of all those employed by the department. There has been some suggestion that convention requires a minister to take responsibility for private conduct, and to resign if there is a scandal. Jaconelli (2005) argues that this is not a 'true' convention, as it does not regulate the business of office. If resignations on such grounds did result from the operation of convention rather than political expediency then, arguably, the principle has become less rigid as the moral boundaries of wider society have relaxed. Hence, while David Mellor resigned in the wake of a sex scandal in 1992, 14 years later, John Prescott remained in office despite revelations that he had had an affair. It is, therefore, doubtful that convention requires Mr Khan to resign due to the scandal regarding the student.[6]

It is clear that a convention exists that requires a minister to be accountable for the actions of the department that they head. A House of Commons research paper lists the options available to a minister who is subject to the convention as: inform and explain; apologise;

[3] It is helpful to adopt a simple structure in which the convention is briefly explained and then applied to the facts of the scenario.

[4] The answer should identify the conventions that are engaged and recognise that a key issue is the difficulty when they are ignored.

[5] You must make sure that you keep relating the legal points to the facts of this problem scenario.

[6] You should ensure that you can provide contrasting examples of how conventions have operated in practice. This is because the answer will suggest that it is not possible to be certain how conventions will operate in the scenario, as the nature of, and enforcement of, conventions depends on many factors.

[7] There are many examples that can be used, and few are essential, but the 'Crichel Down affair' is usually cited when discussing ministerial accountability.

[8] Similarly, there are lots of examples to use, but including something fairly recent will show that you can relate your studies to events in the current political world.

[9] The answer should recognise that there is no clear precedent that shows how a minister must behave.

[10] This is a key point, as it is often suggested that conventions are enforced by non-legal pressures.

[11] Although it is difficult to predict the outcome of any issue concerning conventions, you will receive credit for attempting to draw some conclusions based on the analysis of examples considered in the answer.

[12] This is such an important point that it is worth setting out explicitly.

[13] Marks will be given for including relevant, current examples to illustrate the argument, as this shows real understanding of the material.

[14] Unlike the conventions considered in relation to ministers, there are no examples to draw on here. The examiner is asking for (informed) speculation.

take remedial steps; and, lastly, resign. There are many examples of ministerial resignation due to failings in their department, including, famously, Sir Thomas Dugdale, as a result of the 'Crichel Down affair',[7] despite the fact that he had had no personal involvement in the matter. More recently, Estelle Morris resigned as Education Secretary following delays in marking A-level exams.[8] It is also possible to find examples where a minister has resisted calls for resignation.[9] The Secretary of State for Northern Ireland, James Prior, refused to resign in 1983 after 38 convicts escaped from the Maze Prison, on the basis that policy decisions were not the cause of the escape. Michael Howard drew the same distinction between administration and policy when he too declined to resign as Home Secretary in the wake of prison escapes. Analysis of ministerial responses seems to suggest that resignation depends less on the existence of a conventional rule and more on the political support that the individual can command from colleagues and the media.[10] Here, serious financial anomalies do appear to be issues relating to formulation of policy rather than administration, so the minister may well face sustained pressure to resign.[11]

In all the examples concerning the conduct of ministers, it should be stressed that, as conventions are not enforceable by the courts, a refusal to comply carries no legal sanction.[12]

By convention, the Prime Minister should request the dissolution of Parliament and call a general election following a vote of no confidence. This last occurred in 1979, when James Callaghan was defeated by a majority of one. In 2010, the Conservative–Liberal Democrat Coalition government proposed amending the rules to specify that a majority of 55 per cent should be required to force dissolution, but rescinded from that position following considerable opposition.[13] The refusal to request the dissolution of Parliament is a serious breach of convention that has the potential to trigger a constitutional crisis.[14] The power to dissolve Parliament remains within the personal prerogative of the monarch, but, conventionally, this is done at the request of the Prime Minister. The monarch has not interfered in political matters for centuries, since the refusal of Queen Anne to assent to a Bill in the eighteenth century. Bagehot (1963) described

[15] Bagehot's description of the role of the monarch is important and should be included in this discussion of the constitutional position of the Queen.

the role of the monarch as the right to be consulted, to encourage and to warn.[15] There was speculation that, in the event of a hung Parliament, the monarch might be called upon to take a more interventionist approach, but, in the event, the Queen played no part in the political negotiations that followed the election in May 2010. Should the Prime Minister insist on remaining in office without a democratic mandate, this might demand that the monarch play a greater constitutional role. Marshall (2002) argued that the Crown should act as a 'genuine instrument of residual constitutional protection'.[16] The breach of convention by the ministers is not subject to legal sanction but will create considerable political pressure for the individuals concerned. The consequences of refusing to dissolve Parliament are far more serious and might demand unprecedented action by the monarch if political pressure fails.

[16] The assessment of what could occur in this hypothetical situation should be supported by some academic opinion.

[17] You must make sure that you return to the facts of the scenario and summarise your findings.

While convention appears to suggest that Mr Khan should resign, precedents can be found to support his decision to decline to do so. No such precedent exists for the failure to call for the dissolution of Parliament.[17]

 Make your answer stand out

- By providing current examples of the operation of conventions. If you listen to the news, you will certainly be able to find relevant issues. While writing this edition, there was some controversy over the conduct of a special advisor to the then Culture Secretary, Jeremy Hunt. Arguably, Hunt should have been accountable for any misconduct, according to the convention of ministerial responsibility.

- You could refer to political research and guidance on the use of conventions. For example, a Commons research paper is available: Gay, O. and Powell, T. (2004) 'Individual Ministerial Responsibility – Issues and Examples', Research Paper 04/31. The Cabinet Office Manual, published in 2010, included draft guidance on how conventions would operate in the event of a hung Parliament. Use of these kinds of sources can show real confidence, provided that they are related to the legal issues.

- By referring to academic commentary. There is a useful article considering the enforcement of conventions: Barber, N. (2009) Laws and constitutional conventions *Law Quarterly Review* 125 at 194.

! Don't be tempted to . . .

- Explain the relevant conventions without providing examples of how they operate. There is very little case law concerning conventions, but you still need to provide support for any propositions that you make.

- Write a generalised account of the operation of conventions in the constitution. Students who revise the topic by assuming that it will appear as an essay question can be wrong footed by a problem scenario. Ensure that you use the knowledge you have about conventions to draw conclusions about the events described here.

- Ignore the fact that, when dealing with this topic, there are no clear answers. As the answer shows, it is possible to find examples supporting contrasting outcomes here; you will be rewarded for acknowledging this fact.

Question 4

'In a word, the Queen could by prerogative upset all the action of civil government within the government, could disgrace the nation by a bad war or peace, and could, by disbanding our forces, whether land or sea, leave us defenceless against foreign nations.' (Bagehot, W. (1963) *The English Constitution.* London: Fontana)

Discuss the relevance of the prerogative powers held by the monarch to the modern constitution.

Answer plan

→ Define the prerogative, and briefly outline the historical development of the power within the constitution.

→ Outline the powers thought to be personal to the monarch.

→ Discuss the limitations upon those powers created by convention.

→ Analyse hypothetical situations in which it is said that the monarch might play a decisive role.

Diagram plan

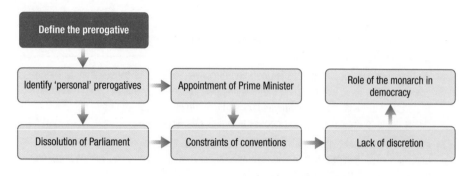

A printable version of this diagram plan is available from **www.pearsoned.co.uk/lawexpressqa**

Answer

[1] Blackstone's definition is usually the starting point for a discussion of the prerogative. If you cannot remember the quote, you do need to make sure that you are able to paraphrase the definition. The key point is that the prerogative is a non-legal power.

[2] This is an important point to make, as the relationship between the two 'non-legal' sources of the constitution needs to be explored.

[3] A strong introduction should signal the direction that the argument is going to take.

[4] It is very important to note that the prerogative is exercised without parliamentary approval, as this emphasises the special constitutional position of the power.

The royal prerogative was defined by Blackstone (1787) as 'that special pre-eminence which the King has, over and above all other persons, and out of the ordinary course of the common law, in right of his royal dignity'.[1] Prerogative powers are still an important source of constitutional power, although few are considered to be within the personal discretion of the monarch. Powers that are personal to the Crown are often constrained by convention to such an extent that it is questionable whether any discretion really exists.[2] Constitutional theorists have hypothesised about situations in which the Queen might be called upon to play a more decisive role in the organisation of the state, but it will be suggested that recent events have demonstrated that the monarch's prerogative is effectively symbolic.[3]

The Bill of Rights of 1689 can be seen as the historical origin of the supremacy of Parliament and, since that point, many of the prerogative powers have been abolished or superseded by statute. Prerogative powers, then, can be described as the residual powers of the state that are not governed by legislation and do not require authorisation by Parliament.[4] They include important matters of governance: the disposition of the armed forces; regulation of the armed forces; the grant of honours; diplomatic relations and making treaties; the appointment of the Prime Minister and the dissolution of Parliament. The majority of powers are now exercisable by the government of the day, acting in the name of the Crown. The Queen retains the personal power to grant certain honours, to assent to Bills passed by Parliament, to appoint the Prime Minister and to dissolve Parliament.

[5] This is an important point to make, as the fact that the monarch does not have a democratic mandate supports the argument that the role is necessarily symbolic.

In a modern democratic state, it would be anachronistic if an unelected monarch were to enjoy free rein to choose the government or to determine the duration of Parliament.[5] The discretion of the monarch is constrained by the operation of constitutional conventions that determine how it will be exercised. The dissolution of Parliament results in a general election, but, by convention, the power is exercised at the request of the Prime Minister.[6] The Crown has not dissolved Parliament on its own initiative since 1835. Dicey (1885) maintained that the power remained and could be exercised in circumstances where the legislature no longer acted in accordance with the 'wishes of the nation' (p. 443). It is, however, almost impossible to imagine a situation in which the monarch could lay greater claim to represent the electorate than the House of Commons. Bagehot (1963) asserted that the possibility of a dissolution instigated by the Crown had 'dropped out of the reality of our constitution' (p. 230), and it is submitted that this is the more tenable argument.[7]

[6] The relationship between the prerogative and conventions is central to the argument, and the answer should be able to provide illustration of how this operates in practice.

[7] A confident approach will be able to include opposing academic arguments, and to draw some conclusions about the merits of the different views.

Bagehot described the constitutional role as to consult, to encourage, and to warn. It would appear that the monarch plays no significant role in taking a political decision. Bradley and Ewing (2010) note that it is recorded that both George V and George VI often insisted on being given the advice of Cabinet in writing if it dealt with contentious issues, suggesting a more active, supervisory, interest in the matters of state (p. 237). More recently, the Queen's private secretary clarified his view that, while the monarch might express opinions to the Prime Minister, ultimately she is bound to act on government advice[8] (*The Times*, 29 July 1986, quoted in Bradley and Ewing (2010)). The monarch has the power to refuse to grant Royal Assent to a Bill, but in practice this has not taken place since 1704. Jennings maintained that George V believed that he had both a legal and a constitutional right to refuse assent but recognised that, were this to occur, this would inevitably result in the dissolution of Parliament and an election contested largely on the issue of the extent of royal power.

[8] As there is little case law in this area, the use of examples to illustrate the points made shows a good grasp of the material.

[9] Here, the answer returns to the central argument: that conventions mean that the personal prerogative of the monarch has little real effect.

The monarch is also empowered to appoint a Prime Minister. Again, this should not be misconstrued as conferring freedom of choice upon the Queen. By convention, the monarch will always appoint the person most able to command a majority in the House of Commons.[9] In the

2 THE UNWRITTEN SOURCES OF CONSTITUTIONAL POWER

'first-past-the-post' electoral system, this is generally straightforward and requires the appointment of the leader of the political party who obtains the most seats at a general election. There has been considerable academic debate about the appropriate course of action that should occur in circumstances where an election does not produce a clear majority for any party, as, in the absence of a written constitution, it could be suggested that the rules are unclear.[10] Bogdanor suggested in 1986 that the situation would raise 'major constitutional questions', although, by 2008, he had resiled from that view and considered the matter to be a purely political issue[11] (cited in House of Commons paper (2010) 'Hung Parliament'). Brazier (1999) felt that the Queen should, in all but the most extreme of circumstances, refrain from involvement in the decision-making process, but did seem prepared to countenance the (albeit remote) possibility that the monarch might need to take action if no political solution could be found. Blackburn (2004) argued that any suggestion that the monarch would have a role to play in the event of a hung Parliament was erroneous and anachronistic.

Prior to the election of 2010, the Cabinet Office published draft guidelines seeking to clarify the position, as the polls suggested that a hung Parliament was likely.[12] It was acknowledged that the monarch would invite the person most likely to be able to command the confidence of the Commons to form a government. It was, however, for the political parties to determine and to clearly communicate to the monarch who that person should be. The guidelines went on to stress that, where a range of possible administrations existed, it would be for the political parties to reach agreement and the monarch would 'not expect' to play a part in deliberations.

In the event, none of the main political parties achieved an overall majority, and negotiations did have to take place to see how a government could be formed. The monarch played no part in negotiations, and appointed the leader of the Coalition government, David Cameron, when asked to do so. This would appear to confirm that, despite academic hypothesising, the exercise of the prerogative power to appoint the Prime Minister is a purely symbolic event.[13] It could conceivably be argued that the extreme position posited by Brazier did not, in fact, arise because the political parties were able to negotiate to form an administration in a relatively short period of time. It is submitted, however, that the matter is now settled, and the guidelines set out in draft will become constitutional practice.[14]

[10] It is important to recognise the range of opinion in this area, and you will need to ensure that you are familiar with the views of at least two academics.

[11] Professor Bogdanor is one of the leading constitutional lawyers, and this is a good point to include, as it demonstrates familiarity with his work.

[12] Reference to these guidelines shows familiarity with the current constitutional position.

[13] It is a fairly commonplace assertion to state that the monarch's constitutional role is symbolic, but can be made more convincing by providing an example.

[14] You will be rewarded for being able to make this kind of assertion, as it shows that you are confident enough with the subject matter to draw your own conclusions.

[15] Here, the answer returns to the suggestion made in the introduction, but, having set out the arguments, a clear and certain conclusion can be articulated.

Perhaps Blackburn (2004) is correct to criticise continued usage of the term 'personal prerogative', as it appears clear that the monarch does not retain any residual powers involving the exercise of discretion. The constitutional relevance of the monarch is now minimal, as the Queen is simply a figurehead of state.[15]

 Make your answer stand out

- Arguably, the publication of Cabinet Office guidance represents a move towards codification of conventions. You could consider whether or not this can be seen as a signal that the 'flexibility' of the constitution is diminishing and the extent of the personal prerogative will become more certain. This would link your answer into broader issues concerning constitutional reform and demonstrate the ability to draw links between different areas of the syllabus.

- By considering some constitutional justifications for reserving the personal prerogative in more detail. You could link this to consideration of the rule of law, and the suggestion that, in the final analysis, the monarch might provide protection against arbitrary government. Again, this shows the confidence to place the discussion into a broader context.

- You could touch upon a more general discussion of royal involvement in the political process and discuss whether or not the exercise of personal prerogatives could be compatible with political neutrality. This would allow you to mention the controversy in 2012 that arose in relation to a journalist's request to see letters sent by Prince Charles to government ministers. The Attorney-General blocked the release, on the ground that neutrality would be undermined. As long as you can ensure that the discussion is relevant to the question, you will be rewarded for being able to draw upon current examples to illustrate your arguments.

! Don't be tempted to . . .

- Make unsupported statements of opinion. This question requires you to use academic viewpoints to support the points that are made. There are, as this answer shows, numerous sources that you can refer to. You must make sure that you are able to refer to a number, and it is advisable to try to reference academics with contrasting views (such as Brazier and Blackburn) because this means that you can provide support for both sides of the argument.

- Discuss the prerogative in general terms. It is crucial that the answer focuses exclusively on the issue of the powers that are said to be personal to the monarch. It is more usual to be asked to consider the use of prerogative powers by the executive. You must make sure that you address the question asked here.

 Question 5

'[C]onventions provide a moral framework within which government Ministers or the Monarch should exercise non-justiciable legal powers.' (Loveland, I. (2012) *Constitutional Law, Administrative Law and Human Rights: A critical introduction* 6th edn. Oxford: Oxford University Press, p. 261)

To what extent do constitutional conventions provide an adequate check on the use of prerogative powers?

Answer plan

→ Explain the meaning of 'conventions' and 'prerogative powers'.

→ Assess the relationship between the two constitutional mechanisms.

→ Describe the alteration to judicial control of the prerogative.

→ Determine whether or not conventions are sufficiently robust.

Diagram plan

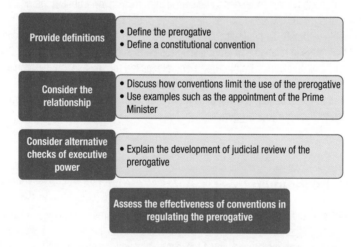

Provide definitions	• Define the prerogative • Define a constitutional convention
Consider the relationship	• Discuss how conventions limit the use of the prerogative • Use examples such as the appointment of the Prime Minister
Consider alternative checks of executive power	• Explain the development of judicial review of the prerogative
Assess the effectiveness of conventions in regulating the prerogative	

A printable version of this diagram plan is available from **www.pearsoned.co.uk/lawexpressqa**

Answer

The United Kingdom constitution is sometimes described as 'unwritten', although, as many sources are in documentary form, 'uncodified' would be more accurate. There are, however, two sources of constitutional power that are unwritten: constitutional conventions and the royal prerogative. Both are products of a constitution characterised by incremental evolution rather than revolutionary change, and it could be argued that conventions have developed to create restraints upon the exercise of the prerogative. Until recently, the use of prerogative powers was not subject to judicial review. Although the list of non-justiciable powers has reduced, conventions still have a role to play in operating a system of checks and balances on the executive.[1]

Dicey defined conventions as 'habits, understandings and practices which . . . are not in reality laws at all since they are not enforced by the Courts'. Conventions regulate the conduct and behaviour of individual members of the institutions of the state. For example, many aspects of ministerial conduct are subject to convention, such as the principle of collective Cabinet responsibility. Once a matter has been decided in debate, the Cabinet should unite behind the agreed policy. Any minister who is unable to do so should resign.[2]

Prerogative powers are areas of executive power that do not originate from statute. Historically, as Blackstone noted, the prerogative belonged to the monarch and denoted 'that special pre-eminence that the King has . . . in right of his royal dignity'. In modern times, although there are some powers that are personal to the monarch, most are exercised by the executive.

The relationship between these two unwritten sources of constitutional power is interesting, because it seems as though many conventions provide guidance as to how the executive powers should be used.[3] The Cabinet, as Loveland notes, 'operates without any appreciable legal structure'[4] (ibid, p. 262), but conventions provide

[1] These two sentences provide a brief outline of the line of argument that is going to be developed.

[2] It is useful to give an example to help explain the kinds of behaviours conventions regulate.

[3] Having provided some definitions, the answer can now refer back to the central issue of the way the two kinds of constitutional power operate in relation to each other.

[4] Using relevant academic references will always improve the quality of an answer. Where the question cites an academic, you should always try to locate and read the source. Here, then, including the relevant quote from Loveland makes it clear to the examiner that this has been done.

the principles under which it operates. The monarch possesses the prerogative to appoint a Prime Minister of her choice, but, by convention, she appoints the leader of the party with a majority in the Commons following an election. Even where there is no majority, the monarch will not exercise discretion, but rather will appoint the leader who emerges from political negotiations (as was shown following the 2010 election).[5]

[5] This is a reasonable point to make, showing how conventions can evolve over time. You do not need to spend long on this, however, as you need to focus on the relationship between the two sources of the constitution.

The importance of the regulatory nature of conventions has diminished, for two key reasons. First, there have been a number of legislative measures that have placed particular prerogative powers and conventions on to a statutory footing (such as the Fixed Term Parliament Act 2011, or the Constitutional Reform and Governance Act 2010). Secondly, the decision of the House of Lords in *Council of Civil Service Unions* v *Minister for the Civil Service* [1985] (the GCHQ case) asserted, for the first time, the courts' power to review the use of the prerogative.[6] Consequently, conventions have less of a role to play.

[6] You do not have time to waste setting out all of the facts and legal issues of this case, and there is no advantage in doing so as long as the relevance of the judgment is made clear.

The GCHQ case marked a moment of constitutional change by asserting the right of the judiciary to scrutinise the legality of the use of executive powers. However, the court held that certain areas of policy (including matters of national security, foreign affairs and the disposition of the armed forces) were non-justiciable and the proper preserve of the executive. It was the nature of the decision being made that was determinative, rather than the source of the power. The case was followed by others that gradually eroded the list of non-justiciable matters: for example, in the case of *R* v *Secretary of State of the Home Department ex-parte Bentley* [1994] the court reviewed the exercise of the prerogative of mercy. Nevertheless, it remains the case that the judiciary will still defer to the executive in areas such as diplomatic relations, the deployment of armed forces and national security (see, for example, *CND* v *Prime Minister of the United Kingdom* [2002][7]).

[7] It is critical that authority is provided to support the statement about the law here, but, again, there is no need to provide detail about the cases.

Where the exercise of the prerogative falls outside of the area of review claimed by the courts, then it could be said that the operation of constitutional conventions continues to be important in setting limitations upon behaviour. It can also be said that the flexible nature of conventions has the advantage of allowing for new guidelines to develop to meet the needs of a changing political landscape. A clear

[8] When dealing with this topic, you will have fewer cases to use and will need to keep up to date with current affairs to find the evidence to support your points.

example is the exercise of the prerogative to declare war. There have been four private members' Bills since 1997, attempting to bring the power under statutory control, but these have failed to win the support of government. Arguably, however, a convention that the executive will not exercise the power without the approval of Parliament has emerged. Tony Blair sought legislative approval for military action in Iraq in 2003, and in 2014 the Coalition appeared to accept that intervention in Syria required a vote in Parliament.[8]

[9] This sentence directly engages with the question asked, and acknowledges the complexity of the argument.

The effectiveness of conventions in acting as a constitutional brake on power is debatable.[9] Of course, the key concern is that conventions can exert only political or moral pressure on the executive. If this is ineffective, there is no possibility of legal enforcement. There have been a number of instances where ministers have chosen not to resign in circumstances where convention suggests that they should: Clare Short, for example, chose to remain in Cabinet despite publicly disagreeing with the decision to declare war on Iraq in 2003.

[10] The use of two examples here reinforces the validity of the point being made.

More recently, the First Minister of Wales, Carwyn Jones, expressed concern that it was not satisfactory to leave aspects of the devolutionary settlement on a conventional basis, as this left open the possibility that Westminster could choose to flout it (*The Independent*, 26/12/2013[10]).

Elliott suggested that formalising the relationship between the central and devolved institutions would undermine the 'implicit trust' created through the use of conventions. The moral and political weight of conventions is difficult to resist. Clare Short did, after all, resign her position some months later, and there have been no instances where Westminster has legislated on matters that have been devolved.[11] Despite the lack of legal redress, the executive recognises the force of constitutional convention in many instances, even if it is primarily motivated by the thought of the ballot box rather than by moral imperatives.

[11] Using the same factual examples here demonstrates how easily an argument can be made on either side of the debate.

[12] Here, the answer refers back to the quote from Loveland given in the title, to make the link between morality and regulation in respect of conventions.

Unless and until all prerogative powers are abolished, it appears that conventions will have a role to play in regulating their use. It is perhaps possible that legislation would provide more formal and robust means of dealing with unconstitutional conduct, but it should be remembered that legal redress would be available only after the fact. The moral framework that conventions provide operates as a means of prior restraint and therefore can exert influence over the use of the prerogative.[12]

Make your answer stand out

■ By incorporating additional academic commentary. A useful reference is Qvortrop, M. (ed.) (2013) *The British Constitution: Continuity and Change – A Festchrift for Vernon Bognador*. Oxford: Hart. This collection of essays covers a variety of issues, but the most relevant chapters here would be those by Feldman, Jaconelli and Blackburn.

■ By expanding the discussion of the changing nature of the constitution and the increasing trend towards codification and the removal of unwritten powers.

■ By spending more time considering the role of political, rather than legal, coercion. How does the continued reliance on 'moral' imperatives governing constitutional conduct fit with a formalistic view of the role of law in society such as that outlined by Raz?

! Don't be tempted to . . .

■ Set out lists of prerogative powers and constitutional conventions. There are no marks for simply showing the ability to itemise these. You must be clear about identifying examples that allow you to discuss the interrelationship between the exercise of a prerogative and the operation of a convention.

■ Answer this question as though it were asking you to explain how conventions and the prerogative have developed and changed over time. This will be too descriptive, and will not contain enough analysis of how they are used in conjunction with each other.

 Try it yourself

Now take a look at the question below and attempt to answer it. You can check your response against the answer guidance available on the companion website (**www.pearsoned.co.uk/lawexpressqa**).

Conventions are meaningless without a method of enforcement. Discuss.

---

www.pearsoned.co.uk/lawexpressqa

 Go online to access more revision support, including additional essay and problem questions with diagram plans, and You be the marker questions, and to download all diagrams from the book.

Parliamentary supremacy

3

How this topic may come up in exams

Examiners will expect students to be able to assess the relevance of the doctrine of parliamentary supremacy in the modern constitution. This will require you to be able to explain clearly the traditional model outlined by Dicey. Questions could focus on specific issues that impact on the role of Parliament: devolution, the role of the European Convention on Human Rights and, of course, the European Union. If you are asked the question in more general terms, you will have to be selective in the areas that you choose to discuss. You could also be asked to discuss the theoretical discussions regarding the nature of parliamentary supremacy itself, notably the 'manner and form' argument.

■ Before you begin

It's a good idea to consider the following key themes of parliamentary supremacy before tackling a question on this topic.

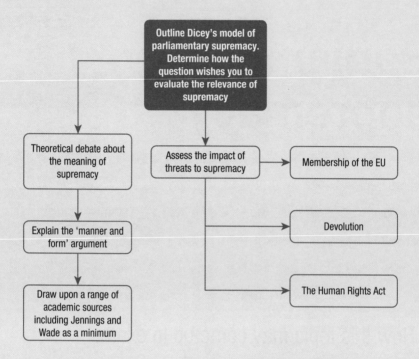

A printable version of this diagram is available from **www.pearsoned.co.uk/lawexpressqa**

 Question 1

'Parliament agreed to join the EU by exercising sovereign powers untrammelled by EU law and I think it would expect to be able to leave the EU in the exercise of the same untrammelled sovereign power.' (*R (Shindler)* v *Chancellor of the Duchy of Lancaster* [2016] 3 WLR 1196 (Lord Dyson MR para 58))

Discuss the constitutional implications of the litigation concerning Britain's exit from the European Union.

Answer plan

→ Outline in brief the factual background to the *Miller* case.

→ Explain the prerogative power of foreign affairs.

→ Identify the contrasting approaches to the effect of the European Communities Act 1972.

→ Assess the significance of the decision on parliamentary supremacy.

Diagram plan

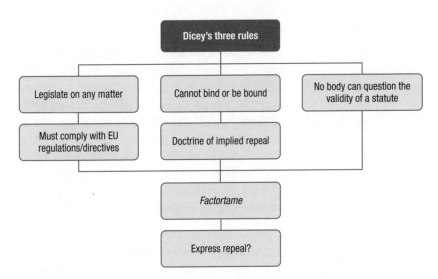

A printable version of this diagram plan is available from **www.pearsoned.co.uk/lawexpressqa**

Answer

The Supreme Court decision in the case of *R (Miller)* v *Secretary of State for Exiting the European Union* [2017] UKSC 5 has been described as 'the most important constitutional case the UKSC has ever heard' (Murkens, 2017). The case generated an unprecedented amount of public interest and media coverage, largely because of the politically controversial vote in the 2016 referendum in favour of the UK's leaving the European Union. It is important to note that the case was not concerned with the merits of that decision, but instead focused on the correct procedure required by the United Kingdom constitution.[1] The issue is complicated by the fact that the constitution is uncodified, and, as a result, the extent of the unwritten prerogative power of the Crown is uncertain. The Supreme Court was required to consider the constitutional effect of the European Communities Act 1972 (ECA) and the status of European Union law in domestic law.[2] Although the case also addressed the role of the devolved administrations in the Brexit process, this discussion will focus on the issues of the constitutional relationship between Parliament and the executive branch of the state.[3]

The United Kingdom's membership of the European Union has long been a politically divisive issue and, following a manifesto commitment from the Conservative government, the European Union Referendum Act 2015 made provision for a public vote. On 23 June 2016, the referendum was duly held and resulted in a narrow victory for 'leave' campaigners who, obtained 52 per cent of the vote. As an immediate consequence of the decision, David Cameron resigned his position as Prime Minister and, following a short leadership contest, Theresa May took office and pledged that the government would begin the formal procedure for exiting the European Union in March 2017.[4]

The constitution of the European Union is contained in a series of treaties prescribing the powers of the institutions and the relationship between the EU and member states. Article 50 of the Lisbon Treaty 2007 specifies the process required to withdraw from the Union, indicating that once irrevocable notice of an intention to leave is given, a period of two years will be available in which to negotiate on the terms necessary to extricate a member state from existing Treaty obligations and agree terms for its future relationship with the EU. The controversy

[1] As the topic of 'Brexit' is so political, it is useful to be clear from the outset that you understand the distinction between the controversy surrounding the referendum result and the legal issues.

[2] It is a good idea to state the constitutional issues briefly, as it reassures your examiner that you have understood the question.

[3] Students sometimes think that they need to discuss every aspect of the case; it is perfectly acceptable to limit the parameters of the answer, as long as this is explained in the introduction.

[4] Take care not to spend too long explaining the background to the litigation. Here, the answer deals with the history as briefly as possible, but reaches the important point concerning the executive pledge to trigger Article 50 within a set timeframe.

since the UK referendum decision has resulted from a dispute over whether or not the government was entitled to 'trigger' Article 50 without parliamentary approval.

⁵ This is an important point. Often, the case is wrongly explained as being about the extent of the prerogative: it is in fact about the correct statutory interpretation of the European Communities Act 1972.

⁶ You need to explain some key issues about the prerogative relevant to the case, and the question of whether or not the ECA alters legal rights is significant only because of the limit this places on the prerogative.

The executive branch of the state has a prerogative power that entitles the government to manage foreign affairs, which includes making and withdrawing from treaties. This was not a matter that was disputed in the litigation.⁵ Prerogative powers are residual; since the Bill of Rights 1688 it has been accepted that if Parliament legislates on a matter that had previously been the prerogative of the Crown, the power is extinguished. For example, the prerogative power to regulate the Civil Service was abolished by the Constitutional Reform and Governance Act 2010. The privileged status of statutory provisions is confirmation of the supremacy of Parliament. It has also been accepted, since the **Case of Proclamations** [1610] EWHC KB J22, that the Crown cannot use a prerogative power to change the common law.⁶ In the case **JH Rayner (Mincing Lane) Ltd & Others v Department of Trade and Industry** [1990] 2 AC 418, the Supreme Court confirmed that, while the prerogative authorises the Crown to enter and withdraw from treaties, it 'does not extend to altering the law or conferring rights upon individuals or depriving individuals of rights which they enjoy in domestic law without the intervention of Parliament'.

⁷ This is such an important point that it is worth reiterating.

Treaty law is not part of domestic law and therefore it would theoretically be possible for the Crown to withdraw from a treaty without contradicting the principle expressed in **JH Rayner**.⁷

Miller argued that the decision to trigger Article 50 would inevitably result in a process that would remove rights enjoyed by citizens in domestic law. The EU has conferred rights on UK citizens, some of which could (and in many cases will) be reinstated by Parliament following Brexit, but also some that are entirely contingent on either the co-operation of remaining member states (such as freedom of movement) or on the right to vote in European parliamentary elections, which cannot continue. The central question, then, concerned the correct interpretation that should be applied to the European Communities Act 1972. Section 2 of the 1972 Act provides that all 'such rights, powers, liabilities and restrictions from time to time created or arising by or under the Treaties . . . are without further enactment to be given legal effect or used in the United Kingdom'.⁸

⁸ Try to avoid talking about legislation in broad, general terms. You should try, where possible, to be precise about the part of the statute in issue.

[9] Students often overlook the significance of dissenting judgments: the fact that three Supreme Court judges did not agree with the ruling makes it clear that the issues are capable of competing interpretation.

The dissenting judgment given by Lord Reed[9] (which the other two dissenting judges approved) argued that the effect of the ECA was 'inherently conditional on the application of the EU Treaties' and 'imposes no requirement and manifests no intention, in respect of the UK's membership of the EU *(R (Miller)* v *Secretary of State* for Exiting the European Union [2017] 2 WLR 583)'. In his view, then, Parliament had not removed or altered the extent of the Crown's prerogative to withdraw from the EU treaties, and an Act was not required.

[10] Reference here to academic opinion shows an ability to engage in critical analysis.

Elliot has suggested that the approach of Lord Reed has considerable force, and that the approach of the majority can in large part be explained by the 'unique' constitutional significance of withdrawal.[10]

The majority found that the ECA had introduced a new process of law making into the UK, and acknowledged the European Union as being a source of domestic law. Lord Neuberger stressed that this was constitutionally unprecedented, in that it created a new source of law that could override domestic legislation (as evidenced in *R* v *Secretary of State for Transport ex parte Factortame Ltd (No. 2)* [1991] 1 AC 603). It had been acknowledged in *Thoburn* v *Sunderland City Council* [2002] EWHC 195 that the ECA could not be overruled impliedly. The majority rejected the suggestion that the fact that the ECA was silent on the issue of withdrawal meant that Parliament had intended to preserve the ministerial prerogative:

> On the contrary: we consider that, by the 1972 Act, Parliament endorsed and gave effect to the UK's membership of what is now the EU under the EU Treaties in a ways which is inconsistent with the future exercise by ministers of any prerogative power to withdraw from such Treaties. (*Miller*, per Lord Neuberger, para 77)

[11] Here, the answer directly addresses the question by summarising the constitutional importance of the case.

Those who voted in favour of remaining in the EU could be disappointed by the Supreme Court decision in *Miller*, as it is clear that the ruling will not alter the decision to withdraw or have any direct impact on the conduct or content of the negotiations about the terms of that withdrawal. The constitutional significance is clear, however. The Supreme Court has reinforced the facts that parliamentary supremacy is, as Dicey said, 'the cornerstone' of the constitution and that the executive does not have the power to change the shape of the constitution without legislative consent.[11]

Make your answer stand out

■ By exploring in more detail the analysis of section 2 of the ECA undertaken in the case. In particular, both the leading judgment and the dissenting judgment of Lord Reed discussed the interpretation of the words 'from time to time'.

■ By including reference to more of the academic discussions of the case. When dealing with current and contentious issues of law, the UK Constitutional Law Association blog (https://ukconstitutionallaw.org/blog/) is a useful resource. In fact, the Supreme Court judges in *Miller* referred to some of the arguments posted here in advance of the hearing.

! Don't be tempted to . . .

■ Treat the question as an invitation to discuss parliamentary supremacy in detail. Weaker students will fall into the trap of setting out in detail the general principles set out by Dicey.

■ Attempt to discuss the merits of the relationship between the EU and domestic law. There is no need, here, to discuss the development of case law since the ECA or to assess the extent to which membership limited supremacy.

Question 2

Since the Human Rights Act 1998, the balance of power has shifted so that it is the judges who are sovereign, rather than Westminster.

Discuss.

Answer plan

→ Outline Dicey's traditional analysis of parliamentary sovereignty and the role of the courts.

→ Assess the effect of section 3 of the Human Rights Act 1998 (HRA) on the powers of the judiciary.

→ Assess the effect of section 4 of the HRA on the powers of the judiciary.

→ Consider whether the HRA has significantly altered the relationship between the two institutions of state.

Diagram plan

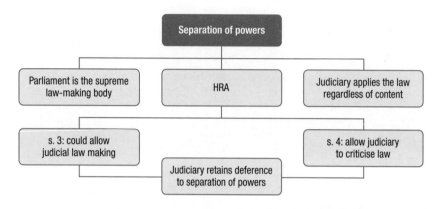

A printable version of this diagram plan is available from **www.pearsoned.co.uk/lawexpressqa**

Answer

[1] The respective constitutional roles of the legislature and the judiciary are central to the answer, and so the introduction should briefly set out the traditional position.

[2] Setting out the central argument about the effect of the HRA in the introduction will give the essay some shape, as the major points can refer back to this statement.

[3] This question requires demonstration of an understanding of the doctrine, but it is not the main focus. Therefore, the definition should be set out as succinctly as possible.

It is commonly understood that Parliament occupies a position of supremacy within the United Kingdom. Dicey described parliamentary supremacy as a 'cornerstone' of the constitution. Under the doctrine of the separation of powers, Parliament has the authority to legislate, and the judiciary applies the law in accordance with Parliament's wishes.[1] The Human Rights Act 1998 (HRA) imposed new obligations on Parliament when creating legislation, and granted the judiciary new powers to interpret and challenge legislation. It is sometimes suggested that this has led to a shift in the constitutional balance; however, it will be argued that the Act has not signalled any significant change.[2]

In considering Parliament's role in the wake of the HRA, it is helpful to begin by considering the traditional doctrine of parliamentary supremacy. Dicey described three constituent elements. First, Parliament is the supreme law-making body, free to make or unmake legislation on any subject matter. Secondly, each successive Parliament is sovereign; no Parliament can be bound by its predecessors, or bind its successors. Lastly, no person or body, including the courts, can question the validity of an Act of Parliament.[3] To address the question, it is necessary to consider Parliament's role as the supreme law-making body in the United Kingdom.

The United Kingdom signed the European Convention on Human Rights (ECHR) in 1950, and it has been possible for an individual to petition the European Court of Human Rights (ECtHR) since 1966, allowing a citizen to claim that legislation infringed one or more of their rights under the Convention and to seek redress in Strasbourg. Although the HRA incorporated the Convention into domestic law, it did not confer any new rights upon citizens, but rather created a new 'procedural mechanism' for enforcing those rights[4] (*R v Lambert* [2001] UKHL 37). The question is whether the procedures established by the Act have impacted upon the constitutional relationship between Parliament and the judiciary.

[4] It is important to recognise that the HRA has not granted new rights; citizens were able to enforce rights under the ECHR prior to 2000, although this would involve the laborious process of taking a claim to the ECtHR in Strasbourg.

In deference to the sovereignty of Parliament, the role of the courts is to interpret and apply legislation regardless of its content. Hence, in *R v IRC ex parte Rossminster* [1980] AC 952, the Lords considered powers conferred by the Taxes Management Act 1970 to be a 'breath-taking' inroad upon rights of privacy and property, but nonetheless felt bound to apply the provisions.[5] The HRA gives the courts new powers. Section 3 requires the courts to interpret statutes in a manner compatible with Convention rights 'in so far as it is possible to do so'. If this is not possible, then section 4 gives the courts discretion to make a declaration of incompatibility. Amending legislation can then be laid before Parliament although this is not mandatory (s. 4).[6]

[5] This case provides a clear illustration of the traditional position, in which the judiciary enforced a law that it plainly felt should be changed.

[6] You need to explain sections 3 and 4 because these are the critical sections of the HRA here, as they confer power and responsibilities on the judiciary.

It is the operation of these sections of the HRA that raises questions about the continued supremacy of parliamentary legislation.[7] Shortly after the Act came into force, the courts had occasion to consider the extent of the power conferred by section 3 in the case of *R v A* [2001] UKHL 25. The courts found that provisions in the Youth Justice and Criminal Evidence Act 1999 conflicted with the rights of defendants under Article 6 of the ECHR, and it was held that the statute should be interpreted to give effect to those rights, despite the fact that this conflicted with the clear words of the offending legislation. Lord Steyn felt this was acceptable as section 3 of the HRA allowed for an interpretation that was 'linguistically strained'. In the dissenting judgment, Lord Hope expressed concern that such utilisation of section 3 ran the risk of the judiciary usurping the role of Parliament. If the HRA allows the courts effectively to rewrite legislation, then it is no longer correct to view Parliament as the sole and supreme legislative authority within the constitution.[8]

[7] It is necessary to display a clear understanding of the mechanics of the Act, and how the particular sections have created powers that could be said to undermine supremacy.

[8] This point refers back to the question by directly addressing the effect of the HRA on parliamentary supremacy.

However, the decisions in cases such as **R v A** and **Ghaidan v Godin-Mendoza** [2004] UKHL 30 should be viewed in the context of the general development of jurisprudence in the wake of the HRA. Lord Steyn felt that section 4 should be used as a 'last resort', but the courts have tended to resile from using section 3 to make radical alterations to statute. In **Re S (Minors)** [2002] UKHL 10, while not directly criticising the decision in **R v A**, the judgment cautioned the judiciary against use of interpretative powers being used 'inadvertently' to stray from its constitutional role into making legislation. In **Wilson v First County Trust Ltd** [2003] UKHL 40, the Court of Appeal refused to impose upon the words of statute a 'meaning which they cannot bear', preferring to make a declaration of incompatibility under section 4. Indeed, despite Lord Steyn's view, it seems that the courts have tended to defer to Parliament where there is conflict, and to invoke section 4 more frequently than he envisaged.

[9] Section 4 can be viewed as undermining supremacy by allowing the courts to declare an Act of Parliament incompatible, but you should recognise that this is less radical than it may at first appear, as the courts cannot disregard legislation.

[10] The case of *A* v *UK* is generally used to highlight the increasing power of the judiciary to challenge Parliament; here, you show a detailed knowledge of the authority and should be rewarded for using the case to make a different point.

[11] This is reiterating the point made in the introduction, giving coherence to the answer.

A declaration of incompatibility does not undermine the legislative authority of Parliament. Section 4 makes it clear that making a declaration has no effect on the parties in the case, as the legislation remains in force unless and until Parliament chooses to amend or revoke it.[9] In **A v Secretary of State for the Home Department** [2004] UKHL 56, a declaration was made in respect of the provisions in the Anti-Terrorism, Crime and Security Act 2001 allowing for the indefinite detention without trial of foreign nationals. Nonetheless, the individuals concerned remained in custody until the Act was repealed by the Prevention of Terrorism Act 2005.[10]

If it is accepted that, where the wording of statute is unambiguous, the courts prefer to use section 4 rather than to attempt an interpretation using section 3, then it is difficult to maintain that the HRA has resulted in a seismic shift in the constitutional balance of power.[11] It seems that the judiciary maintains a position of deference to the sovereign power of Parliament.

Make your answer stand out

- By addressing the argument that the Human Rights Act is a 'statute of constitutional significance' that arguably leads to partial entrenchment. This could be used to suggest that the effect has been to entrench the increased powers of the judiciary, therefore undermining the role of Parliament.
- By referring to the number of cases that still fall to be resolved at Strasbourg, which suggests that the domestic judiciary still defer to Parliament to a large extent. A fairly recent example would be *Gillan and Quinton* v *United Kingdom* [2009] ECHR 28, in which the ECtHR held that section 44 of the Terrorism Act 2000 breached Convention rights, overturning the decision of the House of Lords.
- By discussing the efforts of the Coalition to encourage greater subsidiarity, with reference to the Brighton Declaration of 2012 (http://hub.coe.int/20120419-brighton-declaration).
- You could consider the issue of prisoner voting and the resulting conflict between the will of Parliament and the ECtHR.

 Don't be tempted to . . .

- Make general points about the Human Rights Act (HRA). The question requires you specifically to address the impact of the legislation on the judiciary, so you need to be clear about identifying that section 3 and section 4 are the most relevant.
- Fail to provide evidence of how the courts use their powers. To do well in this question, you will need to be able to use case law effectively to illustrate how the HRA has taken effect.
- Ignore the fact that there are different views that can be taken about the effect of the HRA. You should be able to provide examples of the courts appearing to use the HRA to challenge legislative authority (*R* v *A*) but you will be rewarded if you also provide instances of continuing judicial deference.

Question 3

'If Parliament can do anything, there is no reason why Parliament should not decide to redesign itself, either in general or for a particular purpose.' (Baroness Hale in *R (Jackson)* v *Attorney General* [2006] 1 AC 262 at para 160)

To what extent do you accept the 'manner and form' theory of parliamentary sovereignty?

Answer plan

→ Briefly set out Dicey's view and explain the focus on implied repeal.

→ Outline Jennings' (1959a) argument regarding the rule of recognition.

→ Consider the counter-arguments of Wade (1955).

→ Discuss the effect of the *Jackson* case.

→ Assess whether or not sovereignty is now limited.

Diagram plan

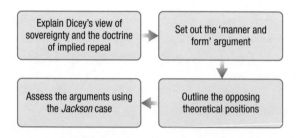

A printable version of this diagram plan is available from **www.pearsoned.co.uk/lawexpressqa**

Answer

[1] Even though Dicey is not mentioned in the question, his view is a good starting point for any assessment of parliamentary supremacy.

The traditional view of parliamentary sovereignty is drawn from the work of Dicey, who saw a legislature able to operate without limits as being the 'cornerstone' of the UK constitution.[1] According to his interpretation of sovereignty, courts will defer to the will of Parliament in applying its Acts, regardless of the subject matter. It is irrelevant that the application of a particular statute will result in injustice, as Parliament can amend or repeal it if it wishes. Crucially, Dicey claimed that no Parliament can be bound by the acts of a predecessor, nor bind a successor, which gives rise to the doctrine of implied repeal.[2] No statute is entrenched, as any can be repealed without the need for specific procedure to protect Acts concerning the constitution. This, it is said, gives the UK constitution a unique flexibility.

[2] The 'manner and form' argument can be understood as a challenge to Dicey's view of supremacy, but <u>it is focused specifically upon the doctrine of implied repeal,</u> so it is helpful to make it clear that your answer will concentrate on this aspect of supremacy.

More than a century after Dicey's analysis, the legal supremacy of Parliament is far less certain. Devolution, membership of the European Union and the incorporation of the European Convention on Human Rights into domestic law can all be cited as evidence of other

[3] The 'manner and form' argument is complex. You can demonstrate your understanding of this difficult area by making sure that you can provide a short, clear explanation.

[4] By referencing the quote in this way, you make it absolutely clear that you have understood the implication of the words Baroness Hale used for the doctrine of implied repeal.

[5] One of the difficulties with this question is that, in order to understand the 'manner and form' argument, a number of issues must be explained. Make sure that you know how to explain this view of sovereignty.

[6] Students are sometimes cautious about referencing the views of numerous academics in their work because they feel that it then looks as if they are not able to think for themselves. When answering this kind of discursive question, this perception is completely wrong. Marks will be awarded to students who demonstrate familiarity with a number of academics and who are able to analyse a variety of arguments.

[7] You must refer to Jennings in your answer, as the 'manner and form' argument is drawn mainly from his work.

[8] Again, these are complicated arguments, so make sure that, before you enter the exam room, you have considered how you are going to articulate them clearly.

institutions encroaching upon the legislative freedom of Parliament. The 'manner and form' theory suggests that, in the modern constitution, Parliament can in fact be bound and a number of statutes are, at least partially, entrenched.[3]

There is an internal contradiction inherent in the doctrine of parliamentary sovereignty. If Parliament is supreme, then, logically, any given Parliament should be able to bind a successor – to 'redesign' itself as Baroness Hale states.[4] By the same token, how can any single Parliament claim sovereignty if it is bound by the actions of a predecessor? Hart's suggestion for resolving this conflict was to acknowledge a distinction between 'self-embracing' and 'continuing' sovereignty.[5] Dicey described a form of continuing sovereignty: each time Parliament convenes it is a new, sovereign institution, free from any limitations, including those created by a previous Parliament. A 'self-embracing' concept of sovereignty, Hart explained, would mean that Parliament is seen as possessing a self-limiting power enabling it to pass laws to alter the way it would operate in the future (Hart, 1994, p. 149). This theory sees 'Parliament' as one single entity, regardless of how many times it dissolves and reconvenes.

Loveland points out that there is little,[6] if any, academic support for the suggestion that there can be entrenchment of any substantive law. He argues that the position in respect of legislation affecting the parliamentary process can be distinguished and considerable support can be found for the 'manner and form' arguments here, with the work of Jennings being foremost (Loveland, 2012, p. 35).[7] Jennings argues that while Dicey was correct to state that there are no limitations on the subject matter that can be addressed by legislation, the doctrine of implied repeal is open to challenge. He acknowledges that the courts will defer to Parliament, but states that as the rule of recognition is a common-law concept and that statute is legally superior, a statute must be able to change the rule of recognition and protect some acts from implied repeal.[8] There does seem to be great logical force to his suggestion that 'its power to change the law includes the power to change the law affecting itself' (Jennings, 1959a, p. 149).

Adherents to the 'manner and form' argument, then, maintain that Parliament is able to entrench statutes that alter its own composition or the law-making process. While we may point to examples such as the Reform Act of 1832, or the Acts of Union, these do not provide

[9] It is important to note the distinction between political and legal possibilities, as this is one of the strongest counter-arguments to the 'manner and form' argument.

[10] The facts of these cases are rather complicated, but there is no need to give any details, as long as you show that you know why ex-colonies are in a peculiar position.

irrefutable support because, arguably, while there may be strong political constraints to consider, there is no legal reason[9] why the franchise could not be withdrawn or the union dissolved. Jennings pointed to three cases in support of his position: *Attorney-General for New South Wales* v *Trethowan* (1931) 44 CLR 394, *Harris* v *Donges (Minister of the Interior)* (1952) 1 TLR 1245 and *Bribery Commissioner* v *Ranasinghe* [1965] AC 172. Each of these cases concerned countries that had previously been British colonies.[10] In each instance, a parliamentary attempt to alter an aspect of the constitution was overruled by the court. The problem with taking these as evidence that constitutional statutes enjoy special protection is that the constitution of each territory was created by the UK Parliament, which continued to exist as a source of 'higher' law.

Wade (1955) argues that the 'manner and form' argument was wrong and that the traditional position was more logical. He maintains that the supremacy of the legislature is self-evident: the rules setting out what constitutes an Act of Parliament are 'a political fact' that cannot be altered by any legal authority – whether by Parliament itself or the courts. Wade does accept that change could be envisaged, but that this would require a revolution and could not be achieved by Parliament. In later years, faced with the reality of the European Communities Act 1972 and in the wake of the *Factortame* legislation, Wade (1996) suggests that there has been a 'technical revolution', which implies acceptance of the 'manner and form' argument.[11]

[11] Always remember the question that you are being asked and ensure that you show how the points you make help reach a conclusion. The main reason for discussing Wade is to show how academic theory appears to have shifted towards acceptance of the argument.

[12] As the question quotes from this case, you cannot avoid discussing the judgment. It was very complicated, so, again, make sure that you are able to set out the key issue succinctly.

The most potent support for the 'manner and form' argument, arguably, is found in the judgment of *Jackson* v *Attorney General* [2005] UKHL 56.[12] The House of Lords considered the argument that the Hunting Act 2004 was invalid, as it was made using the procedure set out in the Parliament Act 1949. The contention was that the 1949 Act was itself invalid, as it was an ultra vires use of the Parliament Act 1911. It was argued that the 1911 Act had granted the Commons the power to make only delegated legislation and certainly did not authorise the use of the Act to extend its legislative competence. The 1911 legislation did not alter the fact that an Act of Parliament requires the consent of the Commons, the Lords and the Queen, and so the 1949 Act could not be lawful. The House of Lords rejected this claim and accepted that the 1911 Act had created a new procedure for making an Act of Parliament.

The judgments in **Jackson** demonstrate a degree of judicial accept-ance of the 'manner and form' argument, although it was directly ref-erenced by only Lords Steyn and Hope. Parliament may have always been constrained by political reality, but the case seems to demon-strate that Jennings' analysis was correct and the constitution has evolved to include some legal limitations on sovereignty.[13]

[13] Do not forget to return to the question and to provide a direct answer in your conclusion.

✓ Make your answer stand out

- By including reference to a wider range of academic theorists. This is a topic that has engendered an enormous amount of debate, so you should read as widely as possible. Additional sources could include: Bradley, A. (2011) The sovereignty of parliament – form or substance?, in J. Jowell and D. Oliver (eds), *The Changing Constitution* (7th edn). Oxford: Oxford University Press; and Elliot, M. (2007) Bicameralism, sovereignty and the unwritten constitution. *Int'l J Const*, 5: 370.

- Consider the judgments in *Jackson* in more detail. The Lords were not in complete agreement in this case, and it would be useful to explore the different approaches adopted in detail.

! Don't be tempted to . . .

- Spend time discussing each of Dicey's three propositions. Students who revise parliamentary supremacy often do so, assuming that any question will require consideration of the orthodox view, and then attempt an answer following that structure.

- Attempt this question without knowing the arguments set out by a reasonable number of academic theorists. Failure to engage with the academic debate will make it impossible for you to obtain high marks.

Question 4

'Now that devolution has allowed the genie of self-government out of the bottle, it would be nigh on politically impossible to put it back in.' (Elliot, M. and Thomas, R. (2014) *Public Law* (2nd edn). Oxford: Oxford University Press, p. 290)

Discuss the impact of devolution on parliamentary supremacy.

Answer plan

→ Define 'devolution' and explain how the devolution settlements attempted to preserve parliamentary supremacy.

→ Describe the growth in devolved powers to the regions, and the independence referendum.

→ Consider the status of the Sewel convention.

→ Assess the potential impact of the 'Brexit' process.

Diagram plan

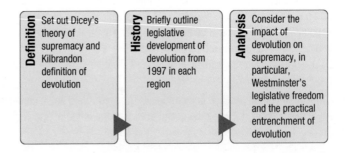

Definition — Set out Dicey's theory of supremacy and Kilbrandon definition of devolution

History — Briefly outline legislative development of devolution from 1997 in each region

Analysis — Consider the impact of devolution on supremacy, in particular, Westminster's legislative freedom and the practical entrenchment of devolution

A printable version of this diagram plan is available from **www.pearsoned.co.uk/lawexpressqa**

Answer

[1] This definition, from the Kilbrandon report, is a good starting point for a discussion.

The Royal Commission on the Constitution defined devolution as 'the delegation of central government powers without the relinquishment of sovereignty'[1] (Cmnd 5460, London: HMSO, 1973). Despite the consideration given by the Commission to the possible models of devolution, the process did not begin until 1997, as part of a programme of constitutional reform instigated by the new Labour administration. The nature and extent of devolution in the UK has been described as 'asymmetrical' (Elliot, M. and Thomas, R. (2014) *Public Law* (2nd en). Oxford: OUP, p. 274) and has occurred incrementally. The 2014 referendum on Scottish independence raised the real possibility of the dissolution of the union. In the wake of the 2016 referendum concerning the UK's membership of the European Union, questions remain regarding the future relationship between Westminster and the devolved powers. Arguably, the delegation of power has led to an irreversible relinquishment of sovereignty. Dicey set out three aspects to Parliamentary supremacy: first, that Parliament is free to legislate

[2] You need to be able to
explain what is meant by
'parliamentary supremacy'
in order to be able to assess
the extent to which devolution
has had an impact. Take care
to do this briefly, however,
as the question is not asking
you to engage in a lengthy
discussion of the doctrine.

[3] You should note the
difference between the
settlements made to each
region, but again, keep this
brief to avoid your answer
becoming overly descriptive.

[4] Make sure that you do
reference the statute here,
as this shows that you
understand how Parliament
has sought to protect
sovereignty.

[5] This is a key point to
highlight, as the suggestion
that Parliament retains only
nominal supremacy over the
devolution process is central
to the argument.

on any subject; secondly, that no Parliament can be bound by a pre-decessor or bind a successor; and, lastly, that no person or body can challenge the validity of an Act of Parliament. The devolution settlements raise questions about the continued applicability of this definition.[2]

Devolution of government power to Scotland, Wales and Northern Ireland followed referenda in each region. Each region did vote in favour of some degree of devolution, but in Wales only a small majority voted for a fairly limited scheme. This difference was reflected in the types of settlements that followed. The Scotland Act 1998 established the Scottish Parliament, and conferred on it the power to make primary legislation in areas encompassed by the Act. Westminster explic-itly reserved certain policy areas, including matters of defence, and created exceptions to legal competence (for example, the Scottish Parliament may not legislate in contravention of the European Con-vention on Human Rights). The Northern Ireland Assembly was given a similar type of legislative competence. The Welsh Assembly was initially given far more limited powers, and legislative competence stretched only to delegated legislation.[3]

In each case, the legislation expressly preserved the supremacy of the Westminster Parliament. Devolution has occurred only through an Act of Parliament, and could be reversed in the same way.[4] The Northern Ireland Assembly has been suspended on four separate occasions, including a five-year period of direct rule from Westminster between 2002 and 2007. This should be placed within the context of the his-torical conflict in Northern Ireland, which created particular tensions in respect of power-sharing between the Unionist and Republican parties. Devolution illustrates the difference between legal possibility and political reality: it is difficult to imagine any government seek-ing to abolish the regional assemblies and return all the legislative power to Westminster.[5] In fact, since 1997, Parliament has ceded additional power to the devolved administrations. In 2006, the Gov-ernment of Wales Act granted the Welsh Assembly additional powers and included the possibility of a future extension to include the power to make primary legislation if voted for in a referendum. In 2011, a referendum was held and a majority voted in favour of the extension of power. In 2013, the First Minister for Wales stated in an inter-view that it was no longer acceptable to rely upon understanding and conventions, and suggested that it was time to enact legislation to

[6] Try not to give too much detail, but the proliferation of extensions to the initial devolution settlements needs to be highlighted.

confirm that Westminster will not take back powers that have been devolved (*The Independent*, 26/12/13). The Wales Act 2017 extended the legislative competencies of the Assembly and recognised the permanence of the institutions.[6]

The Scotland Act 2012 gave further powers to the Holyrood Parliament, including an increased ability to set taxes. In 2014, the referendum on independence was held. Although a majority rejected independence, this was achieved only with a promise of increased devolution being made by all three main political parties. The resulting legislation, the Scotland Act 2016, acknowledged the permanence of the Scottish institutions and formally recorded the Sewel convention in statute. Any doubt as to the constitutional significance of this change, however, was decisively removed by the decision in *R (Miller)* v *Secretary of State for Exiting the European Union* [2017] UKSC 5. Although there was dissent on the question of the scope of ministerial power to trigger the withdrawal process, all 11 judges agreed that the wording of the amended Scotland Act does nothing to alter the legal position that the convention remains legally unenforceable.[7] The acknowledgement of the understanding that Westminster will not 'normally' legislate on behalf of the regions is, then, nothing more than a political gesture, and a rather empty one at that.

[7] This is a key point, and you must reference the *Miller* litigation here. The decision on the status of the Sewel convention provides some evidence to support the view that Parliament can – and will – exert legal control.

In 1997, discussing the Welsh settlement, Davies described devolution as 'a process, not an event', and this has been proven to be true.[8] The process, however, has not been smooth, as it appears that successive governments have attempted to quell political pressures from the regions as they have arisen, rather than implementing a systematic plan to manage the asymmetrical relationships within the union.

[8] The comment made by Davies is useful to include, as it encapsulates the key argument that the answer makes regarding the expansionary nature of devolution.

It is difficult to see how the Brexit process can unfold without further amendments to the devolution settlements and, perhaps, increased pressure from the regions for more control or even independence.[9] The Scotland and Wales Acts oblige the regions to legislate in accordance with European Union law (and the European Convention on Human Rights), making it inevitable that some further amendment to existing legislation is required. The Welsh electorate voted to leave the EU in the 2016 referendum, but Scottish voters were decisively in favour of remaining. The pressure on Westminster from Scotland, then, is unlikely to ease during the Brexit negotiations.

[9] It is a good idea to highlight the likelihood of future tensions within the union, as it helps to confirm that devolution cannot realistically be reversed.

Regardless of the fact that legislation has sought to preserve the sovereignty of the Westminster Parliament, the reality is that it would not be possible to take back those powers that have been given away. Parliament has, then, effectively bound its successors by recognising the permanent nature of the regional administrations. The decades since the initial settlements have seen a steady increase in the devolution of power to the regions, and the pressure on the centre is unlikely to ease. The Supreme Court may have confirmed that Westminster has retained legislative supremacy, but, politically, it is hard to see how Brexit can be negotiated without the consent of the regions.

 Make your answer stand out

- Ensure you keep up to date with developments in this area. At the time of writing, the First Minister for Scotland, Nicola Sturgeon, has suggested that the Scottish National Party is likely to seek a second independence referendum in the wake of the Supreme Court decision in *Miller*.
- Expand the discussion to consider the issue of 'English Votes for English Laws'. Hadfield is particularly helpful in considering the background to the so-called 'English question': Hadfield, B. (2005) Devolution, Westminster and the English Question. *Public Law*, 286–305. Any discussion should assess the impact of the change to standing orders of the House and the review of their implementation: House of Lords Select Committee on the Constitution, Sixth Report of 2016-17, *English Votes for English Laws* (2016, HL 61).
- Focus more attention on Northern Ireland. The majority of students will focus on the question of devolution to Scotland and Wales, while ignoring the issues particular to Northern Ireland.

! Don't be tempted to . . .

- Treat this question as an invitation simply to describe the structure of the devolution settlements. It is quite common for students to answer questions on devolution by setting out, in considerable detail, the types of powers that have been devolved or reserved. Remember that marks will be given for an ability to analyse the law in relation to the question set.
- Approach the question as a generalised discussion of the doctrine of parliamentary supremacy. If you have revised supremacy as a topic, but you have not focused on devolution, avoid this question, as you will not be given marks for dealing with any aspect of the doctrine unless you can relate this to the devolution settlements.

Try it yourself

Now take a look at the question below and attempt to answer it. You can check your response against the answer guidance available on the companion website (**www.pearsoned.co.uk/lawexpressqa**).

'Reform of the House of Lords has done nothing to address the undue power wielded by the unelected chamber.' Discuss.

www.pearsoned.co.uk/lawexpressqa

 Go online to access more revision support including additional essay and problem questions with diagram plans, and You be the marker questions, and to download all diagrams from the book.

Parliamentary accountability

4

How this topic may come up in exams

The topic of parliamentary accountability is an increasingly popular choice for inclusion on the syllabus, as it is highly topical. Following the scandal surrounding Members of Parliaments' expenses claims in 2009, the issue of parliamentary privilege has received a great deal of attention in the media, the courts and Parliament itself. Problem scenarios can be used to examine your understanding of the extent of privilege. Essay questions tend to focus on the constitutional issues raised by the existence of privilege, or on attempts to increase the accountability of individual MPs. There is an overlap between this topic and the constitutional doctrines of the rule of law and the separation of powers. Of course, the House of Commons is ultimately accountable to the electorate, while the House of Lords is not. Questions regarding electoral reform or the reform of the upper chamber are almost invariably dealt with as essay questions.

■ Before you begin

It's a good idea to consider the following key themes of parliamentary accountability before tackling a question on this topic.

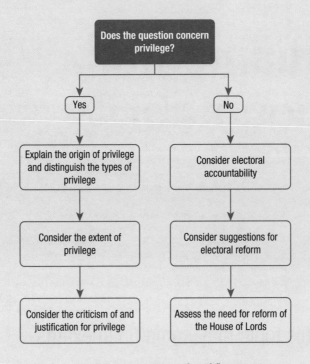

A printable version of this diagram is available from **www.pearsoned.co.uk/lawexpressqa**

❓ Question 1

Michelle Sanders is a journalist who has been writing about the role of commissioning authorities in restricting access to prescription drugs in geographical areas of Britain, creating so-called 'postcode lotteries' for health care. She is invited to give evidence to the parliamentary Select Committee on Health and, during the course of the hearing, she accuses Treyvon Keys, Chief Executive Officer of pharmaceutical companyHearthstone Heart Health, and Dr Louise Anderson, a doctor and advisor to government, of conspiring together to prevent cheaper generic versions of the company's products being available. After publication of the report, Dr Anderson is the subject of disciplinary proceedings by the General Medical Council (GMC) and Michelle is invited to give evidence to the panel. She does so, and repeats the evidence given to the inquiry.

At the end of the proceedings, Dr Anderson is struck off. Dr Anderson applies for a judicial review of the decision. As part of its case, the GMC wishes to use the select committee report. Treyvon Keys brings an action for defamation against Michelle, arguing that the comments made about him before the GMC have damaged his reputation.

Consider the issues regarding parliamentary privileges raised by the scenario.

Answer plan

→ Identify that the problem concerns parliamentary privileges and freedom of speech.

→ Explain the privilege awarded to 'parliamentary proceedings' and its application to select committee hearings.

→ Consider whether 'qualified privilege' applies to the GMC hearing.

Diagram plan

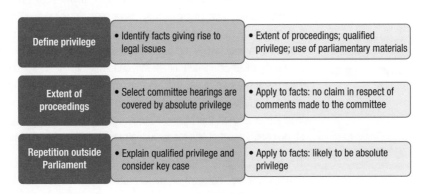

A printable version of this diagram plan is available from **www.pearsoned.co.uk/lawexpressqa**

Answer

Parliamentary privileges are the legal rights and immunities given to individual Members of Parliament, and collectively to both Houses. Freedom of speech during parliamentary proceedings was a key provision of the Bill of Rights 1688, and seeks to defend Parliament from executive interference.[1] The scenario raises three questions: first, the extent of parliamentary proceedings; secondly, whether Michelle may be able to rely on the defence of qualified privilege in respect of the GMC hearing; and, lastly, whether or not the select committee report is admissible as evidence in the judicial review case.

[1] As the scenario is quite complex, it is a good idea to demonstrate that you can identify the key legal issues in the introduction.

Article 9 of the Bill of Rights states that 'the freedom of speech and debates or proceedings in Parliament ought not to be impeached or questioned in any court or place out of Parliament'.[2] This provision creates certain legal rights and immunities; of relevance to this scenario is the protection from civil action given not only to individual Members of Parliament, but to the institution as a whole. This means that comments made during parliamentary proceedings cannot be the basis of a claim in defamation. This is the case even if the maker of the statement knows it to be untrue, or is malicious.[3] In the case of *A v UK* ([2003] 36 EHRR 51) the European Court of Human Rights confirmed the absolute nature of the privilege, and reaffirmed the importance of protection for parliamentary freedom of speech to democracy, to the extent that it outweighed the obvious injustice created for the complainant in that case.

[2] Although it can be tempting to include everything you know about a topic, it is much more effective to select only the relevant information needed to answer the question.

[3] Do not make the mistake of giving factual detail about the case, as you need to identify the reason that the ruling was significant.

There have been a number of cases in which the court has had to determine precisely what is meant by 'parliamentary proceedings'.[4] It is well established that select committee proceedings fall within the definition. Parliament issues a guide to witnesses called to give evidence before a parliamentary committee that confirms this (HC 123, 2016). That guide goes on to say that statements circulated in written form prior to, or following, a committee hearing may not attract that privilege. It seems, then, that Michelle Sanders cannot be sued on the basis of the comments that she made during the committee hearing itself.

[4] It is essential that you give evidence to support the statements that you make, and in this subject the use of sources such as parliamentary briefing papers is acceptable.

The position regarding the comments made to the General Medical Council hearing, however, is more problematic. At first glance, it would seem that, as the hearing is obviously not 'proceedings in Parliament', no privilege can apply in respect of this matter. However,

[5] Although the 2013 Act abolished the *Reynolds* defence, it is worth explaining how it operated, as the courts' approach will be similar in cases like this one.

this fails to take account of the issue of 'qualified privilege'. Qualified privilege cannot provide immunity from court action but rather offers a defence against a claim of defamation. Qualified privilege used to be an issue in actions concerning publication or broadcasts that included details of statements made during parliamentary proceedings. The so-called '*Reynolds* defence' protected journalists against court action provided that reports of parliamentary proceedings were a fair and accurate account of proceedings (see, for example, **Wason v Walter** (1868) LR 4 QB 73).[5] The Defamation Act 2013 formally abolished the '*Reynolds* defence', replacing it with the statutory protection offered by the defence of publication in the public interest set out in section 4 of the Act. However, it is important to note that this change has not removed the common-law defence of qualified privilege in all proceedings. An analogous situation arose in the libel action brought against Lord Triesman, former chairman of the Football Association, who had given evidence to a select committee. At a subsequent Football Association hearing, he was questioned on the same matter, and asked the panel to refer to his previous evidence. The High Court struck out the libel claim, and the Court of Appeal upheld the decision in **Makudi v Triesman** [2014] EWCA Civ 179. In the High Court, the claim was struck out on the basis that Triesman was able to rely on qualified privilege, but the Court of Appeal went further and held that, in fact, absolute privilege could apply.

[6] Here, it is clear to see the factual similarity between the case of *Makudi* and the scenario.

[7] This is one of the rare cases where it is useful to give detail about the authority referred to, as this allows for a comparison with the situation dealt with in the scenario and can help arrive at a conclusion.

The court referred to **Prebble v Television** (1995) 15 LS 204 and confirmed that the purpose of parliamentary privilege is to protect the democratic process, but noted that there is a balance to be struck between two important and conflicting rights: freedom of speech on one hand, but access to justice on the other. Therefore, the court observed that there must be a strong case if Article 9 is to apply.[6] Lord Triesman had been careful not to add to the evidence given to the select committee, and the court felt it important that those giving evidence to select committees could do so freely and without fear of subsequent litigation.[7] It was not, in the court's view, necessary to consider qualified privilege in this particular case. In fact, the court found that it would not make any practical difference if Triesman had in fact repeated the evidence rather than simply referred the panel to it, as absolute privilege would apply.[8]

[8] It is clear here, having set out the previous authority, how the answer has arrived at the advice given in respect of Michelle.

When advising Michelle, then, it appears that provided that she went no further than repeating evidence given to the committee, she would be able to argue that the claim against her should be struck out as her comments would be protected by absolute privilege. If, on the other hand, she altered her evidence, then the question of qualified privilege would apply, as it may then be analogous to a report of proceedings. In **Cook v Alexander** [1974] QB 279 it was held that there was no need for a report of statements made in Parliament to be verbatim, as long as it was generally accurate.[9] The only issue for Michelle would be if she provided fresh or additional information before the panel, as no defence of qualified privilege could apply.

[9] This aspect of the scenario is easy to overlook; ensure that you do cover all the legal issues raised by the question even where the answer appears straightforward.

The final matter to consider is whether or not the select committee report could be admitted into evidence as part of the judicial review proceedings. The answer would appear to be straightforward: Article 9 prohibits the use of privileged material in court proceedings. There have been some exceptions, most notably **Pepper v Hart** [1993] AC 593, in which *Hansard* was admissible to assist with statutory interpretation by allowing the court to consider evidence that could demonstrate what the intention of the legislators had been. However, adopting the report for any other purpose would be a clear breach and the evidence should not be admissible.[10]

[10] Do not make the mistake of speculating too far from the facts of the scenario; you are not expected to give detailed answers to hypothetical questions.

Parliamentary privileges are crucial in protecting freedom of speech in the legislature, to ensure that opinions can be aired freely, with the hope that this will lead to better decisions. This objective would be undermined if Michelle were able to be sued on the basis of evidence given to a select committee.

 Make your answer stand out

- Explore the relationship between Parliament and the court in more detail. There is a useful article on the issues pertinent to the question by Lord Lisvane: Lisvane (2016) The Courts and Parliament' *Public Law*, April: 272–84.

- Expand the discussion to consider in more detail the rationale for protecting parliamentary privilege. You could refer to more examples of occasions where the existence of privilege has, arguably, provided a democratic benefit. Suitable areas for discussion could be the scandal surrounding the company Trafigura, or the use of privilege to highlight the government's role in extraordinary rendition.

- Approach the scenario as a question about the issue of defamation. The question is quite specific in pointing you towards the issue of privilege.
- Include all the information that you know about privilege. This question does not require you to consider the privilege of self-regulation by the Houses of Parliament, or to address the limits of privilege in respect of criminal prosecution.

Question 2

'Parliamentary privilege undermines the rule of law. Specifically it undermines the requirement, which is central to the rule of law, that the law be general. Even worse: it undermines that requirement in a particularly worrying way because it mainly (although not only) has the effect of excusing members of the political elite from conformity with the law.' (Dr Adam Tucker, response to government consultation on the Green Paper, 2012, Cm 8318, Para. 2)

To what extent should parliamentary privilege be reformed?

Diagram plan

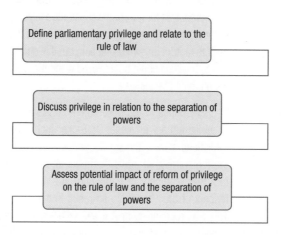

Define parliamentary privilege and relate to the rule of law

Discuss privilege in relation to the separation of powers

Assess potential impact of reform of privilege on the rule of law and the separation of powers

A printable version of this diagram plan is available from **www.pearsoned.co.uk/lawexpressqa**

Answer plan

→ Define 'parliamentary privilege' and its relationship to the rule of law.

→ Consider the need for privilege to maintain a functional separation of powers.

→ Outline previous suggestions for reform.

→ Assess the extent to which further change would impact upon the separation of powers and the rule of law.

Answer

[1] This brief definition is a good way to introduce the answer, as it shows that the key principles have been clearly understood.

'Parliamentary privilege' refers to the legal protections and immunities granted to Members of both Houses of Parliament, individually and collectively. Privilege can be traced back to the Bill of Rights of 1689, Article 9 of which asserted that the freedom of speech in parliamentary proceedings should not be questioned or impeached in any court or place outside of Parliament. Privilege is intended to protect the legislature from undue interference or pressure from the executive branch of the state and has two aspects: freedom of speech, and the right of self-regulation.[1] The European Court of Human Rights has affirmed the fundamental importance of privilege in safeguarding the democratic process (*A v UK* [2002] ECHR 35373/97). There have been a number of instances, however, in which privilege has proved to be controversial, as it gives individual members of the Commons and the Lords protection from legal accountability. While there have been proposals for reform, no substantive legislative change has been forthcoming. This may be partially a result of Parliament's unwillingness to restrict its own protection, but it is difficult to see how alteration to privilege could be achieved without a real risk that democratic debate could be stifled.[2]

[2] It can be helpful to give an indication of the direction the argument will take, as this helps the reader to follow the structure of the argument.

[3] Reference to the quotation helps to demonstrate that you can make the connection between Tucker's view and the relevant aspects of the doctrine of the rule of law.

In his response to the government consultation on possible reform of parliamentary privilege, Dr Tucker highlights the apparent contradiction between the special status awarded to the legislature and the requirement of equal treatment as part of the rule of law.[3] The fact that Members of Parliament are immune from civil action in respect of their conduct can result in injustice in individual cases. This was recognised in *A v UK*, where the court accepted that the statements made about the complainant by a Member of Parliament were capable of being defamatory, and could have been the subject of a successful legal action had they been made in any other context.[4] However, hard cases such as these must be balanced against the need to preserve the integrity of Parliament. The concern must be that the threat of litigation could stifle debate. It can be seen that, in a

[4] There is no need to set out the factual background of the case here.

number of instances, privilege has been used by individual Members of Parliament to force issues into the public domain and allow for them to be addressed. The Labour MP Paul Farrelly used privilege to ask a question regarding the efforts made by the oil company Trafigura to keep information about a civil action it faced over a spillage of toxic waste out of the public domain (HC Deb 13 October 2009, vol. 497, col. 163). The company had obtained an injunction to prevent reporting of the court case, but Farrelly's immunity from an action in defamation allowed him to air the matter. Similarly, the Conservative MP David Davis used privilege to detail allegations against the government of complicity in the process of extra-ordinary rendition (HC Deb 7 July 2009, vol. 495, col. 940).[5] Tucker's response to the consultation went on to note that the rule of law is not absolute and 'must be balanced against the competing claims of other principles' (ibid, para. 3)[6] – in particular, the separation of powers. He argued that the separation of powers exists to prevent one branch of the state interfering with the operation of another. It can be seen, then, that, were the courts able to interfere with the conduct of Members of Parliament, this could lead to an unwarranted restriction of freedom of speech that would be to the detriment of democratic debate.[7]

The issue of privilege was brought to public attention in the wake of the 2009 scandal concerning revelations about fraudulent expenses claims made by a large number of MPs. The case of **R v Chaytor and others** [2010] UKSC 52 concerned an attempt by some MPs to resist criminal prosecution on the basis that the expenses register should be considered to be proceedings in Parliament and, as such, protected by privilege. The court rejected this, and confirmed that privilege can confer immunity from civil action only and will not protect an MP who has committed criminal acts.[8]

Following the scandal, and while still in opposition, the Conservative party pledged to address the issue of privilege, with David Cameron indicating that proposals made for reform in the 1999 report of the Joint Committee on Privilege (HL 43-I, HC 214-I) would be implemented. That report had advocated comprehensive codification of privilege, but the proposals were not adopted. Following election, the government issued a Green Paper querying reform, and a second joint committee was appointed. The committee reported in 2013 (HL 30 HC 100),[9] and argued that statutory regulation of privilege was unnecessary and risked 'unintended consequences' (Para. 277). It was,

[5] Although the point about freedom of speech is often made, it is far more compelling with the examples used to illustrate times when the use of privilege can be seen as positive.

[6] It is always a good idea to read the source that has been quoted, and doing so here has enabled the student to recognise that Tucker's argument was more complex than might have been suggested by simply the part used in the question.

[7] This is the central point of the paragraph, and makes sense to the reader because of the examples that were cited.

[8] This is an important point to note: the case of *Chaytor* demonstrates that privilege is not unlimited, and arguably this restriction confirmed at common law reduces the need for statutory reform.

[9] As the question is about reform, you will be rewarded for demonstrating knowledge of these committee reports.

however, proposed that the 1840 Parliamentary Papers Act should be replaced and updated, and that the highly controversial section 13 of the Defamation Act 1996 should be repealed.

[10] You need to briefly explain the background to this statutory provision in order to make clear why the legislation can be seen as promoting inequality.

Section 13 of the Defamation Act 1996 was passed in order to give an individual Member of Parliament the choice to waive privilege.[10] The legislation was enacted in response to the attempt by the MP Neil Hamilton to sue *The Guardian* newspaper in defamation. To defend the claim, *The Guardian* wished to refer to answers given by the MP in Parliament, but privilege prevented evidence from *Hansard* being adduced, and the case was therefore stayed. Section 13 has been the subject of vociferous criticism, and provides a clear example of how parliamentary privilege has the potential to conflict with notions of equality before the law. The 1999 committee (ibid.) argues that it undermined the basis of privilege, as 'freedom of speech [belongs to] the House as a whole and not of the individual in his own right, although an individual member can assert and rely on it'. The 2013 committee accepted that the waiver had rarely, if ever, been used but nevertheless recommended that it should be abolished.[11] In due course, the Deregulation Act 2015 (Sch. 23 and s. 44) finally repealed the controversial section.

[11] As this is the only aspect of any proposed reform that will result in legislative action, you do need to stress this point.

Although the privilege of freedom of speech can result in cases where individuals are prevented from obtaining redress, and may be open to misuse, it seems clear that the benefit of free and frank debate does indeed outweigh those risks. Abolition of section 13, even if it were rarely used, would appear to be a necessary step in ensuring that MPs are not perceived as being able to use privilege as both a shield and a sword. The issue of self-regulation is more complex; however, the clarification provided by the case of ***Chaytor*** is perhaps reassurance that privilege cannot excuse criminality. It is difficult to see how additional reform could be enacted without undermining the separation of powers.[12]

[12] Where you are not able to reach a definitive conclusion in answer to the question, it is a good idea to summarise the conflicting points made in the body of your answer.

✓ Make your answer stand out

■ By exploring the relationship between parliamentary privilege and parliamentary supremacy. Lakin has suggested the two are coterminous (see Lakin, S. (2013) Parliamentary privilege, parliamentary sovereignty, and constitutional principle. *UK Const. L. Blog*, 11 February available at: http://ukconstitutionallaw.org).

- By exploring the development of attempts to enforce standards of behaviour in Parliament. A good discussion can be found in: Leopold, P.M. (2011) Standards of conduct in public life, in J. Jowell and D. Oliver (eds), *The Changing Constitution* (7th edn). Oxford: Oxford University Press.
- By considering the judgment in *R* v *Chaytor* in more detail. Lord Phillips was careful to distinguish between the privilege protecting freedom of speech under Article 9 and the issue of exclusive cognisance. It seems that the courts are more likely to apply a narrow construction to the latter, whereas the former is seen as inviolable.

! Don't be tempted to . . .

- Give too much information about the history of the parliamentary expenses scandal. If you do include information about how the information came to light, ensure that you link this to the question by explaining how the preservation of privilege in the Freedom of Information Act 2000 hampered the journalistic investigation.
- Ignore the need to discuss exclusive cognisance. Too many students discuss only the immunity from actions in defamation and ignore the broader context.

? Question 3

The Minister for Housing, Mrs Taylor, has recently introduced a Bill to the Commons, proposing a simplification to planning procedures that would make it easier for landlords to convert properties into houses for multiple occupation. An MP, Mr Rafiq, receives a letter from his constituent, Alexia Clements, alleging that Mrs Taylor has been bribed by a student housing company that would benefit from the change, and that the company provides Mrs Taylor's daughter with rent-free accommodation while she is at university.

Mr Rafiq forwards the letter to the Commissioner for Parliamentary Standards, and to the Shadow Minister for Housing. In a debate on the Bill, Mr Rafiq reads out the letter, including a passage which describes Mrs Taylor as an 'odious, slippery character who cannot be trusted'.

Later on, while in a Commons cafeteria, Mr Rafiq is asked about the matter by a fellow MP and reads the letter out again. This is overheard by several of Mrs Taylor's colleagues.

Mrs Taylor is informed, and storms in. She pours a jug of water over Mr Rafiq's head.

Advise Mr Rafiq, Ms Clements and Mrs Taylor about the possible consequences of these events.

Answer plan

→ Explain privilege protecting Mr Rafiq from defamation action.

→ Consider definition of 'parliamentary proceedings'.

→ Discuss the different position of Ms Clements.

→ Consider whether privilege extends to cover criminal activity.

→ Explain the requirements of the register of members' interests and the sanctions for failing to comply.

Diagram plan

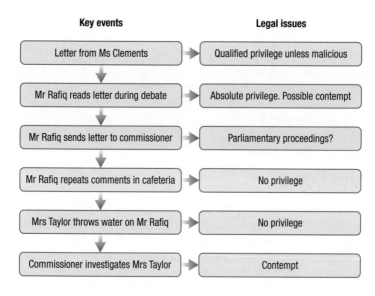

A printable version of this diagram plan is available from **www.pearsoned.co.uk/lawexpressqa**

Answer

[1] You might be tempted to answer this question by focusing exclusively on the privilege of free speech, but the conduct of Mrs Taylor should alert you to the need to consider regulation of conduct.

The scenario raises questions about how far Members of Parliament (MPs) can claim the protection of privilege to excuse conduct that may breach civil or criminal law, and whether non-Members enjoy any similar protection. In addition, the allegations made about Mrs Taylor require consideration of the mechanisms that exist to ensure that MPs comply with ethical standards.[1]

The allegations made in the letter received by Mr Rafiq may be libellous. Mrs Taylor may be able to bring civil proceedings in respect of some of his actions. When Mr Rafiq reads the contents of the letter during a debate, he enjoys absolute privilege. Article 9 of the Bill of Rights enshrined the protection of freedom of speech in Parliament, and no action for defamation can arise in respect of any remarks made during parliamentary proceedings. This would be the position even if Mr Rafiq knew the allegations were false, on the authority of **Wason v Walter** (1868) LR 4 QB 73.[2] However, the protection of absolute privilege only protects Members engaged in parliamentary proceedings. When Mr Rafiq repeats the comments in the cafeteria, it appears that he is not engaged in the business of Parliament and therefore he would not be able to claim immunity from a civil action in respect of this part of the incident.[3] A question arises as to whether any action can result from the forwarding of the letter to third parties, which is, on the face of it, re-publication of the libel. It is debatable whether or not this would enjoy the cloak of privilege, as it is not clear that this could be considered to be 'parliamentary proceedings'. The issue was considered in **Strauss and the London Electricity Board Case** [1958] PL 80 which concerned a letter sent by the MP to the Paymaster General, complaining about methods employed by the London Electricity Board.[4] The Committee of Privileges concluded that the letter was covered by privilege, although a subsequent Commons vote rejected this view. The more recent case of **Rost v Edwards** [1990] 2 QB 460 saw the courts refuse to accept evidence of a letter sent to the Speaker, as it was accepted this did constitute 'proceedings in Parliament'. In any event, the point is perhaps rather academic as, even if absolute privilege does not apply, Mr Rafiq would almost certainly be able to claim qualified privilege. This protects him from an action unless Mrs Taylor can prove that he was malicious. The case of **Breech v Freeson** [1972] 1 QB 14 provides support for the suggestion that sending a letter to the minister on a matter of interest to parliamentary business would attract qualified privilege, although Bradley and Ewing (2010) do suggest that passing a constituent's letter on to a minister without any inquiry as to its truth could be considered malicious.[5] Mr Rafiq should also be advised that, irrespective of any civil action, he may also fall to be censured for contempt as a result of his comments during the debate.[6]

[2] It is unnecessary to give any details about this case, as the only important issue here is the *ratio*, which means that the advice given to Mr Rafiq about this part of the incident can be given with certainty.

[3] Here, you have shown that you understand that the issue here is whether or not privilege affords a defence, and have done so briefly and with reference to the facts. This shows knowledge, and an ability to apply it.

[4] This is an important case to revise, as the issue of whether or not an event will be considered to be part of 'parliamentary proceedings' is a common area for examination. The additional cases are useful, but this is probably essential.

[5] Here, the answer has shown knowledge of case law and academic opinion, and used this to address the problem.

[6] Again, you can gain extra marks by considering the privilege of exclusive cognisance, noting here that the use of 'unparliamentary language' can lead to a Member being rebuked.

[7] While the position of Ms Clements needs to be addressed, you should not need to spend too long on considering this aspect of the scenario, as the position is fairly simple. There is much more debate around the extent of parliamentary proceedings in relation to the letter, and you should concentrate more on that issue.

[8] There is no need to give any more detail about the criminal offence, it is simply important to recognise that a crime has occurred.

[9] This is a good example to include, demonstrating an ability to relate current events to the material that you have studied.

[10] You will be rewarded for expressing an opinion here, as long as you can explain your reasons.

[11] This is a really important point to make, as it shows awareness of the different degrees of culpability that can arise in respect of the register.

The position in respect of Ms Clements is less secure, as non-Members do not enjoy the protection of absolute privilege. She may, however, be able to claim that she can rely on the defence of publication in the public interest set out in the Defamation Act 2013, provided that the letter was sent without malice, on a matter of public interest.[7]

Mrs Taylor has committed the criminal offence of battery when she throws water over Mr Rafiq.[8] Although parliamentary privilege confers a freedom from arrest within the Commons, it appears that this is confined to civil matters. In the case of **Bradlaugh v Gossett** (1884) 12 QBD 271, the courts asserted that there was no authority for the suggestion that criminal jurisdiction was excluded from the House of Commons. In 2012, a Labour MP was convicted and sentenced for common assault following a brawl in a bar in the Houses of Parliament.[9] It is highly unlikely that the fact that the incident occurred in the Commons would protect Mrs Taylor from prosecution, as, if privilege were asserted, this would arguably damage the reputation of the House.[10]

Mrs Taylor may also face difficulties if the allegations are investigated by the Commissioner for Parliamentary Standards and found to be correct. The role of the Commissioner was created in response to the report of the Nolan Committee in the wake of the 'cash for questions' scandal during the 1990s. The Commissioner is tasked with maintaining the register of members' interests, and investigating allegations of breaches. The Commissioner reports findings to the Committee on Standards in Public Life, which can impose sanctions. Mrs Taylor should declare, on the Rregister of members' interests, a connection with an organisation providing her with a material benefit. Registration of the connection would not be sufficient in this case, however, as she has initiated proceedings in Parliament by introducing the legislation and should therefore have declared her connection at the introduction of the Bill.[11] This would be considered an extremely serious breach of the rules regarding the registration of interests, and a clear contempt. Mrs Taylor should be advised that penalties for contempt can include an order to repay money. Following the 2009 scandal regarding MPs' expenses, the Committee ordered a number of MPs to repay large sums of money. In addition, Members

[12] You will be rewarded for being able to demonstrate knowledge of examples of the application of law.

can be suspended from Parliament. George Galloway was suspended for 18 days by the Committee in 2006 for concealing matters on the register.[12] In extreme cases, an MP can be required to stand down at the next election. Since the creation of the office of the Commissioner, doubt has been expressed about the willingness and ability of any parliamentary body robustly to ensure that Members comply with ethical standards. Loveland referred to the response to the Nolan Committee as 'a damp squib' in 2012. This issue arose in the wake of the expenses scandal, and resulted in the Parliamentary Standards Act 2009. This has also been criticised because, during the course of debate, clauses that would have resulted in paid advocacy (of the type alleged here) becoming an imprisonable offence were removed.

[13] While it is important to use the answer to demonstrate a good knowledge of the topic, the information must be utilised to assist in giving an opinion about Mrs Taylor's predicament.

However, given the public concern regarding the conduct of MPs, Mrs Taylor would certainly find herself under considerable pressure to resign, irrespective of any action taken by the House.[13]

[14] As the answer has dealt with a number of individuals and issues, the conclusion should briefly summarise the advice to each party.

Mr Rafiq would be covered by privileges in respect of all actions save for the casual conversation outside the Commons chamber. Ms Clements may be able to utilise the limited public interest provisions in the Defamation Act. Mrs Taylor may face criminal prosecution for the attack on Mr Rafiq. She may also face sanction from the Committee if the allegations are investigated and validated by the Commissioner on Parliamentary Standards.[14]

 Make your answer stand out

- Conduct of parliamentary business is extremely topical. You should ensure you keep up to date with developments that occur during your studies, as you may find illustrative examples to use that are not yet in the textbooks. This will demonstrate that you have a clear understanding of the legal principles and can identify significant issues independently.

- By demonstrating an understanding of how Parliament operates in more detail, for example, by explaining the role that the Speaker would play in each of the possible contempt situations.

! Don't be tempted to . . .

- Spend time explaining the origins of the privileges referred to. Most of the marks in this question will be given for being able to apply the law to the facts given. So, rather than explaining the constitutional justification for absolute privilege, you must instead concentrate on assessing whether Mr Rafiq can claim privilege.
- Explain the background to the 'cash for questions' scandal in any detail. It is worth mentioning to be able to explain the origins of the office of the Commissioner, but you should avoid writing a long, descriptive account of what happened.

🖎 Question 4

The parliamentary expenses scandal focused public attention on the House of Commons, prompting an unprecedented programme of reform that has resulted in a more representative and more accountable legislature.

Discuss.

Diagram plan

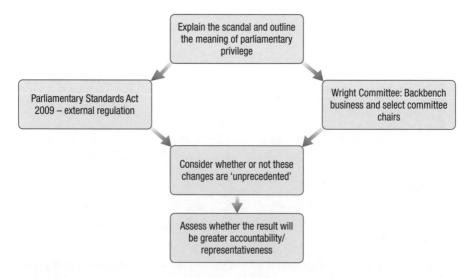

A printable version of this diagram plan is available from **www.pearsoned.co.uk/lawexpressqa**

Answer plan

→ Briefly explain the parliamentary expenses scandal.

→ Define what is meant by 'representativeness'.

→ Outline the reforms that resulted from the scandal.

→ Consider the effect of the Parliamentary Standards Act 2009.

→ Assess the impact of the Wright report.

Answer

[1] There is no need to describe the facts exposed by the scandal in any detail: the focus here must be on the political response.

In 2009, details of expenses claims made by MPs were leaked to the *Daily Telegraph*. The resulting public outcry led to cross-party support for reform to the parliamentary system for dealing with expenses.[1] During the 2010 election campaign, the Liberal Democrats and the Conservatives made much of the need to rebuild trust and the Coalition agreement promised a series of reforms to both the Commons and the Lords. Although some key issues appear to have been removed from the agenda, at least for the time being (reforms to the electoral system and the House of Lords), there have been significant alterations to the system regulating expenses and the conduct of parliamentary business. It will be argued that these reforms are far from unprecedented and that far greater change would be required before it can be claimed that the legislature is either representative, or accountable.[2]

[2] A confident answer will often explain at the outset the direction the argument will take.

[3] Here, the answer explains clearly why the two issues are interrelated.

[4] It is important to link the expenses scandal to parliamentary privilege because you need to consider the events from the perspective of a constitutional lawyer.

The expenses scandal originated in a Freedom of Information Act request that was initially resisted by the Commons and, in particular, the then Speaker, on the basis of claimed privilege. Parliamentary privilege refers to the special protections enjoyed by Members of both Houses, both individually and collectively, enshrined by Article 9 of the Bill of Rights 1689 to ensure that the legislature can act without fear of arbitrary interference by the Crown.[3] Parliamentary privilege protects freedom of speech by granting Members immunity from legal action taken in respect of 'parliamentary business', and grants exclusive cognisance to MPs and peers to regulate their own affairs without judicial interference. In the wake of the scandal, there was an acknowledgement that trust needed to be rebuilt (see, *inter alia*, Fox, 2009), and some argued that privilege (exclusive cognisance in particular) had contributed to a lack of accountability.[4]

Any view regarding the representativeness of the legislature will depend upon how the term is defined. If 'representation' requires Members accurately to reflect the socio-economic, race and gender balance of the electorate, then Parliament (with its concentration of public-school-educated, white males) could not be described in these terms. For the purpose of this discussion, 'representation' will be used to refer to the ability of ministers to act in accordance with the views and opinions of their constituents.[5]

[5] Where there is more than one way of interpreting a particular term, it is important to demonstrate that this is understood. However, it is acceptable to discuss only one meaning, as long as this is explained.

The first legislative response to the scandal was the Parliamentary Standards Act of 2009, which established an external body to regulate MPs' expenses: the Independent Parliamentary Standards Authority (IPSA). It also established the post of Commissioner for Parliamentary Investigations and a new criminal offence at section 10. On the face of it, these measures have the potential to increase accountability and significantly erode the privilege of self-regulation by introducing external oversight of expenses. Some commentators have argued, however, that the changes are largely symbolic. Parpworth (2010)[6] has pointed out that, despite the creation of a regulatory body, decisions of the Commissioner are likely to be immune from judicial scrutiny, given that, in *R v Parliamentary Commissioner for Standards ex parte Al-Fayed* [1998] 1 WLR 669, it was held that 'the activities of Parliament are not the basic fare of judicial review'.[7]

[6] Whenever you say that there are 'some' or 'many' sources of support for a particular point, you should provide at least one example in support of your claim.

[7] Here, it can be seen that reading around the subject can be really beneficial, providing you with material to support a more complex analysis.

In any event, IPSA will only deal with matters relating to expenses claims; all other forms of parliamentary misconduct still fall to be dealt with using systems of internal regulation, and this system depends upon a willingness within the House of Commons to apply enforcement measures. Referral to the Commissioner for Parliamentary Standards for a breach of the Ministerial Code is, currently, a matter for the Prime Minister – a position that has been criticised following the decision not to refer Liam Fox and, later, Jeremy Hunt. The case of Hunt is particularly interesting, as the rationale for declining a referral was the ongoing judicial inquiry headed by Lord Leveson. Lord Leveson publicly stated that he would not rule upon whether Hunt had breached the code or not, as this fell outside the terms of reference of the inquiry. This situation demonstrates a difficulty with the coexistence of internal regulatory bodies with external tribunals – while the latter may appear to promise greater transparency, here it appears to have created an 'accountability gap'.[8]

[8] Similarly, here the answer is assisted by your having a knowledge of current affairs, allowing for the inclusion of more discursive examples.

[9] This is a small point, but crucial for the argument being developed.

Despite all the publicity surrounding the response to the scandal, the MPs in question were dealt with under the pre-existing law.[9] In *R v Chaytor and others* [2010] UKSC 52 the courts held that privilege did not, and had never, indemnified MPs from criminal prosecution.

The events of 2009 did not lead to 'unprecedented' reform. Attempts to restore confidence following a scandal are familiar: reforms implemented after the Nolan report are an obvious example. It is also doubtful that the changes introduced will truly result in increased accountability. It is notable that the most dramatic proposals made prior to the 2010 election are no longer on the political agenda. Electoral reform was abandoned following a referendum notable for its extremely low turnout, demonstrating the public's lack of interest in the issue. House of Lords reform fell foul of a rift within the Coalition.

[10] This point relies on the definition of 'representative' that was set out earlier.

It may be, however, that some measures that followed will be more effective in reforming the Lords to create a more representative legislature. As Russell (2011) has argued, the Wright Committee report resulted in a number of significant changes. Select Committee chairs are now elected using an alternative vote system, which arguably opens the door for more robust scrutiny of government. Importantly, parliamentary time is now set aside to deal with issues raised by backbenchers. It can be argued that this will allow MPs to represent their constituents more effectively, by ensuring that their concerns are aired. As Russell points out, these reforms are not concerned with expenses, but the scandal acted as the catalyst enabling reform.[10]

[11] It is acceptable, here, to set out a strong opinion in the conclusion, because it is supported by the evidence from academic sources and examples drawn from current affairs.

The expenses scandal marked a low point in public confidence in the parliamentary process, but it cannot be said that this was unprecedented. Legislation rushed through Parliament may have been intended to restore trust, but it did not confront the issue of exclusive cognisance. If there is to be real accountability, there must be truly independent external regulation of all aspects of Members' conduct. Although changes in response to the Wright report garnered less publicity than other responses to the scandal, they will arguably have a greater impact in allowing Parliament to hold government to account and better represent the electorate.[11]

Make your answer stand out

■ By expanding the explanation of accountability of government, and considering whether or not the Wright reforms will reinforce the separation of powers. Arguably, a stronger backbench presence in Parliament will lead to a more democratic legislature.

■ By ensuring that you are abreast of developments in this highly topical area of law. For example, a recent decision by the Information Commissioner upheld the refusal of a Freedom of Information Act request for disclosure of the identity of MPs who had been the subject of investigation by the Independent Parliamentary Standards Authority (the decision can be found at https://ico.org.uk/media/action-weve-taken/decision-notices/2016/1624558/fs_50616049.pdf).

■ By incorporating reference to earlier calls for reform of privilege. You could consider, for example, Leopold, P.M. (1999) Report of the Joint Committee on Parliamentary Privilege, *Public Law*: 604. This would allow you to develop the argument that contemporary concerns have, in fact, been part of the political landscape for some considerable time.

! Don't be tempted to . . .

■ Give too much factual detail about the allegations made during the scandal, as this will lead to a descriptive, historical, account rather than a critical analysis of the response.

■ Be distracted by discussion of the debate about the extent of privilege: students sometimes spend a long time on this aspect of the topic, using cases such as *Stockdale v Hansard* (1839) 9 Ad & EL 1 or *Strauss's case*. Unfortunately, marks will not be awarded for demonstrating awareness of the issue of the limits of privilege. The question has a specific focus on criticisms of privilege raised by the expenses scandal.

■ Read the question as being a request to discuss the role of Parliament within the constitution, or to discuss the supremacy of Parliament. Students sometimes make the mistake of providing generalised information about the composition of Parliament, or of Dicey's account of supremacy, but this will not gather marks. The answer must focus on the issues raised.

Question 5

'In a modern democracy it is important that those who make the laws of the land should be elected by those to whom those laws apply.' (David Cameron and Nick Clegg, Foreword to the Draft House of Lords Reform Bill, May 2011, p. 5, available at http://www.official-documents .gov.uk/document/cm80/8077/8077.pdf)

Discuss the need for reform of the House of Lords.

Answer plan

→ Explain the passage of the House of Lords Reform Bill.

→ Outline the constitutional role of the House of Lords.

→ Identify key criticisms of the unelected chamber.

→ Assess the merits of various proposals for reform.

→ Consider whether an elected chamber is an essential component of democracy.

Diagram plan

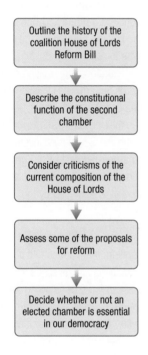

A printable version of this diagram plan is available from **www.pearsoned.co.uk/lawexpressqa**

Answer

A bicameral legislature is a common feature of Western democracies, but the United Kingdom is unique in retaining an unelected second chamber. Proposals to reform the composition and constitutional position of the House of Lords have been on the political agenda for a century but, despite much debate, no consensus has been achieved.

[1] Your introduction should make it clear that you are not going to make the mistake of only considering the reasons for the failure of the Coalition Bill – a common mistake.

[2] Here, the answer describes the constitutional role of the Lords as succinctly as possible. There is no need to give more detail about the functions of the House, as you need to focus on the areas that people have attempted to reform.

[3] There is no need to provide a full account of the passage of the Parliament Acts, as long as the answer makes it clear that you understand the effect of these important statutes.

[4] It is useful to show that you are aware of recent developments such as the Strathclyde review.

[5] Do not spend too much time setting out the detail of these reforms: the key point is that they were intended to be the start of a process.

The arguments for and against reform of the House must be considered in the context of the constitutional role played by the Lords.[1]

The Upper House acts as a constitutional brake on the powers exercised by the Commons, with the power to scrutinise, amend and, in some circumstances, delay legislation.[2] No recent proposals for amendment have suggested any substantive alteration to the role of the second chamber: the foreword to the draft Bill confirmed that these functions should remain unchanged.

The relationship between the two Houses of Parliament has, on occasion, been somewhat fraught. The first Parliament Act of 1911 was a response to a protracted refusal by the Lords to accept a budget endorsed by the Commons. The combined effect of both Parliament Acts was to remove the power of veto from the Lords;[3] effectively, it was a 'statutory confirmation of the Lords' subordinate legislative role' (Lords Reform: The Legislative Role of the House of Lords, House of Commons Research Paper 98/103). Aspects of the relationship between the Houses are still governed by convention, the most important being the Salisbury convention that the Lords will not oppose a Bill that formed part of the government's manifesto pledge. The Coalition government's proposal argued that these conventions should remain, a view endorsed by the Joint Committee on House of Lords Reform.

The need for a second chamber as a scrutinising body in a democratic system, then, appears to be accepted as political and constitutional fact: although the scope of the Salisbury convention was called into question in 2015 following the refusal of the House of Lords to approve delegated legislation introducing cuts to tax credits. The then Chancellor, George Osborne, indicated that the powers of the Lords could be reviewed, but there was little support for the limitations suggested by the following Strathclyde review (2016).[4]

When the Labour government was elected in 1997, the House of Lords had over 1,200 Members, 750 of whom were hereditary peers. The House of Lords Reform Act 1999 reduced this number to 92 and established the House of Lords Appointments Commission, which now has responsibility for selecting cross-bench life peers.[5] The Labour administration saw this move as the first in an extensive programme of reform. Although the Constitutional Reform Act 2005 removed the Law Lords from the legislature, further progress stalled

[6] When discussing the issue of reform, it is really helpful to refer to the specific proposals that have been made rather than simply to discuss the issues in the abstract.

in the absence of political consensus. The Commission on Reform of the House of Lords, chaired by Lord Wakeham, proposed that the chamber should remain largely appointed, with a minority of elected Members (Wakeham, 2000). The Public Administration Select Committee (2002), on the other hand, proposed that at least 60% of the Chamber should be elected.[6] Despite opinion polls showing support for a move to a largely elected Chamber, votes within the Commons and the Lords failed to find an agreed balance between elected and appointed Members. In 2008, the government published a White Paper proposing that 80 per cent of peers should be elected for substantial terms of office, but the Bill that followed was far less radical, containing only a provision to abolish the remaining hereditary peers.

Reform was a manifesto commitment for the Liberal Democrats and became part of the Coalition Agreement. The draft Bill published in 2012 contained proposals broadly in line with those set out in the 2008 White Paper. Following a rebellion by Conservative MPs and opposition from the Labour party, the reform movement has ground to a halt. Changes introduced by the House of Lords Reform Act 2014 did confirm in statutory form that misconduct or lack of attendance could lead to expulsion, but made no substantive changes. This is perhaps surprising given that, once the Coalition Agreement was drafted, there did at last seem to be cross-party support for the need for a largely elected chamber.[7]

[7] You do need to take care that, when dealing with the failed Coalition reforms, you do not spend too much time dealing with the political reasons for failure, as this would take you too far away from the constitutional issues.

Cameron and Clegg appear to endorse the view of the last Labour administration that democratic legitimacy requires at least a degree of electoral approval. Some constitutional observers would dispute this point.[8] For example, McKeown and Thomson (2010) argue that a distinction should be drawn between democratic and electoral legitimacy. If the constitutional role of the Lords is to scrutinise the Commons, they argue that this can be done more objectively and effectively by Members who are not driven by party allegiance or the need for election. The Draft House of Lords Reform Bill did try to counter this kind of criticism by stipulating a single and lengthy term of office.[9] It did not, however, address the suggestion that a chamber consisting entirely of Members appointed by an independent commission (on the basis of experience and expertise) may be better placed to examine legislation and more willing to challenge the Commons in the absence of party allegiance. Phillipson (2004) rejects this suggestion, claiming that the comparison with other unelected bodies such as the judiciary

[8] Do not fall into the trap of vaguely citing 'some' or 'many' sources: you must show your examiner that you can refer to specific examples.

[9] This is a useful point to make and, in addition, demonstrates knowledge of the provisions of the Bill, rather than simply the headlines about it.

[10] Where academic opinion is divided on an issue, credit will be given to students who can acknowledge competing perspectives before reaching their own conclusion.

is disingenuous.[10] He reminds us that no other unelected body is able to exercise such power over the elected House of Commons, pointing to the number of times proposals have been defeated in the Lords (Phillipson, 2004). He does, however, maintain that a partially appointed chamber could be a way to ensure both democratic (electoral) legitimacy and independent expertise. Notwithstanding comments made in the foreword to the draft Bill set out in the question, it should be noted that the Coalition too supported the retention of some appointed peers, albeit in lesser numbers than Phillipson advocates.

It would appear that, following a century of discussion and disagreement, there is now a greater acceptance of the need to reform the composition of the House of Lords and an acceptance that this will require a move to some form of elected representation. The consensus within the proposals put forward since 1999 appears to be that some non-elected peers should remain to challenge executive hegemony in the Commons. It may well be that a move towards an elected chamber will be required in order to preserve the perception of democratic legitimacy, but that the retention of at least some non-elected Members would provide more substantive democratic benefit.[11]

[11] The conclusion must return to the issue of democratic legitimacy, as this is the key point made by the quotation used in the question.

 Make your answer stand out

- Having stated that the Lords will not defeat a Bill that formed part of the government's manifesto, you could address the passage of the Hunting Act 2004. Here, the Parliament Act 1949 was invoked following rejection by the Lords. A report prepared for the Lords concluded that the manifesto commitment was to allow a free vote, not to secure a ban, and that therefore there was no breach of the convention. This will be a good point to make because, not only does it give an example of the use of the Parliament Acts, but you have also demonstrated a more detailed understanding of the case and the issues it raised about the role of the Lords.

- By expanding the comment on the lack of political will to suggest abolition or radical reform. The relatively rare use of the Parliament Acts is worth exploring, as it does seem to suggest that there is an acceptance by the Commons that ignoring the views of the Lords may be seen as unconstitutional, or perhaps undemocratic.

- By expanding on the suggestion that the unelected House of Lords has a democratic function. There is an argument to be made that the second chamber has the potential to act as a protection for constitutional principles. Certainly, this was the argument made by several peers during the debate upon the controversial proposals to limit judicial review in the Criminal Justice and Courts Act 2015. Lord Marks, the Liberal Democrat peer described the Bill as 'an assault upon the rule of law' (HL Deb Vol. 756, Col. 960), while Lord Irvine stressed the importance of judicial review for the separation of powers (ibid., col. 964).

- By using the controversy surrounding the Strathclyde review as the basis for expanding the discussion suggested above. See Chapter 1 for a detailed discussion of this topic.

! Don't be tempted to . . .

- Spend time describing the basic outline of the legislature; you are not required to address the role of the Commons at all in this question.

- Describe reforms that have taken place in respect of the Lord Chancellor, or the establishment of the Supreme Court. You will not be given marks for knowing these details because they do not relate to the specific point of the question, which concerns the relationship of the legislative function of the Lords and ideas of democracy.

- Make general statements about the Lords without providing examples to support what you say. It is not enough to say that the Lords reject legislation that has been approved by the Commons: you need to provide an example.

? Question 6

Megan is a Member of Parliament belonging to the main opposition party. She is very unhappy about government plans to require council tenants to vacate their properties if their household income rises above the national average. The minister for housing has stated that this would allow waiting lists to be reduced by two-thirds and reduce overall expenditure on social housing by £6 million per annum. During a debate about the proposals, Megan attempts to voice her criticism but is shouted down by MPs from the government benches. One backbench MP yells at her to be quiet, calling her 'a stupid woman' with 'the brains of a drunken flea', and accuses her of being a liar. The Speaker does nothing to intervene.

Later on, Megan is approached by a senior civil servant who gives her a copy of an impact statement prepared for the housing minister. The document estimates that overall savings would be less than £1 million per year. Megan leaks the document to a journalist from the *Daily Standard* newspaper.

Figures from the impact statement appear in an article in the *Daily Standard* which is very critical of the government. A week later, Megan is in her office at the House of Commons when police officers arrive and demand to search the room. She is horrified by this and asks why. She is told that she is suspected of a criminal offence of aiding and abetting misfeasance in public office. She asks to see a warrant and is told that none is required as the Speaker has agreed that the search can take place. Megan is then arrested in respect of the offence.

Advise Megan of the implications arising from these facts.

Answer plan

→ Outline the meaning of 'parliamentary privilege'.

→ Explain that there is no legal recompense for comments made in debate.

→ Consider whether or not the Speaker has acted appropriately.

→ Discuss the applicability of privilege to criminal investigations.

→ Assess the legality of the police search.

Diagram plan

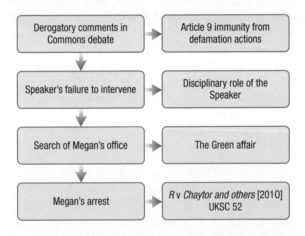

A printable version of this diagram plan is available from **www.pearsoned.co.uk/lawexpressqa**

Answer

'Parliamentary privilege' refers to the constitutional protection given to both Houses of Parliament to protect Parliament from outside interference and therefore to protect the independence of democratic debate. Privilege protects individual Members of either House, as well as applying collectively to each chamber as a whole. Parliamentary privilege can be divided into two main areas: immunity from civil action in respect of parliamentary proceedings; and the privilege of self-regulation. The facts of this scenario raise issues concerning both aspects of parliamentary privilege.[1]

[1] There is no need to provide an account of the historical development of privilege or its constitutional significance in detail. It is important to concentrate on the facts given.

Megan may well feel aggrieved about the personal nature of the abuse suffered during the House of Commons debate. However, there is no legal action that she can take. Article 9 of the Bill of Rights 1689 stated that 'freedom of speech, debates or proceedings in Parliament ought not to be impeached or questioned in any court or place out of Parliament'.[2] The intention was to protect parliamentarians from vexatious legal proceedings designed to stifle democratic debate, but extends in the modern age to confer immunity from any civil action for defamation. It is clear that this protection is absolute in respect of 'parliamentary proceedings', even in circumstances where the person making the statement knows it is false (*Wason v Walter* (1868) LR 4QB). While there has been some debate about what business will be considered to be part of 'proceedings', there is no question that the debate about the proposals will be covered by privilege.[3]

[2] It is always a good idea to refer to Article 9, as this remains the key authority providing the scope of parliamentary privilege.

[3] As this part of the problem is very clear, there are no marks for a broader discussion about activities that may be difficult to classify as proceedings.

The protection given to freedom of speech does not mean that there are no consequences for defamatory or abusive language in Parliaments; only that these must be administered internally rather than through the court system.[4] The parliamentary privilege of self-regulation has been the focus of controversy on a number of occasions where it has appeared that the legislature has not had robust systems to prevent wrongdoing by its members, one of the most recent cases being the MPs' expenses scandal of 2009. The establishment of an independent body to regulate expenses (the Independent Parliamentary Standards Authority) can perhaps be seen as the beginning of a shift towards external accountability.[5] In this instance, however, it is clear that the Speaker, in his role as chair of Commons debates, has the power to enforce discipline on the floor of the house. *Erskine May's Parliamentary Practice* (Millar, 2011) reminds MPs that 'good temper and moderation are the characteristics of parliamentary language'.[6] The Speaker should have intervened during this debate and asked the Member to withdraw the abusive remarks and the accusation that Megan is a liar. Failure to comply would leave open the possibility of the Speaker 'naming' the MP and asking for their

[4] Many scenarios require only a discussion of the protection from actions in defamation in respect of remarks in the chamber. The problem here, however, clearly demands consideration of the Speaker's disciplinary role.

[5] This is a valid point, but you must not spend too long on general discussion about exclusive cognisance as your focus should be on the Speaker's role as chair.

[6] You may not be able to remember quotes in your examination, but it is a good idea to refer to *Erskine May* as this demonstrates that you can provide the authority for your assertions about the Speaker's role.

[7] There is no need to outline the various sanctions available for different forms of contempt, but you will be rewarded for knowing the specific consequences that could arise here.

suspension from the House for five days (for a first offence).[7] It is clear, then, that the Speaker has acted improperly by failing to censure the remarks. There does not appear to be any way for Megan to seek recompense from the Speaker, as there is no clear system to enforce the requirements of the role. In 2009, Michael Martin resigned the position following unprecedented political pressure arising from his handling of the expenses scandal, but this situation is highly unlikely to have a similar impact.

[8] Because the problem scenario mirrors the Green affair so precisely, it would be really difficult to gain high marks if you are not familiar with both the facts and the consequences that followed his arrest.

The facts surrounding the leaked memorandum are similar to those that led to the arrest of Damian Green MP in 2008 and, crucially, the subsequent search of his office in the Houses of Parliament.[8] It is now settled that privilege does not protect Members of Parliament from criminal prosecution (*R v Chaytor and others* [2010] UKSC 52), and therefore Megan cannot make a complaint about the fact of her arrest.[9] The unauthorised disclosure of material by the civil servant can amount to misfeasance in a public office. As with the Green affair, however, there could be concerns here that a report to the police and subsequent arrest are a disproportionate political reaction to the publication of materialthat caused difficulties for the government but fell short of a breach of the Official Secrets Act (Bradley, 2012). The parallels with this scenario are so strong that it seems safe to advise Megan that the arrest is highly unlikely to result in charges. The CPS would be unable to determine that there was a realistic prospect of conviction on these facts.

[9] This is quite an important point to note. Concern about the motivation for the arrest does not affect its legality.

[10] Where you are absolutely certain of the position, do not be afraid to set it out unequivocally. This demonstrates considerable confidence in your ability to assess the facts given.

A second issue arises about the search that has taken place with the consent of the Speaker. This should not have occurred.[10] Following the Green affair, the House of Commons Committee on the Issue of Privilege produced a report, chaired by Sir Menzies Campbell, which criticised not only the decision to arrest the MP, but also the conduct of the search of his office. The report reiterated the need for a warrant to search any part of the precincts of Parliament. Any materials concerning parliamentary proceedings will be covered by privilege and must not be examined by the police (it is usual for the police to instruct independent legal advisors to consider the material and withhold any items deemed subject to privilege).[11] As with the Green case, the actions of the police here should be the source of considerable concern, as they appear to undermine the purpose of Article 9 in ensuring that Members of Parliament can operate without fear of executive interference.

[11] The scenario does not mention whether or not any items were seized, but it is worth noting to show the examiner that you understand the procedures that apply.

Again, any action that Megan may wish to take is circumscribed by the fact that privilege protects not only her but also protects Speaker and his or her assistants in the House. Therefore, while she may be able to make a complaint to the police, she has no obvious means of seeking recompense from the Speaker. This situation is considerably more serious than the first, in light of the Green affair, which resulted in not only the report referred to above but also a declaration of protocol by the Speaker in 2008, confirming that no consent can be given to any search without warrant. Michael Martin was the first Speaker to be forced from office for 300 years, and his resignation was described as being unprecedented. Arguably, however, it does now provide a precedent to show that serious criticism may create unbearable political pressure to relinquish the office. It may well be that this would be such a case.[12]

[12] You will be rewarded for offering this kind of analysis, as it shows that you are able to draw conclusions from the materials you have studied, but do take care not to overstate the likelihood of this as you are only able to speculate.

Parliamentary privilege is often discussed because of the benefits it provides to MPs. Here, it can be seen that operating outside of the ordinary law may, in rare instances, result in an MP having less protection than the average citizen.[13] Megan has no legal mechanism available to her to obtain redress from the Speaker and will therefore be forced to rely upon the far less certain effects of public and political opinion.

[13] This is an unusual but a fair conclusion to make, as the answer has carefully set out the arguments that support it.

✓ **Make your answer stand out**

- By explaining a little more why the Official Secrets Act could not be invoked here. It could be said that the provisions are broad enough to criminalise an extremely wide range of conduct. This could be used to lend more weight to the suggestion that the police action in this case was wholly disproportionate.

- By considering the issue of the extent to which documents in an MP's office should be covered by privilege. It has been suggested that correspondence between an MP and their constituents should be treated as privileged in the same way as communication between a solicitor and their clients.

- By setting the discussion about the need for a warrant in a wider constitutional context. You could draw parallels between this situation and the judgment in *Entick* v *Carrington* (1765) 19 St Tr 1029.

- By considering the constitutional role of the Speaker and whether or not the introduction of external bodies to regulate expenses, and the Martin resignation, has significantly diminished the importance of the role.

! Don't be tempted to . . .

■ Assume that the question is concerned primarily with freedom of expression. The inclusion of information about the leaked report could lead students into a fruitless discussion about Article 10 of the European Convention on Human Rights and press freedom.

■ Spend too long explaining the case law concerning privilege and defamation. There is no need, for example, to consider the Hamilton affair or the Defamation Act 1996. In this case, you are being invited to assess the Speaker's role, rather than the fact of the comments made.

@ Try it yourself

Now take a look at the question below and attempt to answer it. You can check your response against the answer guidance available on the companion website (**www.pearsoned.co.uk/lawexpressqa**).

Mrs Grantham is the Member of Parliament for Knottingley North, and her son is a student. Last summer, during his university holidays, her son asked whether he could work for her. She agreed to employ him as a research assistant, and claimed staffing expenses to pay his salary. He did very little work and spent most of the summer at home, playing computer games.

Mrs Grantham has now been contacted by the local newspaper and asked for comment on a rumour that she faces criminal prosecution for fraud offences. She seeks your advice, and wonders whether she has any grounds to prevent the matter going to court.

www.pearsoned.co.uk/lawexpressqa

Go online to access more revision support including additional essay and problem questions with diagram plans, and You be the marker questions, and to download all diagrams from the book.

The constitution and the Human Rights Act

5

How this topic may come up in exams

This topic lends itself to essay questions that ask you to consider the impact of the Human Rights Act 1998, and the relationship between the UK and the European Court of Human Rights. This issue is pervasive and could overlap with any area of the syllabus. You could be asked to discuss the effect of Convention rights on the constitutional doctrines considered in Chapters 1 and 2, or to assess any number of the substantive rights in connection with laws concerning terrorism, police powers or freedom of assembly. You will see in this chapter that there is no 'correct' position to take in relation to this topic: students can obtain very similar grades for an essay question even if they reach opposing conclusions. The key skill to develop is the ability to use your evidence carefully, to build a persuasive argument. Problem questions could ask you to address the use of the Human Rights Act in challenging or creating domestic legislation.

■ Before you begin

It's a good idea to consider the following key themes of the constitution and the Human Rights Act before tackling a question on this topic.

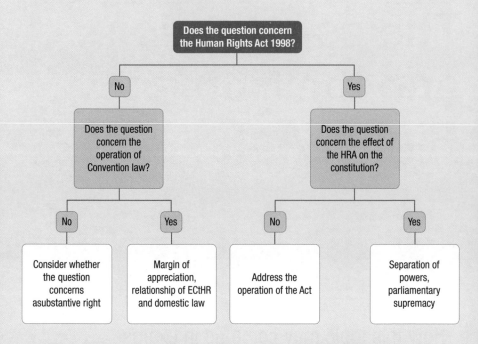

A printable version of this diagram is available from **www.pearsoned.co.uk/lawexpressqa**

🛈 Question 1

The (fictional) University Attendance Act 2010 aims to raise educational standards by ensuring that students take their studies seriously and get enough sleep. Section 10 makes it mandatory for all students to reside in university-managed accommodation during their studies. All universities are required to fit computerised entry systems to residences. The system must record details of any student who returns to their room after midnight. If this occurs more than twice in a seven-day period, all bank accounts belonging to that student will be frozen for one week (s. 13). If the student continues to return late, the penalties increase, and can result in the loss of a university place (s. 15).

Jim is a mature student at university who, prior to starting his course, lived with his wife and family. No university residence could be found to accommodate his family. Therefore, he returns home every weekend from Friday to Monday to see them. He is very disturbed when his bank accounts are frozen, and he is told that he may lose his place. He seeks advice about whether or not the Act of Parliament was made lawfully and whether or not human rights legislation can assist him. Advise Jim.

Diagram plan

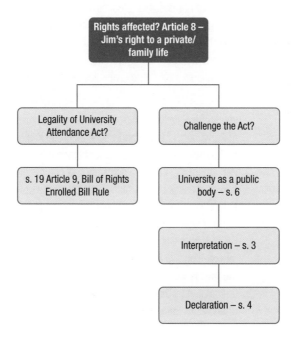

A printable version of this diagram plan is available from **www.pearsoned.co.uk/lawexpressqa**

Answer plan

→ Identify the Convention rights infringed by the legislation.

→ Discuss the legality of the Act of Parliament.

→ Explain the possibility of a claim following the Human Rights Act 1998.

→ Assess the likely approach of the court to the legislation, using sections 3 and 4 of the Act.

→ Draw conclusions about the likelihood of obtaining redress.

Answer

[1] This succinct introduction shows an understanding of the issues that need to be discussed, and also suggests that a particular conclusion will be reached. This shows confidence with the material.

[2] Before launching into a discussion about how the HRA works, it is necessary to be able to demonstrate why the legislation should be challenged, by reference to Convention rights. This can be done swiftly, to ensure more weight is given to discussion of how the matters will be dealt with in the domestic courts.

[3] This gives a clear answer, but more explanation is needed because the question specifically asks for consideration of this issue.

[4] When dealing with the HRA, the answer should refrain from making general statements about the effect of the legislation, and should ensure that specific sections are referenced.

It seems clear that the (fictitious) University Attendance Act (the Act) is in breach of Article 8 of the European Convention on Human Rights. The Human Rights Act 1998 (HRA) provides a mechanism for the citizen to enforce Convention rights in the domestic courts; however, it is not clear that this will provide Jim with effective redress.[1]

Article 8 enshrines the right to a private and family life, and any interference must be justified for one of the reasons specified in Article 8(2). It is not possible to construe the interference with Jim's family arrangements as 'necessary' for the purpose of protecting national security, public safety, health and morals, the rights of others, or to prevent disorder. Therefore, implementation of the Act leads to an unjustifiable interference with Jim's human rights.[2]

Jim queries whether the Act of Parliament is lawful. Regardless of whether legislative provisions conflict with Convention rights, any Act of Parliament is lawful and will be enforced in the courts.[3] Section 19 of the HRA imposes a requirement that a minister introducing a Bill to Parliament must make a declaration of compatibility with the Convention or, if this is not possible, explain that the government wishes the legislation to be passed. Even if this requirement was not met during the passage of the legislation, then it appears that Article 9 of the Bill of Rights will preclude the possibility of judicial interference with 'proceedings' in Parliament. The constitution rests upon the notion of the legislative supremacy of Parliament, which includes the notion (articulated by Dicey) that no person or body may question the validity of an Act of Parliament. The HRA does not alter this state of affairs, and explicitly protects the authority of Parliament by stating that its provisions do not affect the continued validity of any incompatible legislation (s. 3(2)(b), s. 4(6)).[4]

However, Jim may be able to seek a remedy in the domestic courts by bringing a claim against the university for breaching his Article 8 rights. The HRA states that any person who is a victim of a breach of their rights may bring proceedings (s. 7). This will not be problematic for Jim, as he is clearly directly affected. An action can lie only against a public authority (s. 6); this issue requires some consideration. Universities are independent organisations, although they may receive a degree of subsidy from the state.[5] The courts have, in a number of cases, found that if the function of a body can be construed as governmental, then a claim can be actionable. In particular, any body permitted to exercise coercive powers against the individual will almost certainly be considered to be a public body (*R (Munjaz)* v *Mersey Care NHS Trust* [2005] UKHL 58). Considering the punitive powers given to the university, it seems highly probable that it will be dealt with as a public body.[6] In any event, section 6 makes it clear that courts and tribunals are public bodies, creating an indirect horizontal effect.[7] As a result, even if the university is a private body, when dealing with a dispute over the Act, the courts are required to uphold Jim's Convention rights.

The HRA imposes a duty on the courts to interpret existing legislation as compatible with Convention rights 'in so far as it is possible to do so' (s.3). The extent of the interpretative duty has been questioned in numerous cases since the Act came into effect. It is clear that the provision confers considerable powers on the court to interpret statutes as compliant even when the literal meaning of the words is unambiguous. On occasion, the judiciary has utilised the power to impose a meaning that 'linguistically may appear strained' (*R v A* [2001] UKHL 25, per Lord Steyn). This does not, however, extend so far as to allow the judiciary to engage in a process of interpretation tantamount to drafting legislation.[8] This point was stressed in *Re S (Minors)* [2002] UKHL 10, in which the Lords confirmed that the HRA maintains the 'constitutional boundary', and preserves parliamentary sovereignty. The scenario above does not include the precise wording of the statute. However, the effect of these sections is to authorise substantial interference with the domestic and financial affairs of students, and it is hard to see how the courts could read down or read into[9] such provisions to force compliance. Therefore, it would appear unlikely that the courts would be able to utilise section 3 to assist Jim.[10]

[5] Marks will be awarded for noticing that the type of organisation may pose a problem, as it shows familiarity with the procedural issues.

[6] Evidence needs to be provided to support the conclusion that the university is a public body. There are a number of cases that could be cited here.

[7] This is an important point to be aware of, and one that is often overlooked. Reference to 'horizontal effect' shows an understanding of the operation of Convention law. There is no need to provide a detailed explanation, as correct use of the term shows that the issue is understood.

[8] The possibilities afforded by section 3 should not be overstated; marks will be given for recognising that it does not authorise rewriting legislation.

[9] This shows considerable confidence by referring to the judicial terminology.

[10] It is crucial to keep returning to the facts of the scenario and answering the question, which asks you to advise Jim.

Where legislation conflicts with a Convention right, the superior courts have the discretion to make a declaration of incompatibility (s. 4 of the HRA). Referred to in *R v A* (above) as a 'last resort', a declaration will generally be made only where section 3 has been considered and it is deemed impossible to impose a Convention-compliant meaning on the wording. Once a declaration has been made, the government can determine whether any action is necessary. If it is felt appropriate to alter the legislation, this can be done either by introducing a new statute or, under section 10, by taking remedial action and amending the offending provisions by ministerial order. Any order should be limited to removing the incompatible portions of the legislation, and is subject to retrospective parliamentary approval.[11] Jim should be advised that a declaration of incompatibility is likely to be made in this case.

[11] This section demonstrates awareness of the effect of a declaration.

As highlighted above, section 4(6) makes it clear that a declaration does not affect the validity of the Act. Therefore, as expressly stated at section 4(6)(b), it is not binding on the parties to the case. The courts will enforce the law as it exists when dealing with the case. A declaration of incompatibility will not assist Jim in obtaining redress in the domestic courts.[12]

[12] This is an important point, because the answer needs to focus not just on whether or not the courts will approve of the legislation, but on the impact of any decisions on Jim's situation.

If a declaration of incompatibility is made by the superior court, then Jim could consider taking his case to the European Court of Human Rights to seek a remedy.[13] Where a declaration has been made, the government is likely to wish to settle the matter as the outcome of the case would appear to be almost inevitable.

[13] Because the question requires you to focus on advising Jim, you need to acknowledge the fact that he has the option to take a claim to Strasbourg.

The Act includes provisions that infringe Jim's right to a private and family life. However, this does not render the statute unlawful, and it will be upheld by the court unless and until the government repeals or amends the law. Therefore, the HRA does not provide Jim with assistance in the short term, and he may still need to appeal to the European Court of Human Rights in order to obtain redress.[14]

[14] The conclusion needs to refer back to the issues that the question raised, and to summarise the advice given.

✓ Make your answer stand out

- By providing more detail about the redress available in Strasbourg, and explaining the concept of a 'friendly settlement'. This will show the examiner that you have a detailed understanding of the operation of Convention law. You must, of course, ensure that you relate this to Jim's situation.

■ By explaining what is meant by 'indirect horizontal effect', and providing some authority to illustrate this point. A good example might be *Goodwin* v *UK* (1996) 22 EHRR 123, in which (as Loveland points out) the European Court concludes that a state may be in breach if citizens can rely on legal provisions that restrict the access to Convention rights of others. (Loveland, I. (2012), *Constitutional Law, Administrative Law and Human Rights: A Critical Introduction* (6th edn). Oxford: Oxford University Press).

! Don't be tempted to . . .

■ Spend time discussing the limits of Article 8. The focus of the question is not on the extent of Convention rights. It is not necessary, then, to enter into a detailed discussion about the margin of appreciation afforded to states in cases such as *Handyside* v *UK*. You must make sure that you focus on what action Jim may be able to take in this case.

■ Refer to the HRA in general terms. It is very important that you do know which sections are relevant, and why. The more detail you can give, the better. For example, it is clearly right to say that the courts may make a declaration of incompatibility (s. 4). It is more impressive if you can also reference section 4(6) and explain that this has no effect on the case being determined. It is even better if you can highlight that this section serves to preserve the principle of parliamentary supremacy, as this would show that you are making links between the different areas of the syllabus.

Question 2

The Human Rights Act 1998 has strengthened the constitutional position of the judiciary, and weakened the position of the executive.

Discuss.

Answer plan

→ Outline briefly the functions of the judiciary and the executive.

→ Explain the powers given to the judiciary by the HRA (ss. 3 and 4).

→ Provide examples to demonstrate judicial 'strength'.

→ Consider the role of the European Court of Human Rights.

Diagram plan

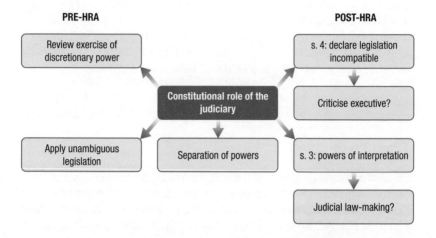

A printable version of this diagram plan is available from **www.pearsoned.co.uk/lawexpressqa**

Answer

The Labour government introduced the Human Rights Act 1998 (HRA) shortly after coming to power, proclaiming that it was 'bringing rights home'. A decade later, senior government figures are highly critical of the Act; Jack Straw, as justice minister, stated that he was 'frustrated' by the Act in late 2008. The Conservative party has stated that it will seek to abolish the Act and replace it with a British Bill of Rights.

[1] The question refers to the clash between the executive and the judiciary, but you will need to recognise that this arises through challenges made in the courts to legislative provisions.

It is clear, then, that the Act is a source of concern to the major political parties. Since 2000, there have been several cases in which the superior courts have utilised powers granted by the HRA in order to challenge legislation.[1] This may lead to the conclusion that the HRA has increased the ability of the judiciary to hold the other organs of state to account. It will be argued, however, that while there are instances in which the judiciary has appeared to challenge legislation supported by the executive, these can be best characterised as political, rather than constitutional issues.[2]

[2] Many answers to this question will be too descriptive. Marks will be available for asserting a clear point of view.

Although the United Kingdom does not have a written document that enshrines the authorities and functions of the organs of state, the doctrine of the separation of powers can be considered to be

[3] You will be rewarded for noting that this question is focused on the impact of the HRA on the separation of powers. You should not spend too long explaining the doctrine, but a brief explanation is needed.

[4] This question does pose some difficulty by requiring the focus to be on the relationship between the executive and the judiciary. The HRA is primarily concerned with approaches to legislation. This section explains why a discussion of the judicial approach to legislation is permissible, as most statute originates from government.

[5] The answer needs to ensure that it does have a clear focus on identifiable legal issues. The discussion must be centred on the provisions of the HRA rather than a broad, political debate.

[6] There are numerous cases dealing with section 3. *R v A* is useful because it represents an example of a very broad use of the interpretative power. The phrase 'linguistically strained' is worth remembering, as it is a useful way of briefly explaining that the power can be used to alter the obvious meaning of a statutory provision.

[7] You should do more than explain the powers given to the courts by the HRA; this needs to be related to the issue of power within the constitution.

an integral part of the constitution.[3] According to the doctrine, the roles of the organs of state are distinct: Parliament is the supreme law-making body, while the executive is responsible for introducing policy and administration, and the judiciary interprets and applies the law. The HRA granted new discretionary powers to the judiciary when considering statute. It would seem that, if there is a shift in the constitutional balance of power, the relationship between the legislature and the judiciary would be the one affected. The question presupposes an acceptance of the view, famously promulgated by Lord Hailsham, that there is the potential for an 'elected dictatorship' if a party of government enjoys a large majority in the Commons. Challenges made to legislation introduced by government could be viewed as, to some extent, undermining the ability of the executive to administer policy.[4]

It is perhaps appropriate to emphasise that the HRA did not increase or alter the rights of the citizen. The right of petition to the European Court of Human Rights has existed since 1966. The HRA aimed to ensure that Convention rights are incorporated into domestic law and accordingly are enforceable in domestic courts.

The HRA gives the judiciary powers to uphold Convention rights. Prior to the HRA, where an unambiguous legislative provision conflicted with a Convention right, the constitutional principle of parliamentary supremacy required the court to apply the statute in accordance with its clear meaning. Section 3 of the HRA grants the courts powers to interpret statutes as Convention compliant 'in so far as it is possible to do so'. It is clear that this allows the courts to read down, or read into, provisions even where no ambiguity is present.[5] The scope of this power is evident in cases such as ***Ghaidan v Godin-Mendoza*** [2004] UKHL 30, where the court was prepared to read additional words into the statute, or ***R v A*** [2001] UKHL 25, where the judiciary were prepared to infer a meaning that was 'linguistically strained'.[6]

Critics of the HRA could argue that section 3 has the potential fundamentally to alter the constitutional landscape, by granting a degree of legislative power to the judiciary, allowing it to subvert the intention of Parliament.[7] Consider the case of ***R v A***, which concerned safeguards against the cross-examination of rape victims contained within section 41 of the Youth Justice and Criminal Evidence Act 1999. The clear aim of Parliament was to ensure that the trial process did not allow questions to be asked regarding sexual history, and yet the judiciary interpreted the provision as meaning that questions were permissible if necessary for a fair trial within the meaning of Article 6. Decisions such as this lend weight to suggestions that the HRA gives power to unelected members of the judiciary in formulating policy.[8] However, this must be balanced against numerous instances where the courts have declared themselves unwilling to impose a meaning that goes 'against the grain' of the statute, as was said in *Ghaidan v Godin-Mendoza*. Therefore, it would seem that, despite the additional powers contained at section 3, the judiciary remains largely respectful of constitutional boundaries and does not seek to stray beyond the 'outer limit' *(Re W (Care Plan)* [2001] EWCA Civ 757) by embarking on a process of drafting legislation.[9]

[8] Here, the developing argument refers back to the issue in the question, to maintain focus.

[9] A preliminary conclusion can be reached here, before moving on to the next part of the argument.

Where it is not possible for a statutory provision to be interpreted as compliant with Conventions using section 3, section 4 of the HRA gives the superior courts the discretion to issue a declaration of incompatibility. This has no effect on the parties in the case, but allows the judiciary to give a clear signal to the executive that the statute requires consideration.[10] The HRA contains a provision for the executive to take remedial action to amend the offending part of the legislation (s. 10). During the passage of the HRA through Parliament, the government envisaged that section 4 would rarely be invoked and this has proved to be the case. In the period 2000–6 the government amended existing law or introduced new legislation in nine cases following a declaration of incompatibility (Joint Committee on Human Rights (2006), 23rd Report).

[10] The answer reminds the marker that the key issue is the relationship between the judiciary and the executive.

The significance of section 4 should not be overstated, however, as the HRA is careful to preserve the supremacy of domestic law. A section 4 declaration cannot compel the executive to review the legislation, and, unless government determines that change is necessary, the courts will continue to enforce the law. It can be argued, then, that the constitutional balance is unchanged. Legislative change occurs not because of coercive pressure from the court, but as a result of political necessity.[11] A series of decisions concerning asylum and terrorism has indeed resulted in the judiciary making strong criticism of particular statutes, and this has resulted in legislative change. In *A v Secretary of State for the Home Department* [2004] UKHL 56, the House of Lords declared that Part IV of the Anti-Terrorism, Crime and Security Act 2001 was unlawful, which resulted in repeal

[11] This is the crux of the argument suggested at the outset, and, at this stage, evidence has been shown to support this assertion.

[12] This is a point worth making, as the courts are not creating new rights, but simply enforcing those protected by the Convention.

and a shift in policy as regards foreign terror suspects. It should be remembered that the courts are guided by Convention principles, and judgments of the court in Strasbourg. If section 4 did not provide a means of resolving the issue domestically, a negative judgment from Strasbourg would inevitably follow. Therefore, the pressure for change is extrinsic rather than domestic.[12]

Political leaders may express concerns about the HRA, but, on closer examination, it seems that the Act does not in fact make radical alteration to the constitutional position of the judiciary. Arguably, pressure on the executive regarding particular policy choices stems not from the judiciary in London, but from that in Strasbourg.

 Make your answer stand out

- By giving more consideration to the issue raised regarding extrinsic pressure on the executive. Some academics suggest that the domestic courts are beginning to adopt a more radical approach than that taken by Strasbourg (see, for example, Fenwick, H. (2016) *Civil Liberties and Human Rights* (5th edn). London: Routledge Cavendish, ch. 4).
- By considering the ramifications of repealing the HRA and replacing it with a British Bill of Rights. Considerable academic comment is available regarding this possibility, and the potential implications for the UK's relationship with Strasbourg. A good starting point would be Elliott, M. (2013) *Law, Rights and Constitutional Politics*, Research Paper 55/2013, Cambridge Faculty of Law (available via: **http://www.law.cam.ac.uk/ssrn/**)

! Don't be tempted to . . .

- Engage in a discussion of issues, without being able to pinpoint examples and cite authorities. A discursive essay of this kind has the potential to lose focus on legal issues and talk generally about the role of the courts. For example, make sure that you can give examples of when the courts have used section 3 to interpret statute in a manner that seems contrary to legislative intention.
- Ignore the fact that the question specifically refers to the clash between the executive and the judiciary. It is fine to use examples that, on the face of it, seem to be more concerned with conflict between the courts and the legislature, provided that this is justified by explaining that the statutes in question represent executive policy.

 Question 3

The wide margin afforded to signatory states undermines the concept of 'fundamental freedoms' in the United Kingdom.

Discuss.

Answer plan

→ Explain the terms 'qualified rights' and 'margin of appreciation'.

→ Outline the supervisory role of the European Court of Human Rights.

→ Consider the justification for differing margins for different rights.

→ Assess the role of the domestic courts in applying margins of appreciation.

Diagram plan

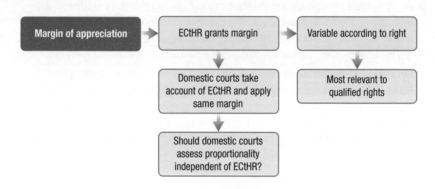

A printable version of this diagram plan is available from **www.pearsoned.co.uk/lawexpressqa**

Answer

The European Convention on Human Rights and Fundamental Free-doms was drafted in the aftermath of the Second World War, as the atrocities that occurred during the Nazi regime became apparent. Signatories to the Convention agree to secure the rights contained within the treaty, and the European Court of Human Rights (ECtHR) is empowered to determine whether an action by a state is compatible with that duty. In so doing, the ECtHR may afford the state a 'margin of appreciation'; it is the effect of this judicial concept that must be examined. It can be argued that the margin of appreciation has, on occasion, allowed the UK government to enact legislation that runs contrary to the spirit of the Convention.[1]

The Convention seeks to set a common standard of rights and freedoms for the signatory states. Article 1 of the Convention places the primary responsibility for securing those rights upon the states. The role of the ECtHR can be seen as supervisory: to review the decisions made by states about how to achieve the objectives of the treaty.[2] The notion of 'margin of appreciation' has emerged over time, as a result of the fact that the language of the treaty permits restrictions on many of the Article rights. Few rights are 'absolute'; the majority are subject to qualification. For example, Article 8 sets out the right to a private and family life, but Article 8(2) recognises that a state may interfere with that right if it is 'necessary' for one of the following purposes: national security, public safety or economic well-being; to prevent crime and disorder; to protect health or morals; or to protect the freedoms of others. In determining whether the action of a state falls within one of the permitted qualifications, the ECtHR acknowledges that the domestic authorities may be better placed to judge what is necessary in the context of their own cultural values and norms; this degree of deference is the 'margin of appreciation'.[3]

Decisions of the ECtHR show that the 'margin' is not fixed, and the degree of flexibility granted to the state may vary according to the nature of the right itself, and also to the reason claimed for qualification.[4] In **Sunday Times v UK** (1979) 2 EHRR 245, the court drew a distinction between issues such as health and morals, and more 'objective' issues such as judicial autonomy (the qualification being claimed in that case). When dealing with an objective issue, the court was not prepared to allow a wide margin, whereas, in **Handyside v UK** (1976) 1 EHRR 737,[5] the court refused to interfere with the domestic government's determination of the moral need for obscenity legislation. A broad margin is also evident when dealing with social policy issues, which are considered to be matters where there can be legitimate political difference and debate. Therefore, in **Hatton v UK** (2003) 37 EHRR 28, the court refused to hold that, in allowing night flights from Heathrow, the state interfered with the Article 8 rights of the claimant. Here, the state was permitted to reach a determination that the interference was necessary for the economic well-being of the nation, and the ECtHR deferred to that determination.

[2] This is a key point to make here, as it makes clear that you understand the respective roles of the signatory states and the ECtHR.

[3] It is essential to be able to give an explanation of the term 'margin of appreciation', and, to do so, reference to the existence of qualifications on Convention rights is required.

[4] The imprecise boundaries of the margin of appreciation needs to be noted, as this forms part of the argument that will be developed about the need for domestic courts to be rigorous in assessing the validity of a particular qualification.

[5] *Handyside* is a useful authority, as it is a clear illustration of application of a margin of appreciation.

It is important to note that the existence of a margin of appreciation does not mean that the court will not review the exercise of discretion. However, as Fenwick (2016) notes, if the margin permitted is wide, the ECtHR will engage in minimal supervision, limited largely to ensuring any discretion was exercised in good faith. If the margin is narrow, there will be a more rigorous examination of the restriction to ensure that it is proportionate to the aim. The notion of a margin of appreciation is controversial. As Loveland (2012) points out, viewed in a positive light, the concept shows an appropriate respect for the autonomy of democratically elected national governments. Alternatively, it could be argued that the ECtHR has, on occasion, abdicated responsibility for ensuring that the rights of minority groups are protected.[6]

[6] A willingness to acknowledge the academic debate ensures that the answer is not overly descriptive; analysis of the issue will be rewarded by the marker.

Matters of national security are conceded to be sensitive, and, historically, the ECtHR has been reluctant to interfere with a domestic determination of necessity. The case of *Brannigan and McBride v UK* (1993) 17 EHRR 539 caused considerable concern when the court upheld the legality of a derogation from Article 5 applied by the government. The derogation arose following the judgment in *Brogan v UK* (1988) 11 EHRR 117, in which the ECtHR held that periods of detention authorised under terrorism legislation were an unjustified interference with the right to liberty. It is difficult to reconcile the decision in *Brannigan* with the ECtHR's role in ensuring robust protection for fundamental freedoms, as there appears to be a tacit endorsement of actions previously considered to be in breach of the Convention.[7]

[7] This is a useful case to cite, as it provides support for the suggestion in the question that fundamental freedoms are undermined by the application of a margin of appreciation.

It is possible to endorse the notion of the margin of appreciation, as it properly emphasises the role of the state in determining how best to balance the freedoms of the individual against the broader public interest. However, the approach of the domestic courts to the margin of appreciation could be viewed as leading to a 'watering down' of the Convention, as Fenwick suggests.[8] Section 2 of the Human Rights Act 1998 requires the courts to give weight to the ECtHR judgments. There are a number of cases in which decisions appear to suggest that where Strasbourg has afforded a considerable margin to the state, the domestic courts should also give judicial deference to the decision-maker. For example, in the case of *Gillan and Quinton v UK* [2009] ECHR 28, the House of Lords had to determine whether the exercise of 'stop and search' powers authorised by the Terrorism

[8] The central argument, that the margin of appreciation has a detrimental effect on the protection of rights in the domestic courts, is being developed here. It would not be sufficient to refer to Fenwick's argument; the answer must also incorporate some illustrative authority to support this view.

Act 2000 breached (*inter alia*) Article 8 of the ECHR. The state claimed that any interference was necessary in the interests of national security. The judgment suggests that, once deference is given on that issue, there can be no interference with the exercise of the power and no circumstance in which the use of the provision would be disproportionate. Fenwick (2007) refers to this as 'double deference'. As noted above, acknowledgement of a margin of appreciation does not mean that the ECtHR will not address the restriction. In the case of **Gillan**, when the matter reached Strasbourg the court was unanimous in finding a breach of Article 8.

There will always be a need to balance individual and majority freedoms, and there is unlikely ever to be a homogeneous culture across Europe. The concept of a margin of appreciation, therefore, is helpful in acknowledging these facts while nevertheless seeking to maintain a common standard of rights and freedoms. It can be argued, however, that if deference to national autonomy is not followed by rigorous examination of executive power in the domestic courts, some of the protection for individual freedoms envisaged in the Convention will be lost.[9]

[9] The conclusion is justified, as the argument has been developed throughout the answer.

✓ Make your answer stand out

- By exploring some of the academic views referred to regarding deference in more detail. Fenwick (2007) is an excellent text (*Civil Liberties and Human Rights* (4th edn). London: Routledge).
- By acknowledging that the decisions of Strasbourg do not always lead to a clear conclusion about the existence of the margin of appreciation in respect of a particular Convention right. Although you have alluded to different justifications for restrictions on a right resulting in a differential approach (through *Sunday Times* and *Handyside*), you could make the point that this somewhat undermines the notion of a 'fundamental' right.
- By exploring the notion of 'double deference' in more detail. Good use has been made of the litigation concerning *Gillan*. You could question whether or not the Strasbourg decision marks a shift towards more stringent supervision from the ECtHR. This would show the ability to draw conclusions about the developing law.
- By referring to the Protocols contained in the Brighton Declaration (2012), which re-emphasise the importance of the margin of appreciation.

> ! **Don't be tempted to . . .**
>
> ■ Assume that the marker will know that you understand the term 'margin of appreciation'. You need to be able to give a definition.
>
> ■ Use terminology incorrectly. A surprisingly large number of students refer to the permitted restrictions on Convention rights as 'derogations', and so lose marks. Ensure that you know the difference between qualifications upon a right for a permitted purpose, and the process of derogation which allows a state to withdraw from the obligation to protect a Convention right in certain limited circumstances.
>
> ■ Fail to explain how the cases you cite support the argument. Too many students make statements along the lines of '*Handyside* v *UK* is an example of the margin of appreciation'. You need to explain that the judgment demonstrates that the ECtHR allowed the state the margin to determine the most appropriate standard of morality for its own population.

Question 4

The government publishes a consultation paper proposing a new Bill provisionally entitled the 'Criminal Trial Bill'. The aim of the legislation is to ensure that more criminal convictions are obtained, by reversing the burden of proof so that defendants will need to prove their innocence in all cases.

Discuss the legality of these proposals, and the difficulties in passing and enforcing the legislation in light of the Human Rights Act 1998.

Answer plan

→ Explain the presumption of innocence in domestic law, and under Article 6.

→ Explain the difference between a legal and an evidential burden of proof, with examples.

→ Consider whether the proposals are in breach of Article 6(2).

→ Outline the effect of section 19.

→ Analyse the likely approach of the courts in enforcing the legislation, in light of sections 3 and 4 of the HRA.

Diagram plan

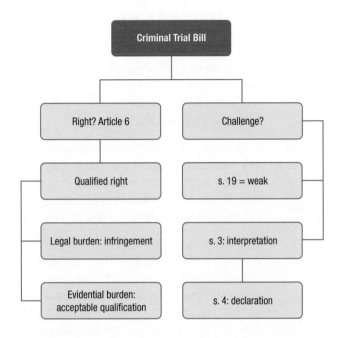

A printable version of this diagram plan is available from **www.pearsoned.co.uk/lawexpressqa**

Answer

[1] The question does not specify the reasons for the Bill being problematic; credit will be given for being able to identify the issue.

The proposals contained in the Bill would, if enacted, remove the presumption of innocence in criminal trials, described as the 'golden thread' running through the English legal system (***Woolmington v DPP*** [1935] AC 462). The presumption of innocence in criminal trials is expressly protected by Article 6(2) of the European Convention on Human Rights.[1] It is probable that these proposals could violate the Convention. The Human Rights Act (HRA) would enable the domestic courts to seek to circumvent the effects of the proposals.

As a general principle, defendants in criminal trials are considered to be innocent until all elements of the crime are proved beyond reasonable doubt. However, the concept of a reversal of the burden of proof is not novel, particularly in relation to defences. A distinction should be drawn between an evidential and a legal burden. The imposition of an evidential burden upon the defendant can be understood as a

[2] Some knowledge of criminal law is needed, to be able to explain the different burdens of proof. This question cannot really be attempted without a specific appreciation of the rights conferred by Article 6, and an understanding of the operation of the burden of proof.

[3] The focus is returned to human rights; it is important to return to the central issue even when referring to other areas of law, to make sure that all material is utilised to answer the question.

[4] Discussion of the European approach was necessary, but the answer needs to move to consideration of the domestic application of Convention law.

[5] This is probably the most crucial case to include in the answer, as the judgment clearly sets out the matters that will be considered when assessing whether placing a burden on the defendant is justifiable.

partial reversal of the burden of proof: the defendant needs to raise some evidence of the existence of the defence; thereafter, the task reverts to the Crown to disprove the claim.[2] Often, all that is required is for the defendant to make the claim. For example, a person accused of an offence against the person can state that they acted in self-defence. It is then for the Crown to provide evidence that their actions were not a legitimate use of reasonable force. An evidential burden does not equate to a presumption of guilt, and would not therefore be considered a breach of Article 6(2).[3]

The imposition of a legal burden is more onerous, and requires the defendant to prove a particular matter. A legal burden upon the defendant is rare at common law (the defence of insanity is a rare example), but may be imposed by statute (generally in relation to defences). A legal burden has the clear potential to violate Article 6.

The European Court of Human Rights (ECtHR) makes it clear that Article 6(2) is not absolute, confirming in *Salabiaku v France* (1988) 13 EHRR 379 that presumptions may be justified, provided that they remain within reasonable limits. When determining whether or not a particular presumption is justified, consideration will be given to what is at stake. The domestic courts have adopted a similar approach and stressed the importance of proportionality.[4] Therefore, whether or not the imposition of a legal burden is justifiable will depend on issues including the seriousness of the allegation, and whether or not the matter is one the defendant can reasonably be expected to prove. In the conjoined appeals *Sheldrake v DPP; Attorney General's Reference (No. 4 of 2002)* [2004] UKHL 43[5] the House of Lords reached differing conclusions in each case. Sheldrake was charged with being in charge of a motor vehicle while under the influence. Statute provided a defence if he could prove that he was not intending to drive the vehicle. The legal burden in this instance was justified, as it was for a legitimate purpose (the protection of road users) and was a matter about which the defendant could reasonably be expected to adduce evidence. This was distinct from the situation in the second case, which concerned the offence of belonging to a proscribed organisation. Section 11(2) of the Terrorism Act 2000 provides for a defence where the defendant can show that they joined prior to the date of proscription and have had no involvement since that time. Here, the House held that this required the defendant to prove a negative, which would be difficult to do, placing the provision in conflict with Article 6.

[6] Having outlined the authority, this must be used to answer the question posed about the suggested legislation.

The suggested legislation, applicable to all offences, would certainly be in violation of Article 6(2), as it is too broad and would encompass a requirement on the defendant to produce evidence about matters that it would be difficult, or impossible, to obtain.[6]

[7] The question requires an explanation of the impact of the HRA on the passage of legislation, so section 19 must be explained. A confident answer can deal with this quickly, as it is not controversial. This allows space to explore the effect of section 3 in more detail.

[8] This is a really useful detail to include, as it shows that you are aware of the practical impact of particular statutory provisions.

If the Bill were to be placed before Parliament, the HRA requires that the minister make a 'statement of compatibility' prior to the second reading (s. 19). This cannot be viewed as creating a particularly onerous obligation.[7] Since the HRA came into force, a declaration of compatibility has been made in almost every case, barring the Communications Act 2003.[8] It should be noted that, where a declaration cannot be made, the minister is only required to state that the government wishes to proceed with the Bill. In any event, no reasons are required to justify either the confirmation of compatibility, or why a non-compatible Bill is still desirable. Section 19 has no relevance once a Bill is enacted, as the principle of parliamentary sovereignty means that the court will not question the legality of proceedings in Parliament and cannot declare an enrolled Act to be unlawful.

[9] Even though you have already discussed *Sheldrake*, you need to give relevant detail from the judgment here, as you are making a different point, which is to do with the procedural approach of the court, rather than the decision that the statute breached Convention rights.

The question of enforcement is more complex. Should the Bill become law, it is likely that there would be numerous appeals against conviction on the basis that the provisions breach Article 6(2). The HRA provides a mechanism for the citizen to enforce Convention rights in the domestic courts. Section 3 confers a power on the court to interpret legislation 'in so far as is possible' to make it compliant with Convention rights. In **Sheldrake**, the courts were prepared to 'read down' into the Terrorism Act that the burden imposed was merely evidential. This was despite the unambiguous wording of the statute, and the fact that elsewhere in the Terrorism Act the legislation listed the provisions that conferred an evidential burden and did not include section 11(2) in that list.[9] Therefore, despite the apparently clear intention of the statute, the courts were prepared to declare that the legislation must have been intended to comply with Article 6(2). It seems possible, then, that the aim of government in enacting the Bill will be thwarted if the judiciary feels able to utilise its powers under section 3.[10]

[10] The answer keeps focus by referring back to the question; you were asked to consider the difficulties that might arise in enforcing the legislation, and your conclusion is that the courts would not enforce the provisions.

Given the extremely broad scope of the proposals, it is possible that no interpretation by the courts will be able to make the legislation compliant. In that circumstance, the HRA enables the court to make

[11] You should not spend too much time on considering possible government responses to a declaration of incompatibility, because that would be beyond the scope of the question, which focuses on enforcement.

[12] All the evidence has been presented, and a clear conclusion can be succinctly set out.

a declaration of incompatibility (s. 4).[11] While this does not impose any obligation on the executive to rectify the incompatibility, there could be political pressure to do so. It would seem certain that any claim to the ECtHR would have a good chance of success, as such sweeping alterations to the trial process would be unlikely to satisfy the requirement of proportionality outlined in *Salabiaku*.

It can therefore be seen that, although the Bill would be 'lawful' if enacted, it would be difficult for it to be enforced, as the HRA would allow the courts to seek to mitigate the effect of the proposals using section 3, or to declare it incompatible with the Convention by using section 4.[12]

 Make your answer stand out

■ By giving consideration to the suggestions raised in the case of *Jackson* v *Attorney General* [2005] All ER (D) 285 that there may be circumstances in which the courts would declare an Act to be unlawful. It could be argued that this Bill, if enacted, would be unconscionable and could spark constitutional rebellion by the judiciary!

■ By referring to some academic arguments on the role of the judiciary in upholding human rights. The journal *Public Law* is a good source of relevant material, including: Hickman, T. (2008) The courts and politics after the Human Rights Act: A comment. *Public Law*, 84. You should make a habit of checking the journal for up-to-date sources of opinion.

! Don't be tempted to . . .

■ Be diverted into a general discussion about the morality, or otherwise, of the aims of the Bill. Be sure to focus on the legal issues raised in relation to the HRA.

■ Be diverted into a discussion about the criminal law. This is a fairly tricky question, because you need to be able to cross-reference your knowledge of the criminal law to explain the issue of burden of proof, but make sure that you bring the discussion back to the HRA.

Question 5

A British Bill of Rights could restore the supremacy of Parliament.
Discuss.

Answer plan

→ Briefly explain the relationship between the Human Rights Act and the European Court of Human Rights.

→ Identify instances in which critics have argued that human rights law has undermined parliamentary supremacy.

→ Assess the validity of such criticisms.

→ Assess the extent to which a British Bill of Rights could address such concerns.

Diagram plan

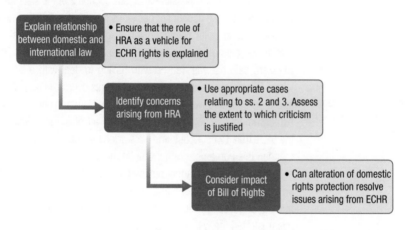

A printable version of this diagram plan is available from **www.pearsoned.co.uk/lawexpressqa**

Answer

In the wake of the Second World War, the United Kingdom government was among the nations forming the Council of Europe that drafted and ratified the European Convention on Human Rights and Fundamental Freedoms (ECHR), seeking to protect the basic rights of all persons present in the member states. The European Court of Human Rights

[1] It is important to show that the relationship between the Convention and the HRA is understood, as this will be a key factor in considering the impact of repealing the domestic statute.

(ECtHR) was also established to settle claims if it was alleged that a member state had infringed the rights agreed.[1] The rights were not enforceable in courts in the United Kingdom until the treaty was incorporated into domestic law by the Human Rights Act 1998 (HRA). The HRA has proved to be extremely controversial, with critics claiming that it has been used to uphold rights for terrorists and criminals, and by the judiciary to subvert the intention of Parliament. The current Conservative administration has pledged to abolish the Act and replace it with a British Bill of Rights. It will be argued that many of the criticisms of the HRA are exaggerated and, in any event, the proposal will be unsuccessful unless the government is prepared to also withdraw from the ECHR.

The HRA creates no new substantive rights, but has imposed obligations on the judiciary to consider Convention rights. Section 3 of the Act created a new rule of statutory interpretation, requiring all legislation to be interpreted in a manner compatible with Convention rights 'in so far as it is possible to do so'. Section 2 of the Act requires the judiciary to take account of decisions made in the ECtHR. The Act quickly became politically unpopular. Wagner (2014) notes that, less than three years after enactment, the Labour Home Secretary, David Blunkett, said he was 'fed up with having to deal with a situation where Parliament debates issues and judges overturn them'. A dec-

[2] This is an important point to make, as often students present a rather one-sided argument.

ade later, Conservative Prime Minister David Cameron announced the establishment of a commission to consider a British Bill of Rights, on the basis that it was 'about time we started making sure decisions are made in this Parliament rather than in the courts' (HC Deb vol. 523, col. 955).[2] While, as Wagner outlined, many criticisms were based on an inaccurate account of human rights decisions, there have been a number of cases in which it is possible to see that a judicial decision has frustrated the will of Parliament.

[3] Although it is never advisable to give extensive factual detail about cases, you need to be able to show how the authority chosen supports the point that you are making. In this case, the facts given show the reasons that critics suggest that the judicial interpretation ignored parliamentary intention.

The interpretative duty imposed by section 3 has, on occasion, led the judiciary to arrive at a decision that appears at odds with parliamentary intention. In the case of *R v A* [2001] UKHL 25, for example, the House of Lords were prepared to imply additional words into section41 of the Youth Justice and Criminal Evidence Act, diluting the ban on cross-examination of complainants in rape cases about their sexual history.[3] The operation of section 2 has also proved controversial. On the face of it, this section did not alter the pre-HRA approach of the judiciary to decisions in Strasbourg, as they were already capable of providing persuasive precedent, and the requirement to 'take account' of the ECtHR falls far short of suggesting that the domestic courts should be bound by it.[4] However, in **Secretary of State for the Home Department v AF (No. 3)** [2009] UKHL 28, Lord Rodgers famously stated: 'Strasbourg has spoken, the case is closed.' This often-quoted phrase fuelled criticisms of the influence of European judges on domestic law. In expressing support for the notion of a British Bill of Rights, the then Lord Chancellor, Chris Grayling, stated that he wished to 'see our Supreme Court supreme again' (Forsyth, 2013). In 2011, Lord Irvine criticised his colleagues for following Strasbourg jurisprudence too closely, arguing that, in doing so, they were failing in their constitutional duty (Lord Irvine of Lairg, 'A British Interpretation of Convention Rights' (Bingham Centre for the Rule of Law, University College London, 14 December 2011)). However, in other cases the judiciary has been careful to point out that it will only follow the ECtHR where there is a 'coherent, evolved and well-established' line of authority (**DSD and NVB v Commissioner of Police for the Metropolis** [2014] EWHC 436 (QB)). In **R v Horncastle** [2009] UKSC 14 it was reiterated that where the court feels that Strasbourg has failed to take account of domestic circumstances, it is permissible to decline to follow the authority.[5]

[5] In this paragraph, the answer is able to use a number of sources to show that there different sides to the argument in a concise fashion.

[6] While it is important not to spend too much time describing historical events, a central part of the argument will be that the plans to repeal the HRA are problematic, and therefore a brief account of the difficulties arising from the report is useful.

Proposals for a British Bill of Rights to replace the HRA were included in the Conservative party manifesto during the elections in both 2010 and 2015.[6] During the period of Coalition government, however, the support of the Liberal Democrats for the HRA meant that little progress could be made beyond establishing a commission to consider the possibility. The resulting report, dismissed by Elliot as a 'damp squib' (Elliott, 2013), reached the cautious conclusion that the HRA probably should be revoked, on the basis that it lacked public support, but that any replacement should broadly model itself on rights contained in the Convention. A Conservative party paper published in 2014 outlined the party's dissatisfaction with 'mission-creep' by the ECtHR and suggested that a new Bill of Rights may restrict the use of human rights law to the most serious cases and may preclude reliance on human rights by certain individuals such as those convicted of taking a life.[7] It also suggested severing the link between the UK court and Strasbourg, and preventing the judiciary from 'effectively rewriting law through "interpretation"'; a clear indication of dissatisfaction with the operation of sections 2 and 3 of the HRA.

[7] It is useful to make this point, as it refers back to the authorities cited earlier.

[8] This is a critical point to make, and one that shows that the relationship between domestic and international law has been understood.

[9] This is a useful source, showing that the student has read a range of current sources.

Since the 2015 election, no concrete proposals have emerged, but some ministers have suggested that, while the commitment to repeal of the HRA remains, it may be an issue that is left until the process of negotiating exit from the European Union is complete.[8] It is difficult to see how a Bill of Rights that essentially replicate the substantive rights in the Convention could have any material impact on the conduct of cases in the domestic courts. Any significant departure from the Convention would be problematic unless the government is also willing to withdraw from the Council of Europe and, therefore, the jurisdiction of the ECtHR.[9] The former Conservative Attorney General Dominic Grieve, a firm supporter of the HRA, notes that its repeal may not be effective in curbing the judicial willingness to oppose the will of Parliament, describing the decision in *R (Evans)* v *Attorney General* [2016] UKSC 21 as a 'shot across Parliament's bows' (Grieves, 2016).

It seems that the desire to repeal the HRA is driven by the perception that it has, in some way, emboldened the judiciary deliberately to undermine the will of Parliament. While there may be instances in which the judiciary has taken decisions that are critical of legislation, it is unclear how a new Bill of Rights could prevent the courts from taking a firm stance in protecting those rights.

✓ Make your answer stand out

- By exploring the issue of subsidiarity in more detail. A good starting point for further reading would be: Spano, R. (2014) Universality or diversity of Human Rights? Strasbourg in the age of subsidiarity? *Human Rights Law Review*, 14(3): 487–502.

- By considering the arguments regarding public perceptions of human rights law in more detail. There is a fascinating discussion of the issue in: Marks, S. (2014) Backlash: the undeclared war against human rights. *European Human Rights Law Review*, 4: 319–27.

- By assessing the implications of failing to comply with ECHtR judgments and the options available to the government. A considerable amount of comment is available about this issue. A useful collection of links is available via the UK Human Rights blog, available here: http://ukhumanrightsblog.com/2014/10/19/tory-plans-to-repeal-the-human-rights-act-the-legal-community-responds-the-human-rights-roundup/

- By exploring the issue raised regarding the judicial use of common law rights. Dr Mark Elliott has written extensively on the issue, and links can be found using his blog, Public Law for Everyone.

! Don't be tempted to . . .

- Treat this as a question about parliamentary supremacy. You are not being asked to explain this doctrine, and you will not be given additional credit for showing that you can do so.

- Ignore the relationship between domestic and international law. It is surprising how many students fail to recognise the difference between the Convention and the Human Rights Act.

- Ignore the need to find support for your arguments. Unfortunately, this is an area of the syllabus where students sometimes resort to making sweeping statements of opinion without providing any evidence.

❓ Question 6

Yvonne and Zahir are both studying law at college and often discuss legal issues during breaks from class. One day, Yvonne appears quite upset, and Zahir asks why. Yvonne tells Zahir that she attended her local authority leisure centre to take part in an exercise class, and was surprised to be greeted by a security guard demanding to search her bag before allowing her into the centre. When she asked why, she was told that it was because the (fictional) Healthy Choice Act of 2012 had come into force, which states that persons wishing to use local authority facilities are required to submit to 'spot checks' to ensure they are not in possession of cigarettes or tobacco. Persons with those items would be required to pay an additional entry fee of £20 or be denied access to the facilities.

Yvonne is a smoker, but she did not have the £20 fee. Therefore she did not go to the class. Zahir is outraged by the story and suggests to Yvonne that she should go to court about the incident, to protest about the infringement of her human rights.

Yvonne is not keen on the idea. Zahir, however, would like to pursue the matter if possible.

Advise Yvonne and Zahir whether or not the Human Rights Act 1998 can assist them.

Answer plan

→ Identify the Convention right that could be engaged.
→ Explain the operation of qualified rights.
→ Consider how sections 3 and 4 of the Human Rights Act 1998 could be applied in this case.
→ Explain the effect of section 7.

Diagram plan

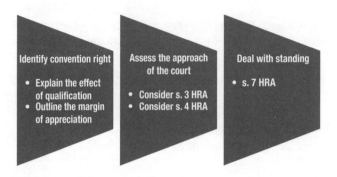

A printable version of this diagram plan is available from **www.pearsoned.co.uk/lawexpressqa**

Answer

[1] It is not necessary to explain the relationship between the Convention and domestic law in detail here, but a brief summary shows understanding of the effect of the HRA.

The Human Rights Act 1998 (HRA) incorporated the European Convention on Human Rights and Fundamental Freedoms (ECHR) into domestic law. As a result, individual citizens who believe that one or more of the rights protected by the Convention have been infringed can seek a remedy in the domestic courts.[1] To advise Yvonne and Zahir, it will be necessary to consider whether any relevant Convention rights are engaged in this scenario, before discussing how the HRA could be applied.

The (fictional) Healthy Choice Act of 2012 (HCA) authorises local authorities to carry out searches of individuals, and impose penalties on smokers by requiring them to provide additional payment. On these facts, the most relevant part of the ECHR is Article 8 (right to respect for private and family life). Although Yvonne may feel that being prevented from entering the building during the search is a restriction of liberty (contravening Article 5), it is unlikely that this would be a successful argument as the time period would be too short. In **Stork v Germany** (2006) 43 EHRR 6, the European Court of Human Rights (ECtHR) held that a deprivation of liberty under Article 5 requires (first) a restriction to a particular place for a 'not negligible' length of time.[2]

[2] Here, even though Article 5 is dismissed, the answer makes it clear how the decision has been reached. You should always try to ensure that your examiner can see your reasoning.

Article 8 is a qualified right, meaning that it is permissible to place restrictions upon the right in accordance with the provisions of

[3] It is really important that you explain what is meant by 'qualified rights', but it is a bad idea to set out all the permissible reasons for restriction. It is far better to identify those that could be claimed in this scenario.

[4] You must remember to keep bringing the focus of your answer back to the facts in the question.

[5] This is a good point, as it shows an ability to use existing material to develop an argument in a different situation.

[6] There is no need to consider the case law around the definition of a 'public body' where the question does not give any indication that this is an issue.

Article 8(2). Restrictions must be prescribed by law, and necessary to achieve a specified aim. In this scenario, the HCA could be intended either to protect 'health and morals' or to protect the rights of others.[3] These are both a legitimate basis for interference with the right, provided that they are a proportionate method of achieving the aim. When considering whether or not the provisions could be considered a legitimate restriction, it should be noted that the ECtHR would apply a 'margin of appreciation'; a degree of deference to the ability of the signatory state to judge the requirements of (in this case) health and morals in their own territory more effectively than the court itself. In this way, the Convention recognises that the signatory states of Europe do not share a homogeneous social or political culture.

The width of the margin may vary, depending on the importance of the right claimed and the reason for the restriction. In **Handyside v UK** (1976) 1 EHRR 737, the claimant was unsuccessful in arguing that a prosecution under the Obscene Publications Act 1959 for distributing pornographic materials breached his Article 10 right to freedom of expression, as a broad margin was applied. In this case, the courts would have to balance the objective of reducing the incidence and financial burden of smoking to the state against the interference with Yvonne's right to make autonomous decisions about her health.[4] The issue of smokers' rights was considered by the Joint Committee of Human Rights during the passage of the Health Act 2006, which introduced a ban on smoking in public places. The committee argued that, although the ban clearly did engage the Article 8 rights of smokers, the restrictions were a proportionate means of protecting the rights of non-smokers to be free from the effects of second-hand smoke. It is worth noting, however, that it reached that conclusion on the basis that the ban did not extend to private homes (Joint Committee on Human Rights, 2005). It may be possible to argue that the provisions in question here are more severe and cannot be similarly justified, as there is no need to balance the rights of smokers and non-smokers.[5]

If Yvonne did decide to bring a claim against the local authority, the court would deal with the case in accordance with the provisions set out in the HRA. Section 6 makes it clear that a claim can be made against any public body which in this case is not problematic.[6] Section 6 makes it clear that where a local authority is merely complying with obligations imposed by statute, it will have a defence.

[7] This part of the answer makes it clear that you understand the procedural application of the HRA.

[8] In any problem concerning the HRA, you will almost certainly have to explain the operation of section 3, so as part of your revision you should ensure that you can do so succinctly and clearly.

[9] Do not forget to use the law that you have explained to reach conclusions about Yvonne's case.

[10] This is such an important point to note about section 4 when advising an individual about the HRA, but one that is often missed. Make sure that you remember to explain the practical impact of a declaration of incompatibility.

[11] There is no need to spend any further time considering a potential claim to Strasbourg, as the question pointed you towards considering domestic human rights legislation.

[12] Although you should not overlook this issue, as you were specifically asked to deal with Zahir's position, the position is very straightforward and needs no elaboration.

The court, however, is also a public body and therefore obliged to comply with the ECHR, creating indirect horizontal effect. In determining whether or not the actions of the local authority were lawful, the court would need to consider the provisions of the HCA for compatibility with Article 8.[7] If, on a literal interpretation, the provisions are found to exceed permissible qualifications, section 3 imposes a duty on the court to apply a compatible interpretation 'in so far as is possible'. The courts have been prepared to use section 3 to 'read down' additional words into a statutory provision, provided that the interpretation can be said to 'go with the grain' of the legislation (***Ghaidan*** v ***Godin-Mendoza*** [2004] UKHL 30).[8] However, where the language of the statute is clear and unambiguous, the courts will be unable to force compatibility through a process of interpretation. In this case, if the courts consider that the imposition of a financial penalty on persons found in possession of cigarettes does infringe Article 8, it is difficult to see how any interpretation of the language could change this and allow the court to find in Yvonne's favour.[9] She should be advised, therefore, that this may be a case in which a declaration of incompatibility is made.

A declaration of incompatibility (s. 4) can be made by a superior court. If a declaration is made, the government may choose to use the procedure set out in section 10 to expedite amending legislation. This would not assist Yvonne in the short term, however, as a declaration of incompatibility has no effect upon the parties to a case (s. 4(6)).[10] To protect the principle of parliamentary sovereignty, the courts must apply the law until such time as it is amended or repealed. If that were to be the case, Yvonne may wish to consider pursuing an appeal to the ECtHR, as the domestic declaration could be said to be a clear indication that an infringement would be found in Strasbourg.[11]

Zahir will not be able to pursue the matter on Yvonne's behalf. Section 7 provides that a claim may be made only by a person who is the victim of an act infringing their rights.[12]

Although the government's aim of reducing smoking may be laudable, it would seem arguable that the imposition of fines authorised by the HCA is an unjustifiable infringement of the Article 8 rights of smokers. Yvonne should be advised that she could bring a claim but that, even were she to be successful, it is unlikely that the HRA could be used to find a remedy in the domestic courts.

Make your answer stand out

■ By considering the case of *R (N)* v *Secretary of State for Health* [2009] EWCA Civ 795, in which the Court of Appeal considered whether or not a smoking ban at Rampton Hospital infringed the Article 8 rights of patients. It is a useful case to consider, as the judges reached differing conclusions about whether smoking is within the ambit of Article 8.

■ By explaining the effect of the margin of appreciation in more detail here, and making clear the relationship between the jurisprudence of Strasbourg and that of the domestic courts. Arguably, when considering an area where Strasbourg has awarded a wide margin, the domestic courts will more readily defer to the executive.

■ By discussing the issue of horizontal effect in more detail. Bamforth (2001) maintains that the courts' position is determined not by section 6, but by the operation of section 3 (Bamforth, N. (2001) The True 'Horizontal Effect' of the Human Rights Act 1998. *LQR*, 117: 34).

! Don't be tempted to . . .

■ Spend too much time considering what the result of any action would be, or the potential remedies that may be available. This is not a question about Yvonne's Article 8 rights; it is one that is designed to test your understanding of the Human Rights Act.

■ Set out the provisions of section 3 or section 4 without making an attempt to analyse how they may be applied in this case. Your examiner wants to see your ability to apply the law, not just your ability to describe it.

Question 7

'The judiciary bears not the slightest responsibility for protecting the public and sometimes seems utterly unaware of the implications of their decisions for our society' (Charles Clarke, former Home Secretary cited by the Rt Hon Lord Phillips in the Gresham Special Lecture 2010).

Discuss the extent to which judicial concern for human rights has undermined legislative efforts to combat terrorism.

Answer plan

→ Outline the provisions that will be the focus of discussion: those dealing with foreign nationals suspected of involvement in terrorism.

→ Set out a number of cases in which the judiciary has considered the human rights implications of legislation.

➜ Identify the response of the executive to judicial criticism.

➜ Assess the extent to which government is restricted.

Diagram plan

Identify issues	Identify key cases	Assess the examples
Set limits on the discussion: Focus on foreign nationals suspected of terrorist activity	Choose cases that can be seen as directly leading to legislative change: ACTA 2001 PTA 2005 Immigration Act 2014	Consider the extent to which the judiciary influenced the executive Note the existence of international obligations

A printable version of this diagram plan is available from **www.pearsoned.co.uk/lawexpressqa**

Answer

[1] The question requires a discussion of the tension between the judiciary and the executive, so it is important to show that this has been understood. In addition, the introduction recognises that the HRA imposes an obligation on the judiciary.

[2] It is perfectly acceptable to limit the discussion in this way, and, indeed, you should, as it is not possible to consider more than one or two areas in sufficient depth.

The Human Rights Act 1998 (HRA) came into force in 2000, one year before the terrorist attacks on New York demonstrated the scale of the threat posed by global extremism. The Terrorism Act 2000 had already been enacted, but further legislation followed to control and contain the threat. The United Kingdom currently has five statutes directly concerned with the prevention, investigation and prosecution of terrorism. The HRA obliges the judiciary to give effect to Convention rights when interpreting statutes. Legislative provisions concerning terrorism have given rise to a large number of human rights cases, and significant judicial decisions that run counter to the intention of the executive.[1] This discussion will focus on key decisions concerning the treatment of foreign nationals suspected of involvement in terrorism.[2]

A v Secretary of State for the Home Department [2004] UKHL 56 considered the legality of provisions made in the Anti-Terrorism,

[3] Although there are a number of areas that can be discussed, this is a useful case to include because it is a clear illustration of the conflict between the executive and the judiciary.

Crime and Security Act 2001, which allowed foreign nationals suspected of terrorist activity to be detained indefinitely without trial.[3] The legislation was designed to contain the threat posed by a number of individuals resident in the United Kingdom, who, if returned to their country of origin, may have faced torture, or inhuman and degrading treatment. *Chahal v UK* (1996) 23 EHRR 413 established that, if the government returns an individual to a nation, knowing that there is such a risk, this will be a breach of its obligations under Article 3. Criminal prosecution could not take place owing to the need to keep sensitive security information secret, but the individuals were felt to be a grave risk. The government felt that the risk to society posed by terrorism constituted a 'national emergency' justifying a derogation from Article 5 in respect of the detainees. Lord Hoffmann felt that the derogation was unjustified, and memorably commented: 'The real threat to the life of the nation . . . comes not from terrorism but from laws such as these. That is the true measure of what terrorism may achieve'.[4]

[4] This is an excellent quote to include, as it is a very strong and clear criticism of the legislation. If you cannot remember the wording, you should ensure that you can paraphrase the comments.

[5] The concept of proportionality is crucial to Convention jurisprudence. Use of the correct terminology demonstrates that this has been understood.

The remaining judges felt that the circumstances did permit derogation, but all agreed that the measures in the Act went beyond those strictly required by the situation and were, therefore, disproportionate.[5] A declaration of incompatibility was made in accordance with section 4 of the HRA. In reaching the decision, the Lords rejected government submissions that it was for the executive to assess the proportionality of legislative responses to terrorism.[6] Lord Bingham stated that the role of the independent judiciary in interpretation and application of statute is 'a cornerstone of the rule of law itself'. The legislation was repealed, and replaced with the system of control orders. The case is perhaps the clearest illustration of the conflict between the judiciary and the executive in respect of measures enacted to prevent terrorist activity, but it is not an isolated example.

[6] It is useful to include this point from the judgment, as it shows that the government and the judiciary were not in agreement about their respective roles.

The control order regime, established by the Prevention of Terrorism Act 2005 to replace indefinite detention, was itself the subject of numerous human rights claims. A control order was a civil order that imposed obligations and restrictions on the suspect to limit the risk of terrorist activity. A series of linked judgments considered the range of conditions applied to various individuals to assess whether or not the orders were in breach of Article 5. Some of the orders were assessed as acceptable; however, in *Secretary of State for the*

Home Department v JJ [2007] UKHL 45, the majority found the orders imposed on the applicants to be incompatible with Article 5. The Lords referred to **Guzzardi v Italy** (1980) 3 EHRR 333, in which it was held that the combined and cumulative effect of restrictions could amount to a deprivation in circumstances falling short of imprisonment.[7] In reaching the decision, the Lords expressly rejected the government argument that the acceptability of the orders must be assessed in light of the serious risk posed by the individuals concerned. Lord Brown stated that such claims must be 'firmly resisted'. As a result, the government redrafted some of the orders, with less stringent conditions.[8]

[7] The ECtHR decision should be cited, as the domestic courts have followed this authority.

[8] The answer should explain the impact of the court rulings to illustrate how judicial decisions have affected government efforts to control terrorism.

The judiciary also assessed the use of 'closed evidence' and the Special Advocate procedure in hearings concerning control orders to consider whether this can be compatible with Article 6 rights to a fair hearing. In **Secretary of State for the Home Department v MB** [2007] UKHL 46, it was held that the Special Advocate procedure provided adequate safeguards for Article 6 rights in all but the most exceptional cases. Two years later, following the Strasbourg ruling in **A v UK** [2009] ECHR 3455/05, the Lords reconsidered the issue and held that an individual must always be told sufficient information about the evidence to enable them to provide instructions to a Special Advocate (**Secretary of State for the Home Department v AF (No. 3)** [2009] UKHL 28).[9] Following the general election, the control order regime was repealed and replaced with new 'terrorism prevention investigation measures' (TPIMs), which are more limited in both duration and scope. Arguably, this is a further example of judicial interference in matters of national security, but it is fair to point out that it was Strasbourg rather than the domestic courts that were the source of criticism.[10]

[9] Here, the answer demonstrates knowledge of how domestic law develops in conjunction with decisions reached in the ECtHR.

[10] It is important to keep linking the points made back to the question of the extent of the constraints the courts place on executive action.

Conflicts in Syria and Iraq have reinforced the importance of maintaining national security and have led to further legislation intended to achieve this. The government has long had the power to revoke citizenship from persons with dual nationality (British Nationality Act 1981). However, the Immigration Act 2014 explicitly extends the power to cover situations in which doing so would render a person effectively stateless.[11] The legislation was a direct response to the decision that the previous provisions did not allow this

[11] Here, the answer demonstrates understanding of recent developments in the law, and the ability to incorporate them into the argument.

(*Secretary of State for the Home Department* v *Al-Jedda* [2013] UKSC 62). It should be noted that rendering an individual stateless may well be in breach of international law, and it remains to be seen how the domestic judiciary will approach litigation arising from these provisions.

It is clear that the judiciary have reached decisions that have forced the executive to revisit measures enacted to combat terrorist activity. In assessing how far this should be viewed as 'undermining' the aims of government, it must be noted that the HRA charged the courts with the obligation to uphold Convention rights.[12] As Lord Phillips noted in the Gresham lecture, Parliament asked the courts to protect the rights, and therefore the judiciary has a specific, democratic, obligation to do so. The domestic courts are now entitled to uphold Convention rights, but it should be remembered that, in doing so, they merely reflect the obligations the UK has under international law.

[12] This is a point worth making, as, arguably, the courts are doing no more than is required by statute.

✓ Make your answer stand out

- There is scope to broaden the discussion to consider the operation of the separation of powers within the constitution. In particular, the case law could be used to show how judicial deference to executive decisions concerning 'national security' has evolved since the *GCHQ case* (*Council of Civil Service Ministers* v *Minister for the Civil Service* [1985] AC 374). You could refer to more recent decisions such as *R (Al Rawi)* v *Secretary of State for Foreign and Commonwealth Affairs* [2007] 2 WLR 1219 to make the point that foreign policy is still held to be non-justiciable; but you can certainly argue that the control order cases suggest that the HRA has resulted in a clearer system of 'checks and balances' among the institutions of state.

- You could spend more time considering the ECtHR jurisprudence regarding *Chahal* and the later case of *Saadi* v *Italy* (2008) (2009) 49 EHRR 30, which appears to confirm that the position regarding deportation and Article 3 has not altered following 9/11.

- By incorporating a broader range of academic opinion. The following article argues that the judiciary is still extremely deferential to parliamentary supremacy: Ewing, K.D. and Tham, J. (2008) The continuing futility of the Human Rights Act. *Public Law*, 668–93. This would link well with the discussion of *Al-Jedda* and the resulting legislation. It could be argued that the Immigration Act 2014 can be viewed as an illustration of supremacy.

! Don't be tempted to . . .

- Engage in detailed discussion of which conditions the judiciary considered incompatible with Article 5 in the control order cases. The detail is not important; only the fact that the judiciary and the government reached different decisions.

- Ignore the effect of decisions made in Strasbourg. The judiciary is, after all, guided by precedent from the ECtHR. Failure to address this fact would result in an overly simplistic approach. It should be recognised that, since becoming a signatory to the Convention, decisions have been persuasive precedent and therefore the impact of the HRA is perhaps less dramatic than the quotation in the question suggests.

- Try to deal with too many different aspects of anti-terror legislation. Here, there has been no attempt to deal with the many provisions aimed at individuals who were born into British citizenship. It is much better to allow yourself to deal with one area in detail than to skim over several without much analysis.

@ Try it yourself

Now take a look at the question below and attempt to answer it. You can check your response against the answer guidance available on the companion website (**www.pearsoned.co.uk/lawexpressqa**).

> Greta lives near a small, regional airport. There is some noise from planes during the day, but none at night. She is dismayed when permission is granted for a second runway with planned night flights. She feels that this will disrupt the sleep of her family and that will be a violation of her rights. She is dismayed when her solicitor advises her that she will not succeed in her claim and confused when she finds reports on the internet about a similar case in Spain where it was held that a similar airport expansion violated the claimant's rights under Article 8 of the European Convention on Human Rights.
>
> Advise Greta whether the initial solicitor gave reasonable advice and why the position may be different in Spain.

www.pearsoned.co.uk/lawexpressqa

 Go online to access more revision support including additional essay and problem questions with diagram plans, and You be the marker questions, and to download all diagrams from the book.

Executive accountability

How this topic may come up in exams

There are various ways in which the executive can be held to account: by Parliament, application for judicial review, the ombudsman system or tribunals. Examiners tend to choose questions focusing on one of these methods. Judicial review is often examined by means of problem scenarios requiring you to provide advice to a hypothetical client, or clients. Most problem questions can be tackled in a similar way by employing a logically structured approach. Although the amount of case law can be intimidating, answers are improved by demonstrating a solid understanding of the procedures necessary to bring a claim. Essay questions will generally require an evaluation of the effectiveness of one of the means of holding the executive to account; this often overlaps with the topic of separation of powers as it concerns the ability of the constitution to restrain the arbitrary or excessive use of power.

■ Before you begin

It's a good idea to consider the following key themes of executive accountability before tackling a question on this topic.

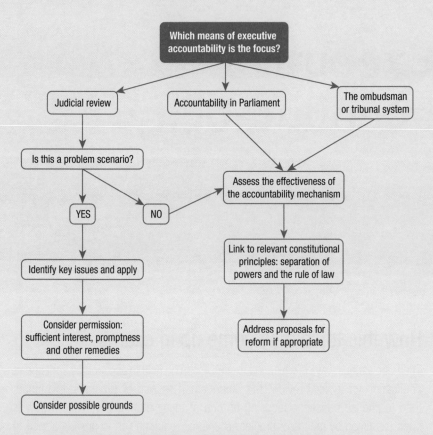

A printable version of this diagram is available from **www.pearsoned.co.uk/lawexpressqa**

❓ Question 1

Marie Chadwick seeks your advice. She has a degenerative illness, and is cared for by her husband. Twice a week, the local authority arranges transport to take her to a daycare facility two miles from her home, so that Mr Chadwick can have some respite. The Chadwicks do not have a car and Marie's disabilities make it impossible for her to use public transport.

Last week, she received a letter from the local authority, informing her that the facility has been selected for closure. A place has been provided for her at an alternative facility 25 miles from her home. Mr Chadwick telephoned the local authority to ask what time the transport would collect Marie and was told that the policy was not to provide transport for journeys over 20 miles long.

The (fictitious) Local Authority (Patient Care) Act 1987 states, at section 12:

> The authority has a duty to provide adequate support for patients with long-term health needs, and their carers. Facilities should be available that are appropriate and accessible for patients and their carers. In determining the appropriate provision, the authority may consider such factors as appear relevant.

Marie tells you that she feels the decision to close the daycare facility is absurd and she wants to know whether she can go to court to change the decision. She would like compensation for the price of the taxi fares to and from the new centre, as well as damages for her distress.

Advise Marie.

Answer plan

→ Explain the process of judicial review.

→ Analyse the available grounds for a claim against the local authority.

→ Discuss the availability of compensation or damages.

→ Mention other remedies that may be available.

→ Outline the effect of a remedy.

Diagram plan

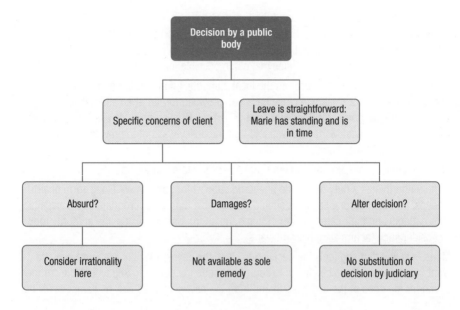

A printable version of this diagram plan is available from **www.pearsoned.co.uk/lawexpressqa**

Answer

Marie may be able to apply for a judicial review of the local authority's decision to close the respite facility and to cease to provide transport. Judicial review is a mechanism that allows the courts to consider the process by which a public body exercising delegated powers has reached a decision. Marie should note that judicial review is a procedure concerned with ensuring that discretionary powers are exercised lawfully and fairly; it is not an appeal regarding the merits of the decision. Marie will need to be advised of the available remedies, as it may not be possible to claim compensation or damages.

The courts may review any decision made by a public body exercising delegated powers. This is not problematic, as the local authority is clearly a public body and therefore amenable to review. It should be noted that leave is required to bring an application. Dealing first with the application to review the local authority's decision: it appears that leave should be granted. Marie is an individual who has sufficient interest in the matter complained of (Senior Courts Act 1981, s. 31) so

[1] You can deal with the leave procedure very briefly, provided that you are able to show how it will be applied to Marie. Because you can clearly demonstrate both timeliness and standing, there is no need to discuss the authorities used to determine the position in more ambiguous cases.

[2] It is important to take note of the wording used in the question. Here, because the word 'absurdity' is used, your examiner is inviting you to concentrate on the ground of irrationality.

[3] Although this is a problem scenario, you will be rewarded for this point which is more analytical and places the topic in the broader context of the study of the constitution.

[4] You need to have at least one authority to illustrate the kinds of situations in which the court has held that a decision is bad for irrationality, as the answer will suggest that Marie has an arguable case.

[5] You need to draw some conclusions about the relative strengths of Marie's case, but you should take care not to speculate too much. The advice needs to be qualified by making it clear that you would need further information.

[6] There are a number of cases you could use here, and there is no need to give any detail. You are simply showing the examiner that you are aware that there are authorities that support the proposition that it is illegal to fetter discretion.

this is unproblematic. An application must be brought promptly and, in any event, no later than three months after the decision complained of (Civil Procedure Rules 1998 (CPR), r. 54). As the letter was received last week, it seems that the application will be in time.[1]

Provided that leave is granted, the courts will need to consider the grounds for the application. There are a number of potential grounds for review, listed in *Council of Civil Service Unions v Minister for the Civil Service* [1985] AC 374 as irrationality, illegality and procedural unfairness. Arguably, the Human Rights Act 1998 has allowed for the development of a fourth substantive ground of review: proportionality. Marie has stated that she believes the decision is absurd. She may wish, then, to consider whether it would be possible to argue that the decision was irrational.[2] The test to be applied is drawn from the case of *Associated Provincial Picture Houses Ltd v Wednesbury Corporation* [1948] 1 KB 223, in which it was held a decision would be irrational only if no reasonable decision-maker could have reached the same conclusion. Successive cases reinforce the point that the test for irrationality is stringently applied, and demonstrate that the judiciary are wary of stepping outside of constitutional boundaries by interfering with executive autonomy,[3] a point stressed in *R v Secretary of State for the Home Department ex parte Brind* [1991] 1 AC 696. Marie should note that an extremely high threshold has been set in respect of claims for irrationality. Judicial support for a claim in similar circumstances can be found in *R (B) v Worcestershire County Council* [2009] EWHC 2915. In that case, the failure to carry out proper assessment meant that the authority had been unable to arrive at a rational decision.[4] Further information would be required regarding the decision-making process, but this could be an arguable ground if it can be shown that the authority has not obtained the information needed to determine whether or not the closure was necessary. The lack of transport may suggest that the authority did not obtain all the material required. While it is for the authority to determine 'relevant' factors, it should be mindful of the statutory duty to consider accessibility.[5]

It is probably worth challenging the decision not to provide transport for Marie as a separate ground of claim, to ensure that, if the centre does close, the authority has to reconsider the issue. Where an authority has discretion, any policy that is a binding rule preventing proper consideration may be considered to be 'fettering discretion' and this will be illegal (see, for example, *British Oxygen Co v Board of Trade* [1971] AC 610).[6]

7 The question specifically directs you to address this point, and it will be hard to obtain good marks if you ignore the issue of damages.

8 You need to include the statutory authority, but you will be rewarded if you are able to refer to relevant case law authority as well.

9 You are only required to discuss the remedy of damages, and that will be the focus of this part of the answer. If you are able to comment on appropriate additional remedies, this demonstrates comprehensive knowledge of the topic.

10 Almost every judicial review answer should note the difference between review and an appeal. Again, close reading of the question shows that this is an issue that you need to explore in more detail because of the client's specific request for advice about whether the court can change the decision.

11 This is a good point to make, as it shows that you not only know that the court will not consider the merits, but understand the constitutional reasons for that.

12 This kind of detailed knowledge of the rules, and relevant case law, will impress your examiner.

As the authority stated that the refusal was on policy grounds, this may well be a point worth exploring.

Marie has instructed that she wishes to obtain damages. Damages may be awarded, and accordingly may be included in a claim (CPR, r. 54.3(2)), but cannot be the sole remedy claimed.[7] Damages will be payable only if they would have been recoverable in a civil claim (Senior Courts Act, s. 31(4)). *R (Kurdistan Workers Party)* v *Secretary of State for the Home Department* [2002] EWHC 644 (Admin) confirmed that damages can be awarded but cannot be 'a good reason for permitting judicial review'.[8] The appropriate remedy to be claimed may be determined in part by the speed at which a claim can be lodged and whether or not the centre is still open at that time. If it is, then Marie should seek a prohibiting order, to prevent the closure, and a quashing order to void the decision.[9] Together, this would have the effect of ensuring that the centre remained open while the authority reconsiders the decision.

Marie has indicated that she hopes the court will change the decision, and she must be advised that this is highly unlikely.[10] The effect and intention of judicial review remedies are, in the main, to make sure that those empowered to exercise discretion do so fairly and lawfully. It would be usurpation of the power conferred on the relevant body for the judiciary to substitute its discretion for that of the decision-maker.[11] A successful judicial review, then, will result in the matter being remitted to the local authority for reconsideration. The CPR and the Senior Courts Act 1981 both state that the court may take the decision itself, but only in circumstances where there is 'no purpose to be served in remitting the matter'[12] (CPR, r. 54.19(3)). This will be appropriate only where the initial decision was taken by a court or tribunal and resulted from an error of law where, without the error, only one result would be possible. In other words, it is only appropriate as a time-saving device, as confirmed in *R (Dhadly)* v *London Borough of Greenwich* [2001] EWCA Civ 8122.

It seems that Marie has good grounds to seek judicial review of the local authority's actions. She may be awarded damages, but the primary remedy will result in reconsideration of the decision.

Make your answer stand out

- By spending more time considering the grounds that could be relevant to both parts of the decision. You do need to focus on irrationality, because the question demands this, but, if space permits, you could open up the discussion to consider whether or not a decision made solely for financial reasons could be classified as having been made for an improper purpose. This would be impressive, as this is quite a narrow point and beyond the scope of generalist text books. It would show real confidence in analysing the law.

- By referring to the Law Commission report (No. 322) on the issue of damages, published in May 2010, *Administrative Redress: Public Bodies and the Citizen* (available at: www.lawcom.gov.uk/docs/lc322.pdf). The Law Commission proposed that damages should be available as a sole remedy in review proceedings. As yet, there has been no governmental response. The prohibition has been criticised as unfair and unjust (see, for example: Malloch, T. (2014) Closing the Gap: Should damages be available for judicial review? *New Law Journal*, 4 July).

- By explaining the available remedies in more detail. There are a number of useful texts you could consider, including: Sunkin, M. (2010) Remedies available in judicial review proceedings, in D. Feldman (ed.), *English Public Law* (2nd edn). Oxford: Oxford University Press.

! Don't be tempted to . . .

- Ignore the wording of the question. Your examiner will provide clues that should help you find the issues that they really want you to talk about. Here, use of the word 'absurdity' should trigger you to consider irrationality. Students who fail to pay close attention to the wording can miss this kind of hint and lose out on valuable marks.

- Not spend enough time discussing the effect of successful review here. The client has raised it, and you need to show the examiner that you can point out the issues that matter to the client and advise accordingly.

- List all the grounds for review that you can remember. You will get more marks for being able to pick out a few that are applicable. It is always important to remember that marks are given for application of relevant law, but judicial review seems to be an area where students are particularly likely to tell the examiner everything they know. It can be daunting, because you don't want to miss a relevant ground. An answer that includes a discussion of two grounds that could be relevant but omits a third will get higher marks than an answer listing every possible ground without explaining how they are relevant.

❓ Question 2

Marcia, who lives in London, is a wildlife enthusiast and is particularly interested in otters. She is horrified, therefore, to read in the newspaper that Northumbria Council is planning to start a cull of otters, as they are blamed for the spread of a rare infectious disease affecting sheep in the area. The cull was authorised by the Minister of Agriculture five months ago, after thousands of sheep had to be destroyed, threatening the livelihood of local farmers. She does some research and discovers that otters are a protected species under the Wildlife and Countryside Act 1981 (as amended), making it an offence to kill them unless it is necessary to prevent the spread of disease. The Animal Welfare Act 1981 confers a power on the Minister of Agriculture to order a cull if it is necessary to eliminate, or substantially reduce, disease (s. 21). Marcia also finds a number of scientific journal articles claiming that, although otters do carry the infection, it is unlikely that they are the primary source of infection in the sheep. She feels that the minister has not taken into account all the scientific evidence.

Marcia has also found that the Otter Preservation Society (OPS) is campaigning against the cull, and she decides to join. She receives her membership confirmation and is given a membership number: 10234.

Marcia would like to know whether she can take action to stop the cull.

Answer plan

→ Explain the function and purpose of review.

→ Consider whether or not a review out of time would be permitted.

→ Consider whether or not the OPS could obtain standing.

→ Assess the strength of the possible grounds.

Diagram plan

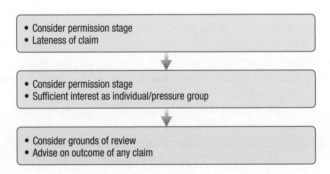

A printable version of this diagram plan is available from **www.pearsoned.co.uk/lawexpressqa**

Answer

[1] It is quite common to
assume that the examiner
always presents a scenario
containing a potentially strong
claim, with arguable grounds.
Here, the case is extremely
weak. A good answer will
realise this and advise
accordingly. Setting this out
in the introduction strikes a
confident tone.

[2] There is no need to give
detail setting out the courts'
approach to the permission
stage here; it is far better to
do this with reference to the
facts given in the problem, as
this shows an ability to apply
the law.

[3] It is obvious that the claim
is out of time and unlikely to
be granted an extension. It is
necessary, though, to explain
the legal reasons for reaching
that conclusion with reference
to the specific considerations
the court would use.

[4] Mention of the issue of
standing here shows the
ability to see the links
between different aspects
of the case, but you should
not discuss the 'sufficient
interest' test in detail here.
It is important to deal with
the procedural requirements
in a logical order rather than
skipping backwards and
forwards.

In this scenario, the only legal action that may be open to Marcia is a claim for judicial review. Judicial review is a process that allows a party to challenge decisions made by or on behalf of the executive. It is important to note that, unlike an appeal, judicial review is not concerned with the merits of the decision – only the manner in which it was made. There are a number of issues that may make it difficult for a claim to be brought in these circumstances.[1]

Judicial review is not an automatic right: leave of the court must be obtained. This is governed by the Senior Courts Act 1981 (SCA) and the Civil Procedure Rules (CPR). Leave will be granted only if the applicant has sufficient interest in the matter complained of and the claim is lodged promptly (SCA, s. 31) and no later than three months from the date of the decision (CPR, r. 54).[2]

In this case, we are told that the Minister of Agriculture authorised the cull five months ago. Any claim, then, would be at least two months late. Even where the claim is within the three-month limit, the court can still refuse leave if, in the circumstances, the applicant has not been prompt. The court may exercise discretion to extend the time limits with 'good reason' (r. 53(4)). In *R v Secretary of State for Trade and Industry ex parte Greenpeace Ltd* [1998] COD 59 it was held that when deciding whether or not to allow a late claim the court should consider whether there is an objective excuse for late application, the possible detriment to third-party interests and the public interest in reviewing the decision. Here, it appears that Marcia can only offer the fact that she has only recently seen the media report.[3] It is doubtful that this would be considered a good enough excuse: in fact, it may simply reinforce the difficulties that she will face in establishing sufficient interest.[4] Conversely, the financial hardship faced by the farmers could be seen as a third-party 'detriment' that would be increased if there were to be a delay.

Even if the court was prepared to extend the time limit, Marcia would struggle to show sufficient interest. The leave procedure is designed to filter out vexatious applications from 'busybodies, cranks and other mischief makers' (*IRC v National Federation of Self-Employed and Small Businesses Ltd* [1982] AC 617) with strong views on a particular issue. Marcia's interest in the welfare of otters is unlikely

[5] Here, the answer refers back to the point made about coming late and gives the explanation for it.

[6] There is no need to repeat the points made above about lateness here, but it is worth pointing out that they do still apply in order to make clear that it is also unlikely an extension would be given to OPS.

[7] The scenario included the information about member numbers. Whenever that kind of detail is provided, you should not ignore it. Ask yourself what aspect of the topic is being suggested to you and make sure you deal with it.

[8] There is no need to set out all the possible grounds for review. Focus on issues arising in the scenario.

[9] Students find it very hard to give negative advice. If you are certain that the case is weak, you should say so.

to meet the test, as she cannot show that the cull would impact on anything other than her feelings. After all, had she not happened to find the newspaper article, she may never have known about it.[5] Her best hope would be to see whether the Otter Preservation Society would be willing to submit an application. Of course, it would face the same obstacles regarding the timing of the claim.[6] It may, though, be better placed to argue sufficient interest. In *R v Secretary of State for the Environment ex parte Rose Theatre Trust Co* [1990] 1 QB 504 it was held that a group could not obtain standing simply by banding together if no single member could have demonstrated it as an individual. In *R v Secretary of State for the Environment ex parte Greenpeace Ltd* [1994] 4 All ER 329, however, sufficient interest was granted to the organisation for a number of reasons. First, Greenpeace had a large membership whom it could legitimately claim to represent. Secondly, some of those members could demonstrate individual standing, but Greenpeace had the resources to mount a more effective challenge. Finally, the decision concerned was one of general public interest, as it concerned the use of nuclear energy. Greenpeace had 400,000 members, so, despite having a membership of over 10,000, the court may not feel that the OPS represents a sizeable section of the public in the same way.[7]

If the OPS were to be granted permission, the court would then consider whether or not any grounds for review were present. The grounds were categorised by Lord Diplock in *Council of Civil Service Unions v Minister for the Civil Service* [1985] AC 374 as illegality, irrationality and procedural impropriety. It is widely accepted that, as he predicted, the increasing influence of the European Convention on Human Rights has led to a fourth ground: proportionality.[8] In this case, Marcia should be advised that it is hard to identify any arguable grounds.[9] Her instructions suggest that she believes the decision to be illegal, on the basis that the minister has failed properly to consider the evidence before reaching his decision and has therefore erroneously concluded that a cull would 'substantially reduce or eliminate' disease. The difficulty here, though, is that the power contained in the Act does not specify any particular factors that must be taken into account. It will, then, be for the court to determine what considerations are necessary to fulfil the purpose of the Act. It may be reasonable to argue that, on any interpretation, scientific evidence

[10] This shows the examiner that the advice given is based upon a logical and careful application of law to facts. Showing this process is actually far more important than the conclusion reached.

must be required to determine necessity. The authorities are clear, however, that it will be for the decision-maker to decide what weight to give to each factor (*Tesco Stores Ltd* v *Secretary of State for the Environment* [1995] 2 All ER 636).[10] Provided, then, that the minister could show that account had been taken of scientific evidence, it is highly unlikely that the court would interfere with the conclusions drawn, unless it could be argued that they were irrational. This is a difficult argument to sustain, as the test for irrationality requires the decision to be one that no reasonable decision-maker could have arrived at. Falling short of this, any criticism of the findings made by the minister would clearly go beyond the constitutional remit of the review process by commenting on the merits of the decision rather than the manner in which it was made.[11]

[11] This point makes it clear that you understand how the topic of judicial review links with other areas of the syllabus.

[12] A brief summary of the identifiable difficulties is helpful, as it leads into the inevitably negative concluding advice.

Unfortunately, the advice given to Marcia will be a disappointment to her. It is highly unlikely that she would be able to bring a claim for judicial review in her own right, as she does not have sufficient interest in the matter. Even if the OPS were to be willing to mount a challenge and able to show standing, it would struggle to persuade the court to permit a late claim in these circumstances. Assuming that permission were to be given, there do not appear to be any arguable grounds.[12] On this occasion, then, there are no legal avenues available to Marcia and she should be advised against attempting to apply for judicial review.

 Make your answer stand out

- By considering some additional cases regarding relevant and irrelevant considerations. You could discuss the case of *R* v *Somerset County Council ex parte Fewings* [1995] 3 All ER 20. The judgment addresses the difficulty in distinguishing between the grounds of relevant/irrelevant considerations and acting for an improper purpose, highlighting the 'grey' areas of the law.

- By recognising the similarities between the facts and those surrounding a court action attempting to challenge the decision to authorise a cull of badgers (*R (Badger Trust)* v *Secretary of State for the Environment* [2014] EWCA Civ 1405). This would allow you to suggest that there is some precedent for permission being given to a wildlife campaigning group, reinforcing the advice that this case would be unlikely to be successful.

> ! **Don't be tempted to . . .**
>
> ■ Give detailed information about the facts of the cases mentioned. Marks are given for showing an understanding of the *ratio*, and an ability to apply this to the scenario given. For example, there is no need to tell your examiner anything about the facts of *Tesco Stores*. In order to explain the facts, you would need to be able to remember a lot of detail about planning law, and it would take up quite a lot of space in your answer.
>
> ■ Incorporate advice regarding the classification of a public body. There is no need to discuss the distinction between *R* v *Panel on Takeovers and Mergers ex parte Datafin plc* [1987] 2 WLR 69 and *R* v *Disciplinary Committee of the Jockey Club ex parte Aga Khan* [1993] 1 WLR 909 in this kind of question, where the decision-making authority is clearly a public body. A good answer will see what areas of discussion are highlighted by the question.
>
> ■ Assume that you must always find grounds for review. Sometimes, the advice that you need to give is negative.

Question 3

'The House of Commons no longer controls the Executive; on the contrary, the Executive controls the House of Commons.' (Low, S. (1904) *The Governance of England*)

Discuss.

Answer plan

→ Explain the constitutional role of Parliament within the system of the separation of powers.

→ Outline the difficulties created by the party political system.

→ Assess the contribution of select committees in ensuring that the executive is accountable to Parliament.

→ Consider the extent to which backbench MPs can exert influence in the legislature.

Diagram plan

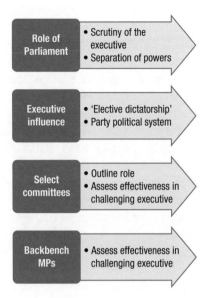

A printable version of this diagram plan is available from **www.pearsoned.co.uk/lawexpressqa**

Answer

[1] This is a useful way to begin the essay, as it shows that you have understood the connection between Low's view and analysis of the constitutional doctrines.

[2] This famous quote is so clearly relevant to the question set that it really should be included.

[3] There are numerous aspects to the work of the Commons that could be discussed: as you cannot deal with all of them you should make clear in your introduction which areas you intend to focus on.

Dicey described parliamentary supremacy as the cornerstone of the UK constitution. Low's comment demonstrates that concerns about executive dominance over the legislature were being aired only 20 years later.[1] More recently, in 1976, Lord Hailsham famously referred to the United Kingdom as an 'elective dictatorship'.[2] If the executive controls the Commons, then this could undermine the ability of Parliament to scrutinise government effectively. The relationship between the executive and the legislature will be assessed by considering the extent to which the Commons resists legislation proposed by government, and the impact of the scrutiny conducted in the House itself and through select committees.[3] Although an executive with a large majority is certainly able to ensure compliance with its legislative agenda, the role of Parliament in influencing policy and scrutinising government should not be underestimated.

[4] You should make the connection between this question and the separation of powers. Make sure that you deal with this briefly, as it is not the central issue.

[5] It is vital that you refer to the whip system, as this is the means by which the party of government primarily controls the House of Commons. It is not enough to talk in general terms; you need to show that you understand the mechanics of the system.

[6] This level of detail is useful, as it gives supporting evidence for the argument.

[7] Here, the answer demonstrates knowledge of the various means of scrutiny by mentioning them, but then explains the reason for the narrower focus.

According to Blackstone, the separation of powers in the United Kingdom exists to ensure that a system of checks and balances exists, ensuring that each branch of government can be held accountable.[4] The democratically elected legislature has a dual role: first, as the primary law-making body, and, secondly, as a mechanism for scrutinising the executive. The ability of the Commons to act as a brake on executive action is limited, however, by the operation of the party political system. First, there is an overlap of personnel between the institutions: the Prime Minister must, by convention, be a Member of the House of Commons, as are the majority of Cabinet Ministers. In addition, the major political parties utilise the whip system: party officials who act as a conduit between the party and Members of Parliament and who are responsible for ensuring that members vote in line with party policy.[5] It can be seen, then, that where a party is able to command a large majority in the Commons, the legislature is likely to follow the government's policy agenda. For example, Labour came to power in 1997 with a landslide majority, allowing the Blair administration to embark on a substantial programme of constitutional reform. In fact, the government was not defeated in a vote on legislation in the House of Commons for eight years (all three defeats of the Blair government in the Commons occurred in 2005). Of course, the possibility of 'elective dictatorship' is far less of a concern where a government has a less stable majority or where there is a coalition. It is perhaps unsurprising, then, to see that the Cameron government was defeated five times between 2010 and 2016, three times in respect of legislation.[6]

The ability of the Commons to scrutinise the executive is not restricted to the legislative process: parliamentary questions, debates instigated by backbench members, and the work of select committees can all be said to be important in holding the government to account in a public forum. Prime Minister's Question Time is the part of parliamentary business that gets the most media coverage, but arguably it is the work of select committees that has the most potential to operate as an effective check on government.[7] Parliamentary select committees are appointed to examine the various policy areas dealt with by government departments. Select committees can determine the specific policy areas they wish to consider and investigate by calling and examining witnesses from both inside and outside Parliament. Select committees are able to report to government and make recommendations.

Government will respond to a select committee report within 60 days. Membership reflects the balance of party membership in the House. It might be thought that the same concerns about the dominance of a party with a large majority would be apparent in the select committee system, but there is evidence to counter this assumption. The Blair government, despite its sizeable majority, faced a backbench rebellion in 2001 when efforts were made to dismiss two Labour MPs from a committee, allegedly because of their perceived hostility to government policy. Following the expenses scandal of 2009, a number of reforms were instigated in an effort to restore public confidence in Parliament, including a change to ensure that the chair of most select committees is now elected by MPs rather than appointed on the recommendation of party whips. The work of select committees has achieved greater public prominence following some high-profile hearings in which not only senior government figures but also key personnel from both public and private bodies have been cross-examined and subject to stringent criticism. For example, the Culture, Media and Sport Committee took evidence while investigating the phone hacking scandal from government ministers, the Director of Public Prosecutions, Rupert Murdoch and other News International executives, and senior members of the Metropolitan Police (*News International and Phone Hacking*, 11th Report of 2010–12, HC 903).[8] This can ensure that those who work in or with government departments can be asked publicly to account for and justify their actions.

It must, of course, be noted that, although select committees are able to issue reports and recommendations, they do not have any legal authority over government. Russell and Benton have examined the work of seven committees over a 16-year period (2011). Remarkably, they found that government accepted and acted upon just under half of the recommendations made. From these figures they estimate that government acts upon approximately 450 recommendations made by all 20 select committees each year.[9]

The report of the Committee on Reform of the House of Commons (the Wright report) proposed not only the election of select committee chairs, but also an increase in the time allocated to the concerns of backbench MPs. It remains the case that the vast bulk of time is given to the business proposed by the government and the leadership of the opposition, but approximately one day per week is now given over to matters decided by the Backbench Business Committee. The

[8] You need to refer to a specific example here to support what you say: there are plenty you could choose from.

[9] This is a really useful piece of research to refer to because these figures provide factual support for the claim that committees are effective.

[10] Again, it can be seen that reference to research helps to make the argument persuasive.

committee is also responsible for assessing online petitions that have received more than 10,000 signatures and determining which of the issues raised should be debated. Foster (2013) assessed the work of the committee in the 2010–12 session and suggests that it had a number of successes in holding government accountable. He points, for example, to the influence of a backbench committee in 'obliging government to clarify its position' on documents held relating to the Hillsborough disaster, and in securing ongoing funding for the BBC World Service.[10]

[11] You should not be afraid to conclude with a clear opinion on the question if you are happy that you have been able to set out the evidence in support of your view.

It would seem that there is evidence that the House of Commons still operates as an important constitutional control over the executive. This is far less obvious when a government has a large majority. However, the influence of select committees in setting the policy agenda and influencing legislation is clear from the response of government to recommendations. The increased independence of both select committees and backbench MPs has resulted in a far stronger Commons than that described by Low.[11]

 Make your answer stand out

- By engaging in a more critical analysis of the work of select committees. For example, Brazier and Fox suggested that committees needed to address their own accountability both to Parliament and to the public, and to be more transparent in their operation (Brazier, R. and Fox, R. (2011) Reviewing Select Committee Tasks and Modes of Operation). *Parliamentary Affairs*, 64(2): 354–69).

- By considering the role of backbench MPs in more detail. There is a reasonable amount of academic comment on the relationship between backbench MPs in the Commons and the executive branch of government. See, for example: Cowley, P. and Stuart, M. (2005) Parliament: Hunting for votes. *Parliamentary Affairs*, 58(2): 258–71. This gives a detailed analysis of how the Labour party leadership dealt with a potential rebellion by MPs, and lends support to an argument that the stance taken by the backbench was ultimately able to influence the government's future policy direction.

- By spending more time assessing the implications of a weak House of Commons upon the effective operation of not only the separation of powers but also the rule of law. You could suggest that a lack of rigorous accountability in Parliament could lead to an increase in the arbitrary use of executive discretion.

! Don't be tempted to . . .

■ Provide an answer that is simply too descriptive. There is a tendency for weaker answers to this question simply to list lots of examples of the various different ways in which the Commons can hold ministers to be accountable without offering any real analysis of their constitutional effectiveness.

■ Treat the question as an invitation to demonstrate a detailed knowledge of the various theoretical interpretations of the separation of powers. You need to make sure that you show that you understand the significance of the relationship between the legislature and the executive as part of the separation of powers. You do not, however, need to outline the historical evolution of the doctrine or analyse the merits of contrasting academic perspectives.

Question 4

In the last 25 years, judicial review has developed as a formidable means of controlling the use of executive power and providing the citizen with redress.

Discuss.

Answer plan

→ Explain the process of judicial review.

→ Explain the relationship between judicial review and the separation of powers.

→ Identify significant changes in the specified time period, including the *GCHQ case*, and the introduction of the Human Rights Act 1998.

→ Consider arguments for and against the suggestion that judicial review is an effective method of controlling the executive.

→ Analyse any problems for the citizen in obtaining review.

Diagram plan

A printable version of this diagram plan is available from **www.pearsoned.co.uk/lawexpressqa**

Answer

Judicial review is the means by which the decision-making processes of the executive can be scrutinised and declared to be incorrect. Therefore, judicial review can be seen as a powerful tool allowing the judiciary to hold the executive to account. It could be argued that this is part of the system of checks and balances that exist between the organs of state to ensure a functional separation of powers, strengthening the constitutional arrangements of the United Kingdom and ensuring that the citizen is protected from the risk of the abuse of discretionary powers.[1] However, this must be balanced against the limitations that the judiciary accepts upon its powers of review, and the difficulties that face the individual wishing to bring a claim.

The right of the court to review the actions of the executive is one that the judiciary robustly defends. The decision in **Anisminic Ltd v Foreign Compensation Commission** [1969] 2 AC 147 confirmed

[2] This is an important authority to cite, but you must make sure that you note the comments are *obiter*, to avoid giving the examiner the impression that you believe that this is a reality, rather than a hypothesis.

that any discretionary power that purports to deny the right of judicial review will be declared unlawful. More recently, in *obiter* comments, the Law Lords suggested that, if Parliament passed an Act abolishing judicial review, the judiciary might countenance the constitutionally unprecedented step of refusing to apply an Act of Parliament (**R (Jackson) v Attorney General** [2005] UKHL 56).[2] The constitutional importance of the procedure, then, is clear.

[3] By asking for consideration of developments in the last 25 years, the question is inviting you to recognise the seminal *GCHQ case* as the starting point for discussion. It would be difficult to get good marks here without outlining the reasons for the case being so important.

The mid-1980s can be selected as a starting point for an analysis of the function and scope of judicial review in modern times, as the seminal case **Council of Civil Service Unions v Minister for the Civil Service** [1985] AC 374 (**GCHQ case**) signalled a shift in the attitude of the judiciary towards the Crown.[3] Previously, there had been an acceptance that the courts had no power to examine the exercise of a prerogative power, and that the role of the judiciary would be limited to determining whether a claimed prerogative did indeed exist. This had the effect of ensuring that the exercise of all discretionary power by the executive can be examined and held to account, whether it derives from the prerogative or is delegated by statute. It is important to recognise, however, that the courts continued to accept that not every action of the government could be scrutinised, as 'excluded categories' remained. These included matters pertaining to the signing of treaties, foreign affairs, the prerogative of mercy, and issues affecting national

[4] Here, the answer refers back to the constitutional considerations outlined in the introduction, ensuring that the focus on the developing argument is maintained.

security. The rationale for the existence of excluded categories is that certain matters of 'high policy' are for determination by the Crown and therefore judicial interference threatens the separation of powers.[4]

Since the decision in the *GCHQ case*, it is possible to argue that the courts have grown more willing to review the exercise of powers in a broader range of areas. For example, in *R v Secretary of State for Foreign Affairs ex parte Everett* [1989] QB 811, it was held that the issuing of passports (previously considered to fall within the area of foreign affairs) is reviewable. The exercise of the prerogative of mercy has been reviewed on more than one occasion, including the case of *R v Secretary of State for the Home Department ex parte Bentley* [1994] QB 349. In *R v Ministry of Defence ex parte Smith* [1996] QB 517, the courts rejected the government assertion that a decision to exclude homosexuals from the armed services was non-justiciable, despite the fact it concerned disposition of the armed forces.[5] It can be argued, therefore, that, in recent decades, judicial review has taken on increased importance in ensuring that the executive utilises its powers correctly.

[5] There are a variety of different cases that could be referenced, but one or two examples are required to support the suggestion that judicial review can be said to be used more effectively to control the executive.

[6] Marks will be given for recognising that the *GCHQ case* has not resulted in review of all areas of executive action.

Nonetheless, it should be noted that the judiciary is unwilling to review the exercise of any government power that concerns matters that are clearly concerned with national security or diplomatic relations.[6] Therefore, in the cases of *R (Abbasi) v Secretary of State for Foreign and Commonwealth Affairs and Secretary of State for the Home Department* [2002] All ER (D) 70 (Nov) and *R (Al Rawi) v Secretary of State for Foreign and Commonwealth Affairs* [2007] 2 WLR 1219 the court refused to interfere with the decision by government not to make representations on behalf of detainees at Guantanamo Bay, and in the case brought by *CND v Prime Minister of the United Kingdom* [2002] All ER 245 the courts refused to interfere with the government's determination of the legal effect of UN resolution 1441. Accordingly, the view that judicial review is able to control the use of executive power can be given only partial endorsement. The judiciary may not accept the existence of any non-justiciable categories, but deference to the executive remains to the extent that significant areas are still deemed to be the province of government.[7]

[7] At this stage of the argument, having looked at some evidence, it is possible to refer back to the question and draw some preliminary conclusions.

It is right to say that relatively few claims of judicial review will now be excluded on the basis that the subject matter cannot be reviewed. The vast majority of cases do not touch on matters of government policy or

[8] The question raises two issues: the role of the courts in controlling the executive, and access to review for the citizen. The answer needs to ensure that both matters are dealt with.

[9] As it is not possible to discuss every aspect of review in the time allowed, it is helpful to set out the parameters of the discussion.

[10] You must keep returning to the question at the end of every point you make.

[11] When answering an essay question, you must ensure that you conclude by addressing the issues that you were specifically asked to discuss. You must be prepared to offer an opinion on the material that you have outlined.

the use of prerogative powers. However, it is not the case that every citizen seeking review of the exercise of a statutory discretion will be able to avail themselves of the assistance of the courts.[8] Judicial review is not a right, and permission of the court is required. It is not possible to consider every aspect of the leave procedure here, but some of the potentially problematic areas can be considered.[9]

Only the actions of a public body are open to review, and, further, only matters concerning public, rather than private, law. This is not always a straightforward determination, as the boundaries between public and private bodies, and, indeed, public and private law, can be indistinct. This can be seen by looking at the distinctions between *R v Disciplinary Committee of the Jockey Club ex parte Aga Khan* [1993] 1 WLR 909 and *R v Panel on Takeovers and Mergers ex parte Datafin plc* [1987] 2 WLR 699. The Jockey Club was declared to be a private body even though it had broad powers to regulate an important activity. The Panel was held to be a public body despite the fact that the organisation was not acting on behalf of the state. The claimant will need to satisfy the court that the body is exercising powers analogous to those available to the state, which may mean that redress is unavailable in some cases.[10]

A claim will be excluded if it is brought out of time. It is fair to say that the three-month limit imposed by the CPR (r. 54) is not overly restrictive, and is indeed more generous than equivalent EU provisions, which allow for two months. However, partial ouster clauses are lawful (*R v Secretary of State for the Environment ex parte Ostler* [1977] QB 122), and these can make it difficult for an aggrieved citizen to lodge a claim. It will also be necessary to demonstrate 'sufficient interest', which can be viewed as a tool to exclude frivolous claims. However, the courts considered the meaning of 'sufficient interest' in *R v IRC ex parte Rossminster* [1980] AC 952 and concluded that it was designed only to exclude 'mischief makers, busybodies and cranks', and, therefore, the majority of individuals who can claim to be affected by a decision will be granted standing.

Judicial review is not capable of challenging every executive action, nor can it protect every citizen. As has been shown, despite an increasing willingness by the judiciary to examine the actions of the state, limitations remain. Nonetheless, it is right to say that the scope of judicial review has increased significantly since the *GCHQ case*, and there is a greater willingness by the courts to scrutinise the use of government powers.[11]

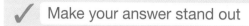

✓ Make your answer stand out

- By expanding the discussion about the 'sufficient interest' test and suggesting that it is less onerous than it once was. You could cite the case of *R (Edwards)* v *Environment Agency* [2004] EWHC 736 (Admin), in which it was held that the applicant had sufficient interest in a decision despite evidence that suggested that he had displayed little interest in the issue during a long consultation process. This could be used to support the argument that the test does not prevent interested parties from lodging a claim.

- By considering the effect of the Human Rights Act 1998 (HRA) on the constitutional role of judicial review. Jowell, J. (2000) Beyond the rule of law: towards constitutional judicial review, *Public Law*, 671–83 is a good starting point for additional reading. You could suggest that the HRA has resulted in a situation where judicial review is able to offer better protection for the citizen. This would show your examiner that you can see the connections between different areas of the syllabus.

- By outlining some of the contrasting academic argument about the role of judicial review in challenging legislation. Waldron has suggested that this poses a challenge to notions of democracy, while Lever has rejected this argument (Waldron, J. (2006) The core of the case against judicial review. *Yale Law Journal*,115: 1346; and Lever, A. (2007) Is judicial review undemocratic? *Public Law*, 280–98). You must remember that it will not be enough to cite the views of academics, however, unless you use the arguments to answer the question that your examiner has asked.

! Don't be tempted to . . .

- Provide statements about the role or effect of judicial review that you cannot support with authority or examples. Marks cannot be given for unsupported opinion. A weaker answer might make the (valid) point that the judiciary will still defer to the executive when matters of foreign policy are in issue. More credit will be given to the student who can state that this can be ascertained from the decisions in *Abbasi* or *Al Rawi*.

- Give a descriptive account of the process of judicial review. Students often expect this topic to appear as a problem scenario, and are therefore unprepared to engage in the kind of analysis needed here. Weak answers, then, tend to explain the various stages of the review process and outline the various grounds of a claim without using knowledge of the subject to offer an answer to the question. If you do not feel able to put together an argument about the role of judicial review, it would be better to avoid answering this question altogether.

❓ Question 5

Taylor wishes to open a bar in the Moorland area of Thurstown. He makes an application to the council's Licensing Committee for permission to sell alcohol for consumption on the premises. The committee meets each month to consider applications, using the power delegated by the Licensing Act 2003, which provides, at section 4, that an application may be refused in order to comply with one of the following objectives:

(a) the prevention of crime and disorder;

(b) public safety;

(c) the prevention of public nuisance; and

(d) the protection of children from harm.

The Act further provides that any appeal against refusal of a licence must be made within four weeks.

Taylor is asked to address his application to Mr Greaves, the chair of the committee. Before posting the form, he decides to telephone Mr Greaves to make sure that he has included everything relevant. During the course of the call, Mr Greaves tells Taylor not to worry, and that there are no reasons why the application should not be granted.

Two days after the committee meets, Taylor receives a letter that simply states that the application has been refused. He telephones the council to ask why, but is told that the minutes will be made publicly available online in two weeks. Five weeks later, the minutes are finally posted online, with a note explaining that they are late due to staff shortages. The minutes regarding Taylor's application state:

> The committee feels that there are too many bars in the area at present, and the commercial viability of existing licensed premises will be undermined if further applications are agreed.

Taylor seeks your advice about any action that he can take.

Answer plan

→ Explain the process of judicial review.

→ Consider the problems raised by the timing of the application.

→ Identify and assess the merits of the potential grounds.

→ Draw some conclusions about the merits of Taylor's case.

Diagram plan

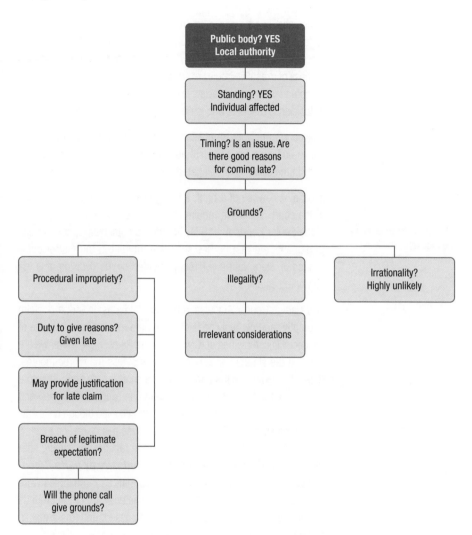

A printable version of this diagram plan is available from **www.pearsoned.co.uk/lawexpressqa**

Answer

Taylor should be advised to consider bringing a claim for judicial review of the decision not to grant a licence. Judicial review is the mechanism that allows the courts to scrutinise the decision-making process of executive bodies exercising discretionary powers. It should be noted that a judicial review is concerned with the manner in which a decision is reached, and is not an appeal on the merits.

The courts are able to judicially review only decisions reached by public bodies. Here, the local authority is clearly acting as a public body in the exercise of delegated power.

Judicial review is not a right, and Taylor will need to seek the leave of the court. The leave requirements are now set out at section 31 of the Senior Courts Act 1981. In order to obtain leave, he will need to demonstrate that he has sufficient interest in the matter complained of. Here, as he is directly affected by the decision, this will be unproblematic.[1]

[1] It is useful to show that all the requirements of the leave procedure are understood, but as standing is not problematic in this scenario, it should be dealt with swiftly.

The Senior Courts Act also requires claimants to lodge a claim 'promptly', and certainly no later than three months from the date of the decision complained of (Civil Procedure Rules, r. 54). Here, we are told that the statute imposes a time limit of less than three months. Rule 54.5 allows for the imposition of a shorter time limit; therefore Taylor is out of time. However, the court can exercise discretion and take the decision to allow the claim to proceed even though he is outside of the time limit. The court may exercise this discretion to allow late application if there are good, objective reasons for coming later (*R v Secretary of State for Trade and Industry ex parte Greenpeace* [1998] ELR 415). Here, it seems that, as the minutes were not available at the correct time, Taylor was unaware of the grounds for the application until the deadline had passed, and it is arguable that this is a case in which the court should exercise its discretion.[2]

[2] The authority cited here allows the answer to draw conclusions about the likely outcome of this case.

Assuming that leave is granted, the court will then have to consider whether there are grounds for judicial review. There are three categories of grounds for judicial review, outlined in *Council of Civil Service Unions v Minister for the Civil Service* [1985] AC 374 as illegality, procedural impropriety and irrationality. Taylor may have grounds falling under the headings of procedural impropriety and illegality.

3 You should attempt some
explanation of 'natural justice',
even though it is a vague
concept. This reassures
your examiner that you do
understand this key concept.

[3] You should attempt some explanation of 'natural justice', even though it is a vague concept. This reassures your examiner that you do understand this key concept.

[4] It is helpful to provide this brief definition. Not only have you shown the examiner that you know what it means, you have also shown you understand something about the legal status of an expectation.

[5] This is a really useful authority to cite, as the facts are similar to those in the problem. It can give a clear indication of the approach that a court is likely to take when assessing the merits of Taylor's claim.

[6] You must remember to keep returning to the facts of the scenario, and using the law you have outlined to draw conclusions about the facts of the problem.

[7] It is a good idea to note the fact that the question has not specified that there is a requirement to give reasons. Some students will assume that there is because reasons have been provided. A better answer will make the point that there is a need to check the legislation carefully, as this is what a lawyer would do in practice.

Procedural impropriety can occur either through failing to comply with statutory requirements, or through a general failure to comply with what are sometimes referred to as the 'rules of natural justice'. This somewhat ill-defined concept deals with the standards of fairness that the courts have seemed to consider demand protection in all proceedings.[3] There have been a number of cases in which a prior indication of the outcome of a decision has been held to create a 'legitimate expectation'. A legitimate expectation is not a 'legal right', but the courts can find circumstances where equity demands that it is given protection, as it would be unfair to thwart the expectation.[4] For example, in *R v Inland Revenue Commissioners ex parte Preston* [1985] AC 835 it was held that it would amount to an abuse to allow the IRC to renege on an assurance given to taxpayers that their affairs would not be investigated provided that certain conditions were complied with. Although it is clear, then, that a legitimate expectation can be created by an assurance, it is not certain that Taylor would be successful. A distinction can be drawn between the situation in the *Preston* case and the authority from *R v Liverpool Corporation ex parte Liverpool Taxi Fleet Operators* [1972] 2 QB 299 concerning an indication given regarding the probable grant of a licence, in which it was held that an undertaking given by a chair of the committee was prima facie unlawful as this would fetter the discretion of the decision-making body itself.[5] The expectation created in the minds of the taxpayers is, arguably, more worthy of protection as, if not honoured, the effect is punitive and potentially a threat to liberty. Here, the facts seem to be more analogous with the *Liverpool* case and it appears that the assurance given to Taylor will not give rise to an expectation that the courts will protect.[6]

There is no general duty to give reasons, so Taylor will be unable to argue that the failure to provide reasons automatically amounts to a procedural impropriety. However, as the council appears to accept that reasons should be given and provide a timescale, the issue requires some consideration and, certainly, further investigation of the provisions of the enabling Act. If the legislation stipulates that reasons must be provided, and gives a timescale, then the failure to comply may be a procedural impropriety.[7] If that is the case, the court would need to determine whether the non-compliance should be considered to be 'substantial', following *R v Immigration Appeal Tribunal ex parte Jeyeanthan* [1999] 3 All ER 231. In this case, it is difficult to

[8] Marks will be given here for noting that the late reasons may provide procedural assistance, even if they are not part of the substantive claim.

[9] It is necessary to show that there are authorities to support this ground, but, here, as there is little controversy about the applicability of the ground, it isn't necessary to explain the ratios or facts in any detail.

[10] Although it will be concluded that this ground is the most appropriate on which to base a claim, little space is given to it in the answer. This is because it is very straightforward, and more marks are available for exploring the more contentious issues in more detail.

see how the late provision of reasons impacts on the decision-making process. This aspect of the case is more helpful in assisting Taylor to persuade the course to allow the late claim.[8]

Taylor may wish to argue that the decision should be considered to be illegal. Illegality can arise in a variety of ways. Where the statute provides that certain factors need to be considered in the decision-making process, it is not permissible to take account of other matters. The courts have been willing to hold a decision to be illegal where it has been taken on the basis of irrelevant matters in numerous cases, including *Wheeler* v *Leicester City Council* [1985] AC 1054 and *R* v *Secretary of State for the Home Department ex parte Venables* [1997] 3 WLR 23.[9] Here, the statute sets out the matters that need to be considered, and the commercial effect on other businesses will therefore be deemed irrelevant. This would seem to be the ground that is most likely to succeed.[10]

If the application is successful, the court has the discretion to provide a remedy, and all remedies will have the effect of ensuring that the decision is taken again. Here, it is probable that a quashing order will be made to void the original decision.

✓ Make your answer stand out

- By spending more time discussing the issue of legitimate expectations, which has attracted considerable academic comment. There is an excellent overview of the topic in Craig, P. (1992) Legitimate expectations: a conceptual analysis, *LQR*, 108: 79–98, which clearly explains the different circumstances in which an expectation could be said to arise.

- By incorporating some more recent case law that has addressed the issue of legitimate expectations. You may wish to start by considering the journal article, Knight, C.J.S. (2009) Expectations in transition: recent developments in legitimate expectations, *Public Law*, 15–24, which discusses a number of important authorities. You will be rewarded if you can incorporate relevant academic comment.

- By giving more detail regarding the late provision of reasons. A clear explanation of this area can be found in Schaeffer, A. (2004) Reasons and rationalisations: late reasons in judicial review, *JR*, 151. This would show the examiner that you have a detailed understanding of the topic.

! Don't be tempted to . . .

- Speculate about the merits of the decision. It may seem self-evident that the licence should have been granted, given the wording of the statute. Students sometimes suggest that, as a result of a review, the decision will be reversed. You must remember, however, that the purpose of judicial review is to assess the manner in which the decision was made, and the effect of any remedy given is to ensure that the decision is made again, using the correct procedure.

- Use speculation to find potential grounds for review. Here, there is no suggestion of any improper purpose or bad faith, and yet a surprising number of students attempt to argue that, as the decision was plainly wrong, it must have been malicious. You must never make assumptions that are not based on facts that you have been given.

Question 6

The constitutional importance of the parliamentary ombudsman in ensuring executive accountability is often overlooked.

Discuss.

Answer plan

→ Explain what the role of the ombudsman is.

→ Discuss the role of the ombudsman in relation to Parliament.

→ Assess the differences between the judicial review system and the procedure used by the ombudsman.

→ Consider the strengths and weaknesses of the ombudsman in controlling the executive.

Diagram plan

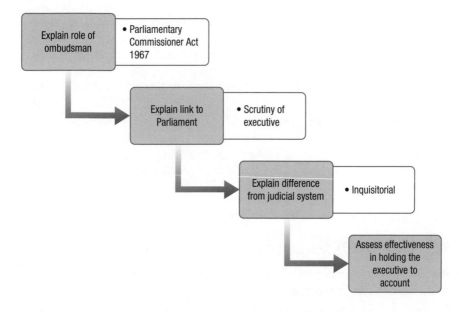

A printable version of this diagram plan is available from **www.pearsoned.co.uk/lawexpressqa**

Answer

[1] You do not have time to deal with the various types of ombudsman in your answer, but it is useful to acknowledge that you are aware of their existence.

[2] This is a good, succinct introduction that sets out the key areas for discussion without going into too much detail.

The Parliamentary Commissioner Act 1967 (PCA) established the role of the Parliamentary ombudsman (PO) for the United Kingdom. Although there are separate ombudsmen dealing with specific government departments in England (such as the Local Government Ombudsman and the Housing Ombudsman), for the devolved regions, the Parliamentary Ombudsman deals with complaints of maladministration made regarding public bodies operating in the UK.[1] The ombudsman scheme was intended to act as an alternative means of obtaining redress outside of the court and tribunal system. In order to assess the effectiveness of the ombudsman, it is necessary to consider how the ombudsman works alongside the legislature, and how the system differs from the possibilities for redress offered by the courts.[2]

The PO is able to investigate complaints of maladministration by public bodies, to reach conclusions and recommend redress, and to make recommendations to the body concerned. The ombudsman was created partly because of pressures on the legislature making it more difficult for MPs to respond to the individual concerns of their constituents (Elliott and Thomas, 2014, p. 584). It is possible to argue that the constitutional role of the ombudsman is best understood as an aspect of Parliament's role in scrutinising the executive. The relationship between the PO and the legislature is clear. The ombudsman is accountable to Parliament, and is required to submit an annual report. The ombudsman can investigate complaints only at the request of a Member of Parliament – a system that is known as the 'MP filter'. It could be argued that the filter is required to reduce the workload of the PO by avoiding unmeritorious claims; perhaps analogous to the leave requirement for judicial review described as a means of excluding 'busybodies, cranks and other mischief-makers' (*IRC* v *National Federation of Self-Employed and Small Businesses Ltd* [1982] AC 617).[3] Studies suggest, however, that MPs are an ineffective filter, as almost all complaints are forwarded to the ombudsman on request (Harlow, 1978).[4] Perhaps the filter simply serves to reinforce the link between the PO and the legislature.

One practical effect of the filtration system is that the ombudsman can investigate complaints that are received and is not able to undertake investigations on her own initiative.[5] The PCA further stipulates that the PO can investigate complaints only where the maladministration alleged is said to have caused injustice of hardship (s. 5(1)(a)).[6] It can be seen that the autonomy of the PO to address areas of concern is more restricted than the powers of scrutiny given to parliamentary select committees, which have free reign to determine areas of consideration within the boundaries of their policy areas. It should also be noted that certain departments cannot be investigated, including the police, the Prime Minister's office, tribunals or commercial transactions. This limitation clearly restricts the extent to which the office can hold the executive to account.[7]

The ombudsman certainly has a quasi-judicial function, in that she can resolve disputes and suggest redress, but there are a number of key differences between the system and the judicial process. First, access to the ombudsman is free of charge; no fee is payable by the complainant. Secondly, while the court system is adversarial, the ombudsman takes an inquisitorial approach. While the judiciary will confine its judgments to the specific issues raised between the

[3] This is a useful point to make. Where you can see links between the topic of a question and other parts of the syllabus, you should make them. Students have a tendency to treat each topic as if it were entirely self-contained, but this is artificial.

[4] It is always helpful to be able to point to research, as this will make your answer far more persuasive.

[5] There are various views about the use of gendered pronouns. Here, the feminine pronoun is used simply for factual accuracy: the current holder of the office is Dame Julie Mellor and her predecessor was Ann Abrahams.

[6] You should refer to specific sections of the legislation rather than simply talking in general terms.

[7] Do make sure that you keep referring back to the question.

[8] This is a good paragraph that itemises the key points fairly concisely but with sufficient detail to make it clear that there is a solid understanding of how the ombudsman system works.

[9] Here, the answer demonstrates an ability to link the different topics and engage in a comparative analysis of different aspects of the constitution.

[10] This is a critical point that goes to the heart of the question of accountability.

[11] Use of the example is very helpful, as it supports your point about the pitfalls of a system reliant upon goodwill.

parties to the case with which it is dealing, the ombudsman can go further and make more generalised conclusions about the government department concerned, including recommendations for better practice in the future. Thirdly, the concept of 'maladministration' is broader than the legalistic grounds available for judicial review.[8] Although the PCA did not give a definition, Ann Abrahams developed the principles of good administration to provide a clearer framework when assessing complaints (Parliamentary and Health Service Ombudsman (London), 2009). The examples provided under each heading in some instances correlate to factors that could constitute grounds for judicial review: for example, examples cited of the first principle, 'getting it right', include matters such as taking into account relevant considerations and taking reasonable decisions. However, they also incorporate examples of behaviours that, while desirable, could not form part of a legal claim, such as treating people with courtesy and asking for feedback.[9] The ombudsman has far-reaching powers of investigation. The PCA makes it clear that she can request the production of relevant documentation, and require members of the department being investigated to attend and answer questions. Should there be non-compliance, section 9 of the PCA allows the matter to be referred to the High Court, which can deal with the matter as if it were contempt of court. Although the ombudsman has coercive powers during investigation, however, the decisions reached are not legally enforceable.[10]

If an ombudsman's report is not acted upon, she can submit a special report to Parliament (PCA, s. 10(3)) and the relevant select committee can determine whether or not to take the matter up. It should be noted that the executive usually complies with the recommendations of the ombudsman and therefore section 10(3) is rarely used (Elliott and Thomas, 2014, p. 600). The problem is, perhaps, that the system is reliant on goodwill. In 2007, the PO issued a report into the mis-selling of pensions and inadequate government regulation (the Equitable Life affair) that included findings of maladministration and recommendations for compensation. The government refused to act, despite support for the PO from the Public Administration Committee.[11] Abrahams described the refusal to accept her findings of maladministration as a lack of respect for her constitutional position (House of Commons Public Administration Select Committee, Sixth Report (HC 219–2008–09) Ev 1, cited in Elliott and Thomas, 2014, p. 603).

The Parliamentary Ombudsman is empowered to scrutinise the executive and must therefore be seen as part of the constitutional framework of checks and balances ensuring accountability. In many respects, the PO is a quicker, cheaper and more accessible means of seeking redress than the courts, and can consider complaints that could not form the basis of a judicial review claim. The weakness, however, is that her findings are not legally binding. The effectiveness of the ombudsman, then, is reliant upon either the goodwill and co-operation of the executive body concerned or, alternatively, the political pressure exerted by the fear of negative publicity.[12] It is probable that, as access to legal aid for judicial review becomes more limited, the constitutional importance of the ombudsman will increase. It is to be hoped that the system is robust enough to provide sufficient assurance of accountability.

[12] The conclusion effectively summarises the opposing arguments that have been referred to in the answer.

✓ Make your answer stand out

- By broadening the sources used to inform your answer. Despite the importance of the ombudsman, there is surprisingly little academic interest in this aspect of the constitution. A good starting point is to read the series of four articles written by the previous holder of the office, Ann Abrahams, which were published in the journal *Parliamentary Affairs* in 2008. The first (The Ombudsman as Part of the UK Constitution: A contested role?, 61(1): 206–15) is a very readable overview of the development of the role.

- By discussing the issues raised by the lack of enforceability in more detail. The pensions scandal referred to in the answer resulted in litigation seeking judicial review of the government's refusal to accept the ombudsman's finding. For a good analysis of the case and the ramifications, see Varuhas, J. (2009) Governmental rejection of Ombudsman's findings: What role for the Courts? *Modern Law Review*, 71(1): 102–15.

! Don't be tempted to . . .

- Answer this question unless you are confident that you understand the ombudsman role. Unfortunately, some students may have revised executive accountability by considering judicial review and/or parliamentary procedures, but not the ombudsman. You will not be able to get good marks for this question by talking in general terms about the importance of accountability: you will need to focus on precisely how the ombudsman system works in order to assess the effectiveness of the office. ▶

■ Answer the question without reference to the relationship between the ombudsman and other constitutional bodies. It is equally dangerous to try to answer the question by simply setting out the mechanics of the ombudsman system and not attempting some comparison with alternative methods of executive accountability.

 Question 7

The changes made to judicial review proceedings risk reducing access to justice and undermining the separation of powers.

Discuss.

Answer plan

→ Briefly explain the function of judicial review claims and the criticisms that led to the Criminal Justice and Courts Act 2015 (CJCA).

→ Identify the key changes introduced by the CJCA.

→ Explain the impact of the legislation on access to justice.

→ Consider the impact of the legislative changes on the rule of law and the separation of powers.

Diagram plan

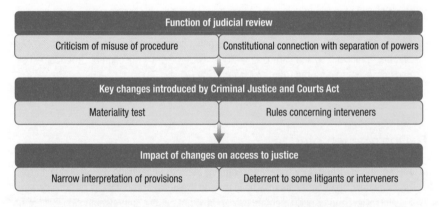

A printable version of this diagram plan is available from **www.pearsoned.co.uk/lawexpressqa**

Answer

[1] Take care not to give a detailed explanation of the process in your introduction: you need to be able to state the constitutional function of the procedure.

[2] It is important to explain at the outset what the key criticism of the pre-CJCA process was.

[3] It is important to keep returning to the constitutional effect of the changes made.

[4] You do not need to list all the provisions in the Act; it is much more effective to give a brief overview and then focus on the issue raised by the question.

Judicial review is the mechanism that allows citizens to challenge the legality of decisions taken by public bodies.[1] Judicial scrutiny of executive action is an important component of a functional separation of powers that ensures that no one branch of the state is able to misuse its powers, and can be seen as an essential requirement of the rule of law.[2] The benefit of judicial review proceedings must be balanced against the risk that unnecessary litigation is costly, and could interfere with the ability of public bodies to work efficiently. The Criminal Justice and Courts Act 2015 (CJCA) aimed to introduce changes to both the procedure required to obtain leave to bring a judicial review claim and the availability of remedies and costs.[3] The changes made to judicial review may have a significant impact on the ability of citizens to challenge government decisions, and this in turn could undermine the constitutional function of the judiciary to operate a system of checks and balances preventing the abuse of executive power.

The legislation caused controversy while it was being debated in Parliament. Lord Marks described the proposed changes to judicial review as 'an assault upon the rule of law' (HL Deb., vol. 756, col. 960), and the Joint Committee for Human Rights warned that restrictions on funding would create a 'chilling effect' that could deter potential litigants (HL 174, HC 868). The Act imposed some restrictions on the courts' discretion at the permission stage, and some limitations on the courts' freedom to provide successful litigants with a remedy.[4] Perhaps, though, the most significant provisions in the Act are those that will impact on the conduct of organisations who may wish to act as interveners in judicial review cases.

The judiciary has always resisted any attempt to limit the availability of judicial review, and is clear that the constitutional importance of the process will be defended as part of the requirements of the rule of law. The decision in ***Anisminic Ltd v Foreign Compensation Commission*** [1969] 2 AC 147 confirmed that any discretionary power that purports to deny the right of judicial review will be declared unlawful. Judicial review is an essential tool in ensuring that an effective separation of powers operates such that there are methods of ensuring that there is accountability for the use of executive power.

[5] You need to be able to explain the pre CJCA procedure briefly, in order to evaluate the impact of changes.

[6] Here, the answer shows understanding of the significance of the change.

[7] It is important to include some of the case authorities here to illustrate the courts' approach to this aspect of the permission stage, as this highlights how radical the legislation has the potential to be.

[8] Although the question specifically requires the answer to address the separation of powers, reference to access to justice should alert you to the need to mention the rule of law.

The constitutional importance of the procedure is clear, but the right to bring judicial review proceedings has never been automatic.[5] Section 31 of the Senior Courts Act 1981 (SCA) sets out the requirementsthat a claimant must satisfy in order to obtain permission; they must show that they have sufficient interest in the matter complained of, and must bring the claim promptly. Lord Scarman noted that the limitations were intended to 'prevent abuse by busybodies cranks and other mischief-makers' (*R v Inland Revenue Commissioners, ex parte Federation of Self-Employed and Small Businesses* [1982] AC 617). The CJCA has added a test of 'materiality' to the leave process, giving the court discretion to refuse leave if it is concluded that it is 'highly likely' that the outcome 'would not have been substantially different if the conduct complained of had not occurred' (s. 84(2)). If the defendant requests it, the court is required to consider the materiality test.[6] The court has always had the option to strike out any case if it concluded that, even without a mistake, the outcome for the claimant would inevitably be the same. The new statutory test, however, sets a lower threshold of likelihood instead of inevitability.[7] In *R (Smith) v North Eastern Derbyshire Primary Care Trust* [2006] EWCA Civ 1291, the Court of Appeal stressed that probability was too low as a threshold at the permission stage. It could also be argued that the increased scrutiny of the applicant's substantive arguments during the permission stage is a significant shift. The joint report on the CJCA prepared by the Bingham Centre for the Rule of Law, Justice and the Public Law Project (BIICL 2015) notes that the court has previously been clear at emphasising the importance of keeping substantive issues and procedure separate. In *R v Secretary of State for the Home Department ex parte Amin* [2006] UKHL 51, Lord Steyn stated it was: 'vital that procedure and the merits should be kept strictly apart otherwise the merits may be judged unfairly' (Para. 51).

It is clear that there will now be more work for applicants to do in demonstrating the merits of the claim at the permission stage.[8] This may well have the effect of deterring some litigants, and this could reduce access to justice, which is a key component of the rule of law. This is particularly worrying when considering limitations to legal aid in judicial review proceedings. The Legal Aid, Sentencing and Punishment of Offenders Act 2012 makes it clear that legal aid payments may be refused if permission is not granted. Legally aided claimants (and their solicitors) may be unwilling to carry the financial risks of completing additional work at this stage.

[9] Credit will be given for the analysis of the impact of the legislation.

The 'materiality test' applied at the relief stage is, if anything, more concerning, as it prohibits the court from granting relief where it seems highly likely that there would have been no substantial difference in outcome except in cases of exceptional public interest.[9] The legislation, then, can be seen as marking a constitutional shift away from a model in which judicial review is concerned with insisting on procedural fairness as part of natural justice. It is important to note, however, as Elliott has done (2015, 2), that the judiciary is likely to interpret provisions that limit rights extremely narrowly.

[10] Take care not to give too much descriptive detail from the statute.

The CJCA has also introduced a number of provisions that will have an impact on organisations who intervene in judicial review proceedings. During the passage of the legislation, Lord Faulkner argued that the changes were intended to encourage organisations to 'pause long and hard' to consider whether or not to intervene in proceedings.[10] The court now has a statutory duty to award costs against an intervener who has, in effect, taken over the case or whose evidence was irrelevant or of insignificant assistance. The duty can be set aside in the Supreme Court in exceptional circumstances. The Bingham Centre suggests that, provided that is interpreted narrowly, this part of the legislation does not make significant changes to current practice, but notes that nevertheless the formal statement of costs risks could act as a deterrent to organisations struggling to manage their resources.

[11] You should take care to refer back to the question in the conclusion.

Changes to judicial review have undoubtedly created additional challenges for potential litigants.[11] If interpreted broadly, the legislation could restrict access to the process and this would be an alteration to the operation of the separation of powers. It seems likely, however, that the judiciary will apply a narrow interpretation to legislation in order to preserve the constitutional effectiveness of the procedure.

Make your answer stand out

- By ensuring that you remain up to date. The legislation is fairly recent, and you will be rewarded if you are able to discuss the application of the new provisions. For example, a case decided in late 2015, **R (on the Application of Hawke) v Secretary of State for Justice** [2015] EWHC 3599, demonstrates how the courts use a narrow construction of the provisions concerning relief.
- By examining in more detail the connection between legal aid changes and limitations on judicial review. It is worth keeping up to date with cases and materials posted by the Public Law Project.

 Don't be tempted to . . .

- Treat the case as an invitation to set out in detail the changes made by the statute. Weak students tend to include long quotes from legislation rather than selecting a few key points that are the most useful to them in answering the question.
- Provide detail about the substantive grounds of review in any of the cases that you refer to: this question is about procedure, not grounds.

@ Try it yourself

Now take a look at the question below and attempt to answer it. You can check your response against the answer guidance available on the companion website (**www.pearsoned.co.uk/lawexpressqa**).

> 'Natural justice' is a vague, imprecise concept that can be interpreted in so many ways, it is impossible to provide any certainty of advice to participants in judicial review proceedings.
>
> Discuss.

www.pearsoned.co.uk/lawexpressqa

 Go online to access more revision support including additional essay and problem questions with diagram plans, and You be the marker questions, and to download all diagrams from the book.

The individual and the state: police powers, public protest and surveillance

How this topic may come up in exams

This is a broad area and some universities will deal with these issues as separate topic areas in your syllabus. Here, they have been collected together as all deal with the intrusive powers that the state has to interfere with the liberty and the privacy of individual citizens. This topic can overlap with several others: clearly, the exercise of these types of powers can involve consideration of executive accountability. There is also scope to assess the relationship between the use of state powers and the doctrine of the rule of law. It is quite common for examiners to set problem questions dealing with the use of general police powers and the policing of public protest.

Before you begin

It's a good idea to consider the following key themes of the individual and the state: police powers, public protest and surveillance before tackling a question on this topic.

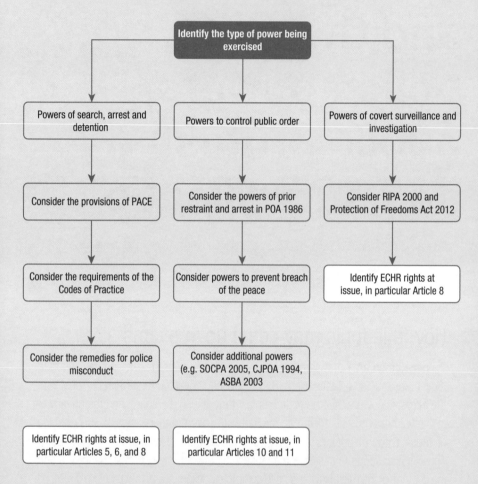

A printable version of this diagram is available from **www.pearsoned.co.uk/lawexpressqa**

Question 1

The creation of offences of aggravated trespass, and the use of civil injunctions have led to a situation where greater weight is given to the rights of businesses than to the right to protest.

Discuss.

Answer plan

→ Explain the rights at Articles 10 and 11.

→ Distinguish between protest and disruptive action.

→ Explain the need to balance the rights of competing interest groups.

→ Assess the effect of section 68 of the Criminal Justice and Public Order Act 1994 (CJPOA).

→ Consider the use of injunctions under the Protection from Harassment Act 1997.

Diagram plan

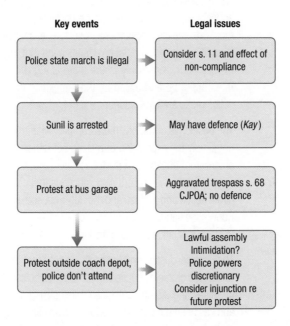

A printable version of this diagram plan is available from **www.pearsoned.co.uk/lawexpressqa**

Answer

Freedom of expression, association and assembly are expressly protected by the European Convention on Human Rights at Articles 10 and 11. These rights are considered central to the democratic process, which should tolerate and encourage the expression of minority views. There are limits upon such freedoms, however, as any government may legitimately seek to keep order and ensure that individuals can go about their business without fear of criminal interference.[1]

Article 11 protects only peaceful assembly; therefore, there is no protection for violent protest.

In the United Kingdom, despite numerous statutory and common law provisions that entitle the state to control public processions, and assemblies, the basic right to engage in political protests of this type is supported. The Public Order Act 1986 provides the key legislative framework, and although the police have powers to impose conditions on processions or static assemblies in public places, the assumption appears to be that they should be permitted to proceed save in the most extreme circumstances.[2] For example, section 11 states organisers of a procession must give notification, but they are not required to seek permission. Only where there is a grave risk to public order that cannot be addressed by the imposition of conditions can the police make an application for a ban (s. 13).[3]

The position is, arguably, more complex when the aim of a protest is not simply the expression of a view, but rather, to disrupt or prevent others from engaging in lawful activity. Here, there has been a tension between civil and criminal sanctions that can be invoked to curb direct action and protest, and the duty imposed on the court to uphold Convention rights by the Human Rights Act 1998. The courts are asked to strike a balance between the rights of competing interest groups.[4]

The Criminal Justice and Public Order Act 1994 introduced measures to address problems caused by protesters who sought to enter land or premises and disrupt activity by criminalising 'aggravated trespass', and has been utilised to prosecute individuals and groups engaged in protests regarding, *inter alia*, foreign policy in Iraq, experimentation on animals, and genetically modified crops. The case of *R v Jones* [2006] UKHL 16 involved defendants who trespassed on to military bases with the intention of disrupting activity, to protest against

[1] By referring to the two separate interests (business and protest), the examiner is asking you to consider the balancing act that the judiciary has to perform when considering Convention rights, and, by raising this in the introduction, you demonstrate that you have understood the question.

[2] This question asks for a discussion of provisions in the Criminal Justice and Public Order Act 1994, and civil injunctions. An explanation of the main statutory controls on protest demonstrates knowledge and gives the discussion some helpful context, but must be brief.

[3] It is always a good idea to give an illustrative example of the law in operation, as this will provide support for the point raised, and show that you really understand the issue.

[4] You need to keep returning to the balancing exercise conducted by the courts, as you have identified this as the central issue. All the points you discuss should be related to the central argument.

[5] It will be difficult to obtain good marks for this question without a reasonably detailed knowledge of some key cases, as you must show how the courts have addressed the balance to be struck between competing interests.

[6] Having considered the case law under section 68, the discussion needs to return to the central theme, which is whether the balance between competing interests has been struck appropriately.

[7] The question does not explicitly specify the Protection from Harassment Act 1997 but reference to injunctions implies that you should discuss it.

[8] Here, a detailed knowledge of case law is key, as this will help you to identify a relevant aspect of civil law and this will be rewarded.

[9] The use of the contrasting cases is helpful here, as it allows the answer to examine the key argument, which is how the courts have attempted to balance business interests and article rights. You must ensure, though, that you use the case law to help you draw some conclusions about the development of the judicial approach.

involvement in the war with Iraq.[5] The defendants sought to argue that the conflict was an 'aggressive war', and therefore illegal under international law. If there was no 'lawful' activity taking place, it followed that there could be no intention to commit the offences outlined in section 68. The House of Lords were not prepared to entertain the argument. Lord Hoffmann plainly considered that the argument was simply an attempt to gain further publicity during the court case, a form of protest through litigation. The majority of case law decided regarding section 68 has rejected a claim that interference with the activities of others is justifiable. It is submitted that this is not contentious, as the offence seeks to protect the rights of individuals going about their lawful business, and therefore the legislation falls squarely within the qualifications permitted by Articles 10 and 11. Civil disobedience may, or may not, have a moral or philosophical justification in any given instance, but there appears to have been no compelling legal excuse promulgated by the protesters in these cases.[6]

More controversial is the use of civil injunctions to restrain or prevent protest under the Protection from Harassment Act 1997.[7] The Act was designed to address the problem of 'stalking', and permits a civil injunction to be granted where a course of conduct creates harassment, alarm or distress. Breach of the injunction is a criminal offence. There have been a series of cases involving protests about animal experimentation, in which civil injunctions have been obtained to restrain the activities of both individuals and groups.[8] In an early case, *Huntingdon Life Sciences Ltd* v *Curtin* (1997) *The Times*, 11 December, the judge refused to allow the Act to be used to injunct a group, stating that it could not have been Parliament's intention that the statute would be used to suppress public protest. However, later cases have sanctioned the use of the Act to restrain the activities of protesters, including placing limitations on protesting at a laboratory save at specified times in the case of *University of Oxford* v *Broughton* [2008] EWHC 75 (QB). In the latter case, the judiciary was clearly mindful of the need to balance the competing rights of protesters with the Article 8 rights of employees and contractors of the university. A recent decision was more supportive of the rights of protesters, and refused to allow an injunction to prevent protesters outside a facility using megaphones, wearing blood-spattered clothing and masks (*Novartis Pharmaceuticals UK Ltd* v *Stop Huntingdon Animal Cruelty* [2010] HRLR 8).[9] It was held that, while there could be occasions when protest crossed a line and became harassment,

[10] If you can, it is worth revising a few short quotes such as this one, which neatly encapsulate an idea.

opinions that some find offensive should nevertheless be able to be expressed. As was said in **Redmond-Bate v DPP** [1999] Crim LR 998: 'Freedom only to speak inoffensively is not worth having.'[10] The courts continue to take a dim view of civil disobedience when this infringes upon the rights of others.

It is hard to see why the right to protest should extend into the curtailment of the liberties of others, by allowing protest to prevent individuals or companies carrying out their business. It is important, however, that the right to protest, and to protest robustly, is supported and upheld. If this does not occur, then there is a danger that the interest and opinions of businesses and corporations will be afforded undue weight in any debate, and those of minority groups may not be heard. This was a point stressed in the judgment of the European Court of Human Rights in **Steel and Morris v United Kingdom** (2005) 41 EHRR 22, in which it was held that refusing to grant the applicants legal aid to defend a libel action instigated by McDonalds infringed Article 10. The public interest demands that those 'outside the mainstream' can disseminate information and ideas. It is submitted that the judicial approach in response to section 68, and the Protection from Harassment Act, has sought to strike an appropriate balance by supporting the right to air controversial opinions, but preventing behaviour that unduly interferes with the lawful activity of others.[11]

[11] It is important to conclude by offering a view regarding the central argument. There is no 'correct' answer, as such, but you should ensure that the conclusions you reach are supported by the evidence provided in your argument.

✓ Make your answer stand out

■ By considering the implications of the use of the Protection from Harassment Act in more detail. Is it appropriate that it has been utilised to deal with public protest, when this was not the problem Parliament had in mind? For a detailed analysis of the issue you should refer to the discussion of the use of the Act in: Fenwick, H. (2007) *Civil Liberties and Human Rights* (4th edn). London: Routledge-Cavendish, pp. 787–98.

■ By incorporating academic comment in your answer, as well as assessment of relevant case law. This will add weight to your arguments. Fenwick is an excellent starting point, as is: Stone, R. (2012) *Textbook on Civil Liberties and Human Rights* (9th edn). Oxford: Oxford University Press.

■ By assessing the relationship between commercial interests and individual freedom in more detail. There is an excellent analysis of the changing priorities of regulation of protest in Mead, D. (2013) A chill through the back door? The privatised regulation of peaceful protest, *Public Law*, Jan: 100–18, which also contains details of several other key cases and journal articles.

! Don't be tempted to . . .

- Talk generally about powers to restrain protest; this question is focused on two particular provisions. You should not attempt this question if you have focused your revision on the application of the Public Order Act 1986. 'Question spotting' is a dangerous revision strategy. Students who expect this topic to be dealt with by a problem scenario focusing on the POA will be in trouble if forced to attempt this question!

- Attempt this question without knowledge of a range of cases that illustrate how the courts approach protests that impinge on business interests. Without this, you will not be able to obtain good marks, as your answer will lack analysis.

? Question 2

'Trainers not traffic' is the name given to an event that takes place once a month in Fetcham City Centre, to protest against pollution caused by too much traffic. The participants, all joggers, congregate outside the Town Hall on the last Friday of the month, and at 5 pm set off jogging for one hour. They take up as much room on the road as possible, to disrupt the traffic. Sunil organised the first event, and pays for a notice in the local paper inviting people to attend. The route is never decided in advance, as whoever jogs the fastest decides where to go.

One Friday, as the joggers congregate, the police hand out flyers that state: 'This is an illegal procession, because no notice has been given. Therefore, taking part is a crime.'

One of the joggers, a law student, says that this is rubbish, and the event goes ahead. After 20 minutes, the police arrest Sunil.

The following day, several joggers climb over a wall into the local authority bus garage, and chain themselves to a bus. They are carrying placards that state 'Pollution is a crime. Prevent crime'. It is several hours before the chains are cut and the buses can set off. All the protesters are arrested.

The next day, 20 joggers congregate on a patch of land outside a privately owned coach garage and shout at coach drivers as they arrive for work. The police are called but decide not to attend. Several coach drivers are too frightened to go into work, and a considerable amount of money is lost. The coach company is considering whether or not to take legal action against the police for failing to act, and to prevent the protesters from attending again.

Consider the legality of the activities described, and whether the police have acted properly.

Answer plan

→ Outline the notice requirements in section 11 of the Public Order Act.

→ Analyse the legality of the police actions, and consider the case of *Kay*.

→ Assess the legality of the protest at the bus garage, in the light of section 68 of the CJPOA.

→ Discuss the conduct of the assembly at the coach depot.

Diagram plan

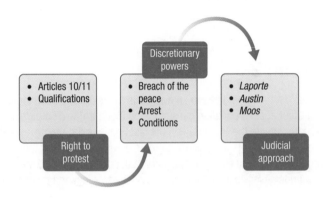

A printable version of this diagram plan is available from **www.pearsoned.co.uk/lawexpressqa**

Answer

This scenario deals with the freedom of individuals and organisations to engage in forms of protest. Articles 10 and 11 of the European Convention on Human Rights protect the rights of expression, and assembly, in recognition of the fact that tolerating protest and dissent is seen as one of the hallmarks of a democracy. It is accepted, however, that a state may have legitimate reason to limit these rights, and the permitted qualifications are listed within the Convention. In order to advise the joggers, it will be necessary to consider the restrictions on protest contained in the Public Order Act 1986 (POA), the Criminal Justice and Public Order Act 1994 (CJPOA), as well as civil sanctions created by the Protection from Harassment Act 1997 (PHA).[1]

[1] The facts of this problem raise issues about several different legal provisions. Setting them out in the introduction shows the marker that the key issues have been identified.

The monthly event in Fetcham City Centre is a procession, as defined in ***Flockhart v Robinson*** [1950] 2 KB 498 as 'a body of persons moving along a route'. The Public Order Act 1986 imposes obligations

² You don't need to list all the processions listed at section 11 here; far better to mention those that are relevant to help you advise the joggers, as this shows that you can pick the parts of the statute that are applicable.

³ It is important to note this, as the question asks for comment on the police conduct. To do well in this question, you need to have read the scenario closely, as there are a lot of details that are all included for a reason. The distribution of the flyer is one of these and there are marks available for dealing with the issue.

⁴ The facts of the first part of the scenario are based on those in the case of *Kay*. The answer is greatly assisted by having a good knowledge of this case, and, because the facts are analogous, it is worth giving more detail than is normally required.

⁵ It is critical to make sure that, having set out the facts of *Kay*, you make sure that you do relate this to the facts of the scenario.

on the organisers of most processions including those that are designed to publicise or show support for a campaign, as is the case here.² Section 11 requires the organisers of such processions to give written notice to the police, six days in advance, including details of the route. Failure to do so renders the organisers liable for a criminal offence. The flyer distributed by the police, however, does not accurately reflect the legal position. Section 11 requires the organisers of particular processions to give notice, but failure to do so does not render the procession itself unlawful. Those in the procession are not committing an offence simply by taking part.³

Following the decision in **Kay v Commissioner of Police of the Metropolis** [2008] UKHL 69, Sunil may be able to deny liability for an offence.⁴ That case concerned an analogous event: the monthly 'critical mass' cycle ride in London that took place on the last Friday of every month at a specific time, with no particular route. The House of Lords was only asked to consider whether or not the event was 'customary' and therefore exempt from notice provisions at section 11. Lord Phillips also made a number of *obiter* statements regarding the applicability of notice requirements to such events. The case turned on whether or not a procession with a route that varied each week could be considered to be customary. It was held that, despite a variable route, each monthly event shared sufficient common features to be able to state that it was a common event. Therefore, Sunil may be able to argue that the 'Trainers not traffic' events are exempt from the notice requirements at section 11.⁵

Further, Lord Phillips rejected the submission that, unless customary, it would be impossible to arrange a procession of this type that did not have a planned route. The submission was based on the proposition that section 11 imposes a requirement to give notice of the route, and criminal liability if a different route is taken. This was, in the view of Lord Phillips, 'draconian'. It would seem, then, that the event was lawful, and Sunil will have an arguable defence.

The position of the joggers who enter the bus garage is less certain. It is likely that the bus garage is private land, and therefore, entry will constitute civil trespass. Section 68 of the CJPOA creates an offence of 'aggravated trespass', which is committed by entry onto private land with the intention of disrupting or obstructing lawful activity. Here, the offence appears to be made out. It would appear that, based on

[6] Marks will be given for noting the significance of the wording on the posters. This is a further example of the value of making sure that you consider every detail of the scenario to ensure that you maximise your marks.

[7] *Jones* is probably the key case regarding the application of section 68, and certainly is the leading authority regarding the attempted defence argument that the activities disrupted are unlawful.

[8] You need to note that there are distinct types of protest, and explain how each event will be classified.

[9] The question states that the company is considering legal proceedings against the police; there will be credit for a brief discussion of the form this might take. This is linked to the analysis required of whether the police have acted correctly.

[10] *Police* v *Reid* is a really useful case, as it provides assistance with the interpretation that should be applied to the statutory provisions that allow conditions to be imposed on assemblies that intimidate.

the posters, the joggers may seek to argue they were acting in order to prevent a crime, but there is no precedent that would support this.[6] Although section 3 of the Criminal Law Act 1967 authorises 'public defence' to prevent criminal activity, *Blake* v *DPP* [1993] Crim LR 586 rejected a similar claim on the basis that the section was designed to excuse conduct involving a degree of force. It will also be difficult to point to a particular criminal offence alleged against the owners of the bus garage. Similar arguments were explored in detail, and comprehensively rejected, by the House of Lords in *R* v *Jones* [2006] UKHL 16, who declined to support direct action as a form of legitimate protest where this involved interference with the lawful activities of others. Therefore, the joggers will be liable for the offence of aggravated trespass and do not appear to have a defence.[7]

The protest outside the garage appears to take place on public land, and will therefore constitute an assembly as defined at section 16 of the Public Order Act.[8] There is no requirement to give notice of an assembly. Once called, the police could impose conditions on the conduct of the assembly if satisfied that these are necessary to combat a serious risk of public disorder, damage to property, disruption to the life of the community, or if the purpose of the gathering is to intimidate others. The police choose not to take action despite the fact that the protesters are shouting at drivers. The coach company may seek judicial review of this decision, on the basis that the police did not exercise their discretion correctly.[9] This is unlikely to succeed because, first, there may not be grounds to impose conditions on the assembly due to the abuse; as the case of *Police* v *Reid* [1987] Crim LR 702 is authority for the fact that 'intimidation' is more than 'mere discomfort'.[10] Secondly, the courts are unwilling to interfere with police discretion, as evidenced in *R* v *Chief Constable of Devon and Cornwall ex parte Central Electricity Generating Board* [1982] QB 458, where the courts refused to criticise an operational decision not to police a demonstration.

It would be open to the company to seek an injunction under the Protection from Harassment Act 1997 to restrain future protest, but the authorities do not provide support in these circumstances, as this protest is unlikely to be considered to be harassment. The decision in *Novartis Pharmaceuticals UK Ltd* v *Stop Huntingdon Animal Cruelty* [2010] HRLR 8 upheld the right to protest outside a facility in blood-stained clothes, with megaphones, despite the fact that this would cause some offence. Despite the inconvenience caused to the company, this would appear to be a legitimate protest.

To summarise, it appears that the actions of the joggers in the original event, and outside the coach garage, are lawful. However, those who enter the bus garage and physically prevent the company from conducting business will be liable for aggravated trespass.

✓ Make your answer stand out

■ By discussing whether or not the police could arrest the joggers for obstruction of the highway, including a discussion of *Hirst and Agu* v *Chief Constable of West Yorkshire* (1987) 85 Cr App R 143. That case suggested that the courts have been willing to accept that protest may be a legitimate use of the highway. Although this is not the key issue raised by the question, a thorough answer should note all matters of relevance.

■ When discussing the protest outside the coach company, outline the powers of arrest under sections 4 and 5 of the Public Order Act, and the common law power to prevent a breach of the peace. This would show a comprehensive knowledge of the available powers.

■ By including academic comment to expand the discussion. You could consider the assessment of the use of section 5 of the POA as a restraint on free speech in Geddis, A. (2004) Free speech martyrs or unreasonable threats to social peace – 'insulting' expression and section 5 of the Public Order Act 1986. *Public Law*, 853.

! Don't be tempted to . . .

■ Ignore the detail you are given in this question. All the information you are given will be included for a reason. Therefore, consider the significance of every piece of information. For example, the examiner has told you the precise wording on the placards used. This is because you are being invited to consider cases in which protesters sought to argue they acted in the legitimate prevention of crime.

■ Fail to explain your reasoning fully. Students often make the mistake of thinking that because a particular argument cannot succeed, there is no need to address the issue. Here, you are told that the coach company are considering legal action. It is clear that there is no basis for judicial review here, but you need to show the examiner how you have reached that conclusion in order to get full credit for this point.

Question 3

Since the case of *Laporte*, the courts have demonstrated an increasing willingness to sanction broad use of the discretionary powers to prevent a breach of the peace.
Discuss.

Diagram plan

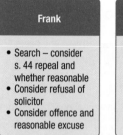

Frank

- Search – consider s. 44 repeal and whether reasonable
- Consider refusal of solicitor
- Consider offence and reasonable excuse

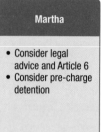

Martha

- Consider legal advice and Article 6
- Consider pre-charge detention

A printable version of this diagram plan is available from **www.pearsoned.co.uk/lawexpressqa**

Answer plan

→ Identify breach of the peace as the main focus of discussion.

→ Consider the effect of *Laporte*.

→ Contrast *Laporte* with recent 'kettling' cases.

→ Conclude that the courts are unwilling to interfere with police discretion.

[1] It is important to use an example here, as otherwise the statement about the effect of protest movements is simply an assertion of opinion. You should always try to provide evidence in support of a proposition.

[2] The relevance of Article 10 to questions about the freedom to protest is often overlooked, so it should be specifically mentioned.

Answer

The right to protest is seen as a necessary part of the democratic process. Protest movements can ensure that an issue receives media and public attention and can also exert a powerful influence on government policy. In the United Kingdom, for example, protest against the community charge led to its abolition.[1] The European Convention on Human Rights obliges signatory states to protect that right by Articles 10 and 11. Article 10 protects the right to freedom of expression, which includes the right to express ideas and support or opposition for a cause.[2] Article 11 protects the right of peaceful assembly and association. Both rights are qualified and can therefore be restricted to the extent required to achieve a specific objective such as the maintenance of public order, or the protection of the rights of others (Art. 10(2) and Art. 11(2)).

There is a balance to be struck between allowing peaceful protest and the need to prevent public disorder and minimise disruption. The police use discretionary powers granted by statute and at common law to control protest. Statutory powers are largely contained in the Public Order Act 1986, but these are supplemented by (*inter alia*) the Criminal Justice and Public Order Act 1994, the Anti-Social Behaviour Act 2003, the Serious Organised Crime and Police Act 2005 and the Police Reform and Social Responsibility Act 2011. Despite the numerous legislative provisions, the police often rely upon the common law powers to prevent a breach of the peace. It is these powers that confer the broadest discretion and that have attracted the most academic criticism. There have been a number of significant cases considering the use of these powers, which can be examined in order to assess how the judiciary attempts to assess the balancing exercise between protecting protest and supporting public order controls.[3]

At common law, the police have the power to take steps to prevent a breach of the peace. This includes arrest, but also allows an officer to take other steps to keep the peace such as the imposition of conditions upon a protest, dispersal or containment through the use of police cordons (commonly referred to as 'kettling'). It is not possible to provide a comprehensive list of actions that can be taken to prevent a breach of the peace because there is no statutory framework governing the common law powers; instead, the judiciary has had to determine what sort of conduct constitutes a breach of the peace and assess the legality of the police response on a case-by-case basis. This lack of definition has attracted criticism. For example, Fenwick (2009) described the powers as 'bewilderingly imprecise'.[4]

In *R v Howell* [1982] QB 416, it was said that a breach of the peace occurs whenever a person (or in their presence, their property) is harmed, or caused to fear such harm by 'an assault, an affray, a riot, unlawful assembly, or other disturbance.[5] It would not be sufficient, therefore, for the police to take steps to prevent unruly conduct falling short of this: there must be a threat of violence or damage to property. Where a disturbance is already in progress, there is little difficulty in endorsing arrests made in order to bring it to an end

[3] Although the question requires you to concentrate on breach of the peace, it is worth mentioning the statutory provisions here. This is not simply to impress your examiner with the extent of your knowledge, but to allow you to make the point that the police have ample powers that could arguably be invoked in circumstances where the common law power is relied upon.

[4] It would not be enough to simply state that there is criticism; you must provide some evidence of this by citing one or more sources.

[5] You must include this definition, but do not be diverted into a lengthy discussion about the judicial debate surrounding the meaning of the term. Your answer needs to focus largely on the legality of responses to a breach.

[6] Here, the answer explains why the focus of the answer will be on one particular aspect of the topic, which then enables the discussion to ignore authorities that deal with matters outside of those parameters.

[7] As the answer is not going to focus on the power of arrest, there is no need to list the conditions contained in *Bibby*.

[8] Having set out the relevant law, it is crucial to explicitly relate the authority back to the question so that the examiner can see that law is being applied to develop the argument.

[9] You do not need to set out the facts surrounding *Austin* or *Moos* in any detail. It is far more important to set out the legal issue common to both cases.

[10] The question specifically mentions 'recent' decisions, so the answer should discuss the most up-to-date authorities.

(although, arguably, there are other statutory offences that could be used instead). The more contentious use of the power, however, arises when the police take steps to prevent an anticipated breach of the peace.[6]

Where a breach of the peace has not yet occurred and the detainee has not yet engaged in any unlawful conduct, the courts have stressed that the discretionary power of arrest must be used sparingly and only if certain conditions are met (outlined in **Bibby v Chief Constable of Essex**, The Times, 24 April 2000).[7] However, steps falling short of arrest may be taken that effectively curtail protest. These were considered by the House of Lords in **R (Laporte) v Chief Constable of Gloucestershire** [2006] UKHL 55. In that case, the police stopped three coaches carrying individuals to a planned protest and after searching the vehicles ordered them to return to London. The coaches were escorted by police and were not permitted to stop en route. The House of Lords, on this occasion, declared the police actions unlawful and disproportionate. Powers can only legitimately be used to prevent an imminent breach of the peace and imminent means in the immediate future. This authority, then, is an example of the judiciary placing clear limits on the use of police discretion in order to uphold the right to protest.[8]

Since that case there have been highly publicised uses by the police of the use of police cordons to contain protesters in a geographical area (sometimes for long periods) to prevent a breach of the peace. These have been challenged by claimants, arguing that the detention was unlawful and a disproportionate use of the power that failed to discriminate between protesters whose conduct threatened the peace and those who were acting lawfully.[9] Despite the decision in **Laporte**, such challenges have failed. In **Austin v Commissioner of Police of the Metropolis** [2009] UKHL 5 the House of Lords declared that 'kettling' had not constituted a breach of Article 5 in the 'unusually difficult' circumstances the police had faced. The Court of Appeal in **R (Mclure and Moos) v Commissioner of the Police for the Metropolis** [2012] EWCA Civ 12[10] also endorsed the use of kettling and made it clear the consideration will be whether or not the police decision was reasonable in the circumstances, rather than the court reaching its own conclusion. These two cases can be seen

[11] Here, the answer again refers back to the central question.

as something of a retreat from **Laporte** and a restatement of judicial deference to the operational discretion of the police.[11] It should be noted that in **R (Mengesha) v Commissioner of Police for the Metropolis** [2013] EWHC 1695 (Admin), the Divisional Court made it clear that the court would only endorse actions that met the Laporte requirements of necessity and proportionality in the circumstances facing the police.

Given the plethora of statutory controls, it is perhaps surprising that the police still rely on the common law in public order situations. It seems that one explanation may well be the extent to which the judiciary has been prepared to approve of the use of such a vague, and broad, power. Although **Laporte** is an example of judicial attempts to impose limitations, more recent authorities do suggest that the courts are prepared to countenance significant restrictions on the freedom to protest in order to prevent a breach of the peace.[12]

[12] This conclusion can be clearly and briefly stated because the arguments have been set out in the body of the answer.

✓ Make your answer stand out

- By providing a more detailed discussion of the case law. More detail could be given about the kinds of conditions endorsed in *Austin* v *Commissioner of Police of the Metropolis* [2009] UKHL 5. This could allow for a broader debate about the role of the judiciary in supervising the executive under the Human Rights Act. If you are able to use this material to comment upon the separation of powers, then you will be showing the examiner that you can consider the topic of freedom of assembly in the context of your study of the constitution.

- By incorporating additional academic comment into your answer. Comment on the *Austin* case can be found in: Mead, D. (2009) Of kettles, cordon and crowd control – Austin, Commissioner of Police for the Metropolis and the meaning of 'deprivation of liberty'. *EHRLR*, 376.

- By discussing the approach of the European Court of Human Rights, and contrasting the decisions in *Gillan and Quinton* v *UK* [2009] ECHR 28 and *Austin and others* v *UK* (2012) 55 EHRR 14. The latter case endorses the deference to police discretion, whereas the former criticised powers seen as disproportionate and indiscriminate.

! Don't be tempted to . . .

- Include too much detail about 'old' authorities dealing with breach of the peace. As the question specifies 'recent' decisions, you should avoid explaining cases such as *Beatty* v *Gilbanks* (1882) LR 9 QBD.

- Try to deal with too many areas of discretionary power. It is far better to identify one or two topics that you wish to discuss and deal with them in detail than to skim the surface of a large number of issues.

- Ignore the issue of Convention rights. Although the question does not expressly reference the Convention, you cannot do well in this question without considering the application of Article 5.

? Question 4

Alisha is a final year student studying law at the University of Northton. She is also a member of the Northton Student Union branch of an organisation called Action for Sustainable Energy (ASE). The group advocates direct action protests to draw attention to the damage caused to the environment by the use of fossil fuels, in the hope of persuading the government to support the expansion of wind farms and other sources of renewable energy. In recent years, the group has organised a number of controversial protests targeting companies they have identified as 'climate criminals', staging direct action protests intended to disrupt business activities. For example, two months ago, members of the group barricaded the doors of the UK headquarters of an airline company, using welding equipment to chain themselves to the doors, preventing employees from entering, or leaving the building. Several members are facing charges including conspiracy to commit criminal damage, public order offences, and assaults against police officers.

Alisha organises a fundraising event to contribute to the legal fees for those defendants, and invites a prominent member of the group, Sam Grace. Sam has an extensive criminal record in respect of his protest activities, and is an incendiary speaker. Alisha places fliers for the event around the student union.

Rosemary is a senior lecturer in the Law Department, and she sees the flier. She has heard about the activities of ASE and has some concerns about the event. She carries out an internet search about Sam Grace, and finds a video of him speaking at an event in which he urged his audience to 'take no prisoners' in the 'fight against corporate capitalism'. In the question and answer session at the end of the video, he is asked if he would advocate violence and he replied 'sometimes there is no way to reach the end if we will not contemplate the means'.

Rosemary takes the view that she has no choice but to report her concerns about the event, and Alisha, to the university and the police. The university bans the event from taking place on their premises, and the police interview Alisha, although she is not charged with any offences. Alisha had hoped to join the Crown Prosecution Service on graduation and is now concerned that her police interview will mean that she is unable to do so.

Consider whether or not Rosemary acted appropriately in contacting the university and the police, and whether the university's response was appropriate. Advise Alisha whether she has any grounds to ask the police to delete the information about her arrest, in the light of the fact that she was not charged.

Answer plan

→ Explain the responsibility that Rosemary and the university have under the Counter-Terrorism and Security Act 2015.

→ Assess whether or not the activities of ASE could be said to fall within the definition of terrorism.

→ Consider whether or not the decision to ban the event was compatible with Article 10 of the European Convention on Human Rights.

→ Consider whether or not the police are entitled to retain the data they hold regarding Alisha's arrest.

Diagram plan

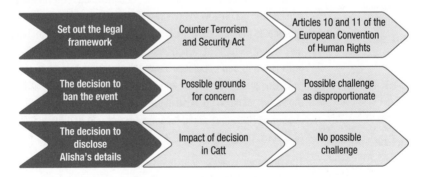

A printable version of this diagram plan is available from **www.pearsoned.co.uk/lawexpressqa**

Answer

One of the most important duties of government is to ensure that the public are protected from the threats posed by terrorism. In recent decades, it has become clear that young people, in particular, could be targeted by extremist groups seeking to encourage the spread of radical ideologies and recruit members willing to participate in terrorist activities in the UK and overseas. In response to this, the UK government strategy for countering terrorism, CONTEST, aims not only to prosecute those who participate in or plan attacks, but also to prevent people from becoming or supporting terrorist activity. [1]The Counter-Terrorism and Security Act of 2015 imposes specific duties on educational institutions requiring them to share information and take steps to reduce the spread of extremist ideologies. Difficulties can arise when determining precisely what kinds of ideologies should fall within the 'prevent' duty, and in balancing the statutory requirements with the rights that individuals have under the European Convention on Human Rights.

[1] It is helpful to make clear that you understand the key legislation that you will need to consider when providing advice.

[2]Section 26 of the Counter-Terrorism and Security Act 2015 (CSA) imposes an obligation on Northton University to have 'due regard to the need to prevent people being drawn into terrorism'. [3]Section 1 of the Terrorism Act 2000 gives the statutory definition of terrorism as the use or threat of one or more of a number of specified actions (set out at s. 1(2)(a)) designed to influence the government, an international governmental organization, or to intimidate the public or a section of it, with the aim of advancing a particular political, religious, racial or ideological cause. The guidance provided for further education institutions on how to comply with the 'prevent' duty set out in the CSA states that terrorism 'includes not just violent extremism but also non-violent extremism, which can create an atmosphere conducive to terrorism and can popularize views which terrorists exploit' (*Prevent Duty Guidance: For further education institutions*, 2015). In light of the broad definition provided in the statute and the guidance, it would seem that Rosemary could reasonably conclude that the activities of ASE could be categorised as 'terrorist activity'.[4]

[2] When referring to legislation it is important to be specific in identifying the relevant sections.

[3] It is not necessary to include the whole section; it is far better to precis the key requirements as concisely as possible, as this shows that you understand the meaning of the statutory language.

[4] The definition provided in the Terrorism Act 2000, and the breadth of activities caught in the Prevent guidance, has been the subject of debate. In dealing with a problem scenario, though, you may not have the space to engage in a discussion of the merits of the law: your main objective is to apply the law to the parties.

The guidance makes clear that Universities are required to ensure staff have sufficient training to allow them to understand the types of conduct that may pose a risk, and to be able to identify individuals vulnerable to radicalization, and policies in place to allow them to manage those risks and share information with other agencies if it is necessary and proportionate to do so (Revised *Prevent* Duty Guidance for England and Wales, 2015).

In complying with the obligation set out in section 26 of the CSA further education institutions are required to also have regard to the

[5] You will be rewarded for understanding the relationship between Convention rights and the 'prevent' duty.

[6] The issue of proportionality is key, as it is clearly the aspect of the problem that creates the most scope for debate.

[7] It is always useful to refer to recently decided cases, but it is important to ensure that authorities are used to consider the appropriate advice to the parties in the scenario.

need to respect freedom of speech (s. 31). [5]Although the Act does not specifically refer to Article 10 of the European Convention on Human Rights, this is the legal protection for freedom of expression that will apply, as the Human Rights Act 1998 has incorporated the Convention into domestic law. Article 10 is a qualified right, which does permit interference with the right as long as it is prescribed by law and necessary to achieve a specified aim. This can create a difficulty for Rosemary and the university when assessing the risk posed by the planned event and deciding how to balance this against the need to protect Article 10. [6]While the university could almost certainly demonstrate a realistic fear that the event could encourage public disorder or crime (in addition to the potential to encourage extremism), it may be more difficult to argue that the decision to impose a ban would be considered a proportionate response to the risk. The proportionality test was set out in *R (on the application of Quila)* v *Secretary of State for the Home Department* [2011] UKSC 45 and requires the decision maker to ask whether the measures taken are 'no more than necessary' to limit a fundamental right. In this case, it could have been feasible to require the presence of a speaker to challenge Sam Grace and provide an opposing view as suggested in the government's guidance on the 'prevent' duty. [7]In the case of *R (Ben-Dor)* v *University of Southampton* [2016] EWHC 953 (Admin) it was held that there was no breach of the applicant's Article 10 or 11 rights where the university had delayed a conference to ensure that safety and security matters could be addressed. Here, it seems that the university has given no thought to whether any measures could be considered that could deal with the risks posed by the meeting falling short of a ban.

Alisha may wish to argue that, in passing on information about her activities to the police, the university has failed to comply with the obligation to protect personal information about her in breach of the Data Protection Act and her right to respect for a private and family life set out in Article 8 of the European Convention on Human Rights. The Data Protection Act does give exceptions when disclosures are made in order to facilitate the 'prevention and detection' of crime and therefore the university may be able to argue that the disclosure is neither a breach of their statutory duty or a disproportionate measure in respect of Article 8.

[8] Where you are able to give definite advice, you should not be afraid to do so.

In the circumstances of this scenario, Alisha does not have any basis on which to complain about the police retention of the information regarding her arrest.[8] This would appear to be the effect of the decision in **R (Catt) v Metropolitan Police** [2015] UKSC 9, in which the retention of data concerning a peaceful protestor did not breach Article 8 provided that the decision to keep that information was subject to periodic review. Unfortunately, the police will be able to disclose data concerning arrest or other intelligence if required to do so by the Disclosure and Barring Service. [9]This may well have an impact for Alisha should she apply for a position that requires her to obtain an enhanced criminal record certificate. However, there is no legal basis upon which she can challenge this.

[9] It is important to acknowledge the impact that disclosure could have for Alisha, but be clear that there is no possibility of challenge.

It is unlikely that the university decision to share information about Alisha and the ASE event with the police would be found to be in breach of her Convention rights, or of their statutory duty to protect her personal data. [10]It would appear, though, that the decision to ban the event may be open to challenge as the university may not have taken steps to ensure that its actions were a proportionate response to the risk that Sam Grace would promote extremist views. The Counter-Terrorism and Security Act and accompanying guidance make it clear that alongside the 'prevent' duty, universities have an obligation to preserve freedom of speech and academic freedom.

[10] It is helpful to give a brief summary of the advice given in your conclusion.

✓ Make your answer stand out

- By keeping up to date with developments in this area. At the time of writing, the CONTEST strategy is due to be updated and it will be important to take note of any additional requirements placed upon universities.

- By incorporating additional academic comment in support of the propositions you make. For example you could explore some of the issues concerning the tension between freedom of speech and the 'prevent' strategy in more detail. You can find source material not only in legal journals but in some specialist academic journals such as the British Journal of Education Studies.

- By assessing the issue of proportionality in more detail. The test used is set out in *Bank Mellat* v *HM Treasury (No 2)* [2013] UKSC 39, [2014] AC 700.

Don't be tempted to . . .

■ Speculate about whether or not the disclosure will significantly impact on Alisha's career prospects: you are not expected to consider the view the CPS may take of her involvement, only to advise on whether or not she has any legal basis to complain about the actions of the university.

■ Spend any time discussing the merits, or otherwise, of the views of the organisation or Sam Grace. Ensure your focus is on the legal obligations of the university to prevent radicalisation and protect freedom of speech.

Question 5

The approach taken by the courts in applying section 78 of PACE arguably endorses unlawful behaviour on the part of the police, and provides no remedy for the suspect who is treated unlawfully.

Discuss.

Answer plan

→ Explain the meaning of section 78, and highlight the distinction between this and other exclusionary powers.

→ Analyse the exercise of the discretion under section 78, with reference to case law.

→ Identify alternative remedies for the suspect.

→ Draw a conclusion about the approach taken by the judiciary.

Diagram plan

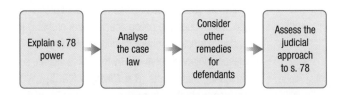

A printable version of this diagram plan is available from **www.pearsoned.co.uk/lawexpressqa**

Answer

The Police and Criminal Evidence Act 1984 (PACE) regulates the use of police powers to investigate crime. Section 78 sets out circumstances in which the court may exclude evidence from criminal trial as a result of conduct during the investigation. Case law suggests that, in exercising discretion, the primary concern of the court is the reliability of evidence, rather than the conduct of officers.[1]

Section 78 gives the court a discretionary power to exclude any evidence at trial if 'having regard to all the circumstances, including the circumstances in which it was obtained'[2] admission would have an adverse effect on the fairness of the proceedings. On the face of it, the powers conferred by provision are wide; the legislation applies to all types of evidence and, in considering fairness, there is no requirement to show bad faith. This contrasts with the courts' common law power to stay proceedings for an abuse of process, or to exclude confession evidence under section 78 PACE.[3] Proceedings can only be stayed for an abuse of process where prosecution would be 'an affront to justice' (*R v Abu Hamza* [2006] EWCA Crim 2918). Confession evidence must be excluded under section 76 if it has been obtained by oppression, or in circumstances that render it unreliable. Confession evidence that would not breach these standards could, in theory, be excluded under section 78.

However, case law demonstrates that the courts seldom invoke the power to exclude physical evidence even where the circumstances in which it was obtained amount to serious illegality by the police. The leading authority comes from the case of *R v Khan* [1997] AC 558. The prosecution case rested on evidence obtained by illegal surveillance.[4] The House of Lords held it was proper to admit the evidence even though the police actions were probably in breach of the defendant's Article 8 rights. Other examples of evidence being admitted despite unlawful behaviour by the police include secretly recorded incriminating statements (*R v Chalkey* [1997] EWCA Crim 3416), and evidence obtained from illegally retained DNA (*A-G's Reference (No. 3 of 1999)* [2000] UKHL 63).[5] In the case of *R v Keenan* [1989] 3 All ER 598, it was held that, where there has been a breach of the rules under PACE, the court should consider first whether the breach was 'substantial or significant',[6] and only then continue to

[1] This part of the introduction reassures the examiner that the answer will take an analytical approach to the subject.

[2] You need to make the point that exclusions under section 78 are discretionary; this is a critical point that is occasionally overlooked.

[3] The answer needs to explain the difference between this power, and other powers of exclusion.

[4] *Khan* should be included. When outlining these cases, you should highlight the conduct of the police but avoid lengthy explanations of the facts.

[5] There are lots of cases that could be used to demonstrate that the courts often admit evidence obtained illegally. You should try to use a few examples to reinforce the argument, but, apart from *Khan*, it does not really matter which cases you cite.

[6] *Keenan* deals with a slightly different aspect of the point, as it is specific to breaches of the codes of conduct. It should be cited, as the 'significant and substantial' test is important.

assess the impact of the breach in the particular circumstances of the case. It may appear that the courts do indeed send a signal to the police that endorses unlawful behaviour while investigating criminality, through the reluctance to exercise their discretion. Wortley and Stockdale (2014) commented on the unreported case of *R v Howe* (2013), which was heard at Newcastle Crown Court. In that case, evidence of a footwear impression was excluded at trial, on the basis that it had been obtained in breach of section 61 PACE. The section states that a footwear impression can be taken for a speculative search, but stipulates that the defendant must be informed. During cross-examination, a custody officer commented that it was possible the defendant would not have been aware as it was common practice to take footwear (which is left outside police cells) for the purpose of taking an impression. This was assessed as being a flagrant breach of PACE justifying exclusion, and it must surely be of concern that deliberate flouting of legislation appeared to have become a routine part of conduct at that station.[7]

[7] This is an important point, as the conclusion will suggest that failure to enforce the law leads to the possibility of abuse of power.

[8] It is important to briefly explain what you understand by 'due process'.

It could be suggested that the courts, as an emanation of the state, must insist on due process. On this view, the courts have a duty to maintain the standards expected of the police, and to punish those who fail to meet them by making sure they cannot benefit from illegal behaviour.[8] Undoubtedly, though, there is a difficult balance to be struck. PACE was implemented to provide safeguards for the public by setting down clear standards of conduct. However, the courts are wary of endorsing an acquittal where there is clear evidence pointing to guilt. The courts have sought to strike the balance by focusing primarily not upon the manner in which the evidence was collected, but on whether or not as a result the evidence has been rendered unreliable.[9] This point was stressed by Lord Steyn in respect of the illegally obtained DNA evidence in *A-G's Reference (No. 3 of 1999)* [2000] UKHL 63, when he noted that if admitted, the defendant would still have the opportunity to challenge the reliability of the evidence. The first concern of the court, then, is to determine the guilt or innocence of the accused, and it is not part of the judicial role to police the police. If, however, the police conduct has led to evidence that could result in a miscarriage of justice, then the courts will not countenance reliance upon it. This position is understandable. It would be disturbing if in a case such as *A-G's Reference (No. 3 of 1999)*, a rapist had been allowed to walk free despite DNA evidence proving guilt. There is,

[9] This is the crux of the argument that is being advanced, and needs to be carefully explained.

[10] Where you are able to point to academic comment to support the argument being advanced, you should do so, as it makes the answer more authoritative.

[11] Where you can make connections between different areas of the syllabus, you should do so. Here, you would be rewarded for understanding how executive misconduct links to the rule of law. You do not have to spend time outlining the doctrine, however.

[12] You should highlight the mechanisms that are available to obtain redress, but do not spend time explaining these as this is not the focus of the question.

[13] The earlier examples used have already made this point, which lends weight to the conclusion.

however, a danger in using the seriousness of the offence alleged to be a determinative factor for the court in exercising its discretionary power, a point noted by Carney (2013) commenting on the case of **Plunkett** [2013] EWCA Crim 261: 'The emphasis on the seriousness of the crime and the fact that its victims were still in danger in this case allowed the courts to be willing to accept a technique that undermines many of the important protections that the 1984 Act has given to suspects.'[10] Arguably, the rule of law requires an insistence on legality and to allow the police to ignore their legal obligations is to endorse arbitrary conduct on behalf of those exercising executive power.[11]

The exclusion of evidence from a criminal trial is not the only remedy available to a defendant who complains of police maltreatment. Where breaches of PACE or the codes of conduct have occurred, complaint can be made to the IPCC. In the most serious cases, this could result in criminal prosecution of the officer(s) involved. Alternatively, where police behaviour constitutes a tortious wrong, redress can be sought in the civil courts.[12]

It is correct to say that the courts have not been willing to use the discretion given by section 78 as a means of disciplining police officers who fail to follow procedure. In many cases this is unobjectionable where guilt has been established on the basis of reliable evidence. It is perhaps troubling, however, to suggest that the ends will always justify the means where no miscarriage of justice has occurred, as a law that is not routinely enforced may well become one that is routinely ignored.[13]

 Make your answer stand out

- By referring to ECtHR decisions in this area. Consider *Schenk* v *Switzerland* (1988) 13 EHRR 242, in which it was held that it was for the national courts to determine admissibility of evidence. Admission of illegally obtained evidence does not necessarily breach Article 6.

- By expanding the discussion of the procedure that applies to section 76. The case of *R* v *Dhorajiwala* [2010] EWCA Crim 1237 confirms that, once a representation is made to the court that a confession *may* have resulted from oppression, then it shall not be admitted unless the Crown can prove that it did not. You should use this point to reinforce the distinction between section 76 and section 78.

- By reinforcing the point that the role of the court is not to police the police. You could cite *R* v *Smurthwaite and Gill* [1994] 1 All ER 898, in which Lord Diplock stressed that the criminal court is not there to exercise a disciplinary role over the police.

! Don't be tempted to . . .

- Include general information about PACE, or the codes. That is not relevant here. There is no need to demonstrate that you know the different aspects of procedure governed by the codes, for example.
- Explain in detail the facts of all the cases referred to. You do need to highlight how evidence was obtained to illustrate the argument about the courts' reluctance to use section 78, but that is all. This may require some explanation, such as in the discussion of Howe, as it is important to understand how the illegal collection of footwear impressions has been obtained.

? Question 6

PC Binner is on foot patrol when he sees a group of three youths standing on a street corner. He instinctively feels that they look suspicious. He approaches the youths, and asks what they are up to. One of the youths, Silvio, begins to walk away.

PC Binner takes hold of Silvio by the elbow and says 'We'll see about that when I search you'. Silvio punches the officer in the chest. PC Binner uses his radio to call for assistance, and handcuffs Silvio. He then goes through Silvio's pockets, and finds a tablet loose in his trouser pocket. A police car arrives and PC Binner places Silvio in the back of the car, and Silvio is taken to the police station.

On arrival, the custody sergeant books Silvio into custody at 9 pm. Silvio asks 'why am I here?' PC Binner tells Silvio he has been arrested for dealing drugs. Silvio immediately asks for a lawyer and is told this will be arranged. He is placed in a cell.

PC Binner asks the custody sergeant for permission to search Silvio's address. The custody sergeant calls for the duty inspector, who authorises the search. PC Binner and a colleague search Silvio's flat. No drugs are found, but a large quantity of car radios are seized.

At midnight, Silvio is told he can wait for a lawyer, or be interviewed immediately. He decides to be interviewed. In interview he is asked to explain about the car radios, and admits that he stole them. He insists that the tablet found is an aspirin.

Silvio is charged with assaulting a police officer and with theft. However, a friend of his who is studying law has told him that he will be able to have the case thrown out because of PC Binner's actions.

Advise Silvio.

Answer plan

→ Consider the legality of asking questions in the street.

→ Outline the requirements of sections 1–3 of PACE and consider legality of the search.

→ Assess the legality of the arrest, and consider whether this provides a defence.

→ Briefly consider the search of premises.

→ Consider the applicability of section 78.

Diagram plan

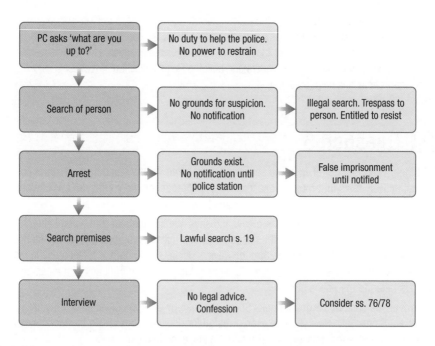

A printable version of this diagram plan is available from **www.pearsoned.co.uk/lawexpressqa**

Answer

[1] The introduction avoids repeating the facts of the scenario, and, instead, demonstrates that the key issues have been understood.

The validity of the police actions needs to be assessed in order to advise Silvio of any options available to him. It appears that the stop and search and initial arrest were unlawful. This may provide Silvio with a defence to the charge of assaulting a police constable. It is unlikely that he will be able to avoid the consequences of the theft as the interview is likely to be admissible.[1]

On being approached and questioned by PC Binner, Silvio is lawfully entitled to walk away. It is a long-established principle that, as stated in **Rice v Connolly** [1966] 2 All ER 649, there is no general duty to assist the police.[2] Therefore, unless the circumstances are covered by a specific statutory provision (for example, the duty to give details under the Road Traffic Acts), the police have no power to detain a person for questioning falling short of the power to arrest. Accordingly, Silvio should be advised that the officer has no lawful authority to take hold of him by the elbow, and that this may constitute a battery at common law.[3] The facts of **Collins v Wilcock** [1984] 3 All ER 374 were similar, and are authority for the proposition that 'the slightest touch can constitute a battery'.[4] Therefore, arguably, Silvio is entitled to use force to defend himself from the unwarranted interference with his person. **Kenlin v Gardiner** [1967] 2 WLR 129 confirms that a person can resist an unlawful detention. However, Silvio should be advised that the level of force used here may not be proportionate.[5]

PC Binner states his intention to search Silvio. There are no grounds disclosed in the scenario that would give rise to the power to search. Section 1 of the Police and Criminal Evidence Act (PACE) author-ises a police officer to stop and search if he has reasonable grounds to suspect that the person is in possession of one of the specified items (stolen goods, offensive weapons, fireworks, or items made or adapted for use in criminal damage). We are not told whether or not PC Binner suspects that Silvio is in possession of such articles; however, the facts do not disclose any reasonable grounds for any such suspicion. The Codes of Practice, Code A 2.2, makes it clear that suspicion must be based on objective factors, and cannot arise purely on the basis of personal factors such as age, appearance or previous convictions. We are not told of any objective basis for the officer's concerns. The subsequent search is illegal as it is not justified, and in addition, the notification requirements of sections 2 and 3 do not appear to have been complied with.[6]

The initial arrest is unlawful, as PC Binner does not advise Silvio of either the fact of, or the grounds for arrest as required by section 28 PACE.[7] The case of **Christie v Leachinskey** [1947] 1 All ER 567 made it clear that failure to inform a person of the fact and reason for arrest renders it illegal.[8] The more recent case of **Lewis v Chief Constable of the South Wales Constabulary** [1991] 1 All ER 206 demonstrates that an illegality can, in effect, be 'corrected' when the

[2] *Rice* v *Connolly* is the leading authority here, and it is important to include the case.

[3] The answer must use the authorities to provide specific advice regarding the facts of the scenario.

[4] You should note the similarity with *Collins* v *Wilcock* but you don't need to rehearse the facts. It is useful to remember the wording from the judgment, which stresses the minimal degree of contact required for the offence.

[5] Take care not to be diverted into a discussion regarding criminal law. There is no need to consider the elements of private defence in any detail here.

[6] The facts of the scenario are very clear, and credit will be given for providing unambiguous advice in these circumstances, as it shows confidence.

[7] Again, it is possible to give very definite advice here.

[8] Despite the fact that section 28 PACE deals with the same issue, the case remains good law, and is usually cited.

[9] It is important to consider any remedies that Silvio may have, as this would form part of the advice to a client.

detainee is properly notified. It seems that Silvio is notified once at the police station. Although detention after unlawful arrest constitutes an actionable false imprisonment, any claim would be limited to the time period prior to notification as from that point, the detention is rendered lawful.[9]

Once in custody, Silvio's treatment is governed by statutory provisions and Code C. The custody sergeant is responsible for ensuring that Silvio's detention is necessary, and for ensuring that his welfare and his rights are protected. It is his responsibility to ensure that Silvio is advised of his rights, including the right to have someone notified of his arrest (s. 56, PACE) and of his right to free legal advice (s. 58). We are not told whether or not the sergeant complies with this, only that Silvio makes a request for legal representation. Equally, it is not clear whether or not a lawyer is ever contacted. If this has not occurred then this will be a clear, and potentially significant, breach of PACE.[10]

[10] The answer should not make assumptions where the facts are silent or unclear.

[11] The answer should deal with the search, as it is mentioned in the scenario. As it is clearly lawful, this issue should be dealt with briefly.

Before considering the effect of such a breach, it is worth noting that the search of premises appears to be lawful. Section 18 of PACE provides for the search of premises occupied or controlled by a person in custody for evidence connected with the offence for which he has been arrested.[11] Although the extent of the search must be limited to that which is necessary for the nature of the items sought, section 19 (as amended) makes it clear that it is permissible for the officers to seize any items discovered in the course of the search that they reasonably believe are connected with any offence. The seizure of the car radios is, therefore, legitimate.[12]

[12] It is important to note the effect of section 19, as this is often overlooked by students.

[13] The reference to 'having the case thrown out' should be a clear signal that the answer needs to address the possibility of excluding evidence.

During the course of the interview, Silvio admits the offence of theft. He may seek to have the confession evidence excluded at any subsequent trial,[13] under either section 76 or section 78 of PACE. Section 76 provides for such exclusion if the confession was obtained by oppression, or if it was obtained in consequence of things said or done that, in all the circumstances, would render it unfair if admitted. On the facts provided, neither of these conditions appears to be met. Section 78 allows for the exclusion of any evidence (including confessions) if, having regard to all the circumstances in which it was obtained, it would be unfair to admit it. In this case, Silvio may seek to argue that either the initial illegal stop and search, or the denial of legal advice would render the confession unfair. While both these breaches are serious, the authorities suggest that the courts are unwilling to

[14] When considering section 78, the leading case of *Khan* should be cited.

exclude evidence unless it appears to be unreliable (see, for example, **R v Khan** [1997] AC 558).[14] Therefore, Silvio should be advised that an application under section 78 is unlikely to succeed and that therefore, contrary to the advice of his friend, the case will proceed.

[15] The conclusion should summarise the advice provided.

In summary, it appears that the police have acted unlawfully. Silvio may wish to consider claims in tort for trespass to the person, and false imprisonment.[15] The illegal search and arrest may afford Silvio a defence to the charge of assaulting a police constable. It is doubtful that confession evidence would be excluded in this instance, as it would seem the reliability of the evidence is unaffected.

✓ Make your answer stand out

- By including additional authorities in the answer. You could cite *DPP* v *Blake* [1989] 1 WLR 432 as part of the discussion regarding the illegal search, or any number of cases concerning the application of section 78. While you should include authorities only where they are relevant, you will certainly be rewarded if you can provide an authority for as many propositions of law as you can.

- By using recent case law to reinforce the fact that Silvio is likely to have a defence to the charge of assault PC Binner. You could cite *R (Michaels)* v *Highbury Corner Magistrates' Court* [2010] Crim LR 506, in which the Divisional Court stressed that the notification requirement of section 2 will be strictly enforced. In that case, a conviction for obstructing a police officer was set aside. You could demonstrate an ability to use analogous cases to form conclusions about the outcome of a scenario.

- By discussing the potential remedies in more detail; in particular, the answer does not address the potential for a formal complaint through the IPCC. It would be useful to show that you are aware of this procedure, as it would demonstrate that you are familiar with all aspects of this topic.

! Don't be tempted to . . .

- Show the examiner that you have revised all aspects of PACE. For example, many students will give detail about how and when powers to search premises may arise under section 17 or section 32. More credit will be given for demonstrating an ability to recognise that section 18 is the one that is relevant here. ▶

■ Discuss the requirements of the criminal law. It is fairly common for students to make the mistake of thinking it is helpful to outline what the Crown would have to prove to obtain a conviction for theft. There are no marks available for demonstrating knowledge of the components of criminal liability. You must ensure your answer focuses on the public law aspects of the scenario.

? Question 7

Shamila is a young woman aged 19 who suffers from anxiety. She is extremely claustrophobic and has panic attacks in confined spaces.

One evening, she is waiting for a bus when a fight breaks out. The police arrive on the scene quickly. Someone points towards Shamila, saying 'She started it'. Shamila is immediately arrested for affray and is taken to the police station.

She is booked into custody and the custody officer asks her whether she would like anyone to be notified of her detention. She nominates her father. She declines legal advice. When she is told she will have to go into a cell, she becomes very distressed, citing her claustrophobia. The custody officer assures her that it will be for only a few minutes. He then telephones Shamila's father, who asks to attend the interview. The custody officer states that this is not possible because Shamila is an adult.

Officers investigating the fight watch the CCTV footage of the incident, which is unclear but shows a woman throwing a bottle. It is believed this resulted in serious injury to someone.

At midnight, an officer takes Shamila into a small interview room. At the start of the tape-recorded interview, she is told that she is being further arrested for an offence of causing GBH (s. 18 of the Offences Against the Person Act 1861). She is properly cautioned. During the interview, she is shown the CCTV footage and the interviewing officer says: 'It is definitely you here, throwing that bottle. If you don't admit what you've done you'll be in a cell for years, not just a couple of hours.' Shamila continues to deny the offence while the officer repeats the assertion that she threw the bottle. When he does so for the twentieth time, she begins to cry and admits that it was her.

She is charged with an offence under section 18 of the Offences Against the Person Act.

Advise Shamila of the legalities of the police conduct and the possible consequences.

Answer plan

→ Consider whether the arrest is lawful.

→ Identify the issues raised by the custody officer's conduct.

→ Assess the legality of the interview.

→ Discuss any remedies available.

Diagram plan

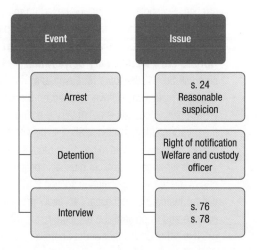

A printable version of this diagram plan is available from **www.pearsoned.co.uk/lawexpressqa**

Answer

The police are granted extensive powers over the citizen to facilitate prevention and investigation of crime. Many powers are exercised with the authority of a judicial warrant. There are a large number of steps, however, that can be used without warrant. It is important that such powers are carefully regulated as, inevitably, officers will need to interfere with the liberties of citizens in order to carry out their work. In this scenario, all of the officers concerned should be exercising powers regulated by the Police and Criminal Evidence Act 1984 (PACE) and the associated Codes of Practice. It appears that the custody officer and the interviewing officer have failed to carry out their functions in accordance with PACE so Shamila will need to be advised of the potential ramifications of this.[1]

The power of arrest exercised in this scenario is governed by section 24 of PACE (as amended by the Serious Organised Crime and Police Act 2005).[2] Officers present can lawfully arrest Shamila if they reasonably suspect that she has committed an offence (s. 24(2)). The courts have, on a number of occasions, considered what is meant by 'reasonable suspicion'. The leading case is ***Castorina v Chief***

[1] A general introduction to the topic is helpful, but make sure to set out the key issues that are raised in the problem.

[2] Most students fail to note that not every arrest is authorised by PACE. You do not need to outline alternative powers, as PACE does govern this arrest, but you will be rewarded for showing you are aware of this.

Constable of Surrey [1988] NLJ 180, which set out a three-part test. First, the officer must suspect that the person is guilty of an offence. Secondly, this must be based on reasonable grounds and, lastly, the arrest should be assessed in accordance with the principles used to assess irrationality in *Associated Provincial Picture Houses Ltd v Wednesbury Corporation* [1948] 1 KB 223. A decision will be '*Wednesbury* unreasonable' if it is one no reasonable decision-maker could have reached on the same facts. As Zander (1995) has noted, this is not 'a very exacting standard'. In this case, the purported identification of Shamila by a person at the scene would almost certainly be held to meet the requirements.[3] In addition to the grounds for arrest, the officer must also believe that it is necessary for one of the reasons specified in section 24(5). In this case, the arrest will be justified as necessary to allow prompt investigation of the offence and to prevent the disappearance of a suspect (s. 24(5)(e), (f)). It is not clear whether or not Shamila has been properly informed of the fact of, and grounds for, her arrest (s. 28).[4] If these requirements have been met, the arrest will be lawful.

The custody officer is responsible for Shamila while she is detained at the police station. He must decide whether to authorise her detention or, alternatively, release her without charge, or on bail, or charge her with an offence. In this case, the decision to authorise detention is unlikely to be challenged as section 37(2) states that a reason to do so will be to preserve and secure evidence.[5]

The custody officer also takes responsibility for Shamila's welfare; he must ensure that her rights are protected and the conditions of detention meet the standards set out in Code C of PACE. The immediate requirement is to inform her of her right to legal advice, to have someone notified of her detention and to read the Codes of Practice (Code C Para. 3.1). The facts do not state whether or not she was informed of her right to read the Codes, but she is correctly offered legal advice and to have her nominated person informed.[6]

As Shamila is over 18, she will not be treated as a juvenile in police custody. However, the custody officer is required to take steps to protect a vulnerable adult in custody (Code C Para. 1). Here, there are clearly grounds that should have led him to treat her as such: her visible distress in the custody area and the fact she informs him of her claustrophobia. It is not a breach of PACE to place her in a

[3] The quote from Zander here provides support for the assertion that the arrest will be considered lawful.

[4] Ensure that you do provide statutory authority for every point made here, rather than simply referring to 'section 24'.

[5] Where you are certain that an action is lawful, or unlawful, do not be afraid to state your postion confidently (as long as you can explain your reason).

[6] Do not make assumptions about facts that are not stated; instead, point out the areas that require more investigation.

cell in these circumstances, but he should have considered obtaining an appropriate adult to support her while in custody and during the interview. He would not have been obliged to allow her father to carry out the role if he felt a qualified person would be more appropriate, but there is no suggestion that this has been considered.[7]

When Shamila is interviewed, the procedure appears to have initially complied with the requirements of PACE and the Codes. She is properly cautioned and the interview is tape-recorded in accordance with section 60. It is not clear whether or not she was reminded of her right to legal advice. The questioning, however, appears to be a clear breach of Code C, which precludes the use of oppression, or of attempting to elicit information by indicating what is likely to happen to the detainee dependent upon their answer (Para. 11.5). Repeated assertions of guilt coupled with the threat of a prison sentence are, therefore, a serious breach of the Codes of Practice.[8]

The custody officer and the interviewing officer have breached the Codes of Practice during Shamila's detention. This can give Shamila grounds to make a formal complaint to either the local police force or the Independent Police Complaints Commission.[9] The misconduct will also have implications for any subsequent trial for the section 18 offence, as it appears likely that some or all of the evidence obtained in the interview will be inadmissible. Section 76 of PACE imposes a mandatory duty on the court to exclude evidence of a confession if it is obtained through oppression or in circumstances which render it unreliable. In *R v Fulling* [1987] 85 Cr App R 136 the court found that although 'oppression' would almost certainly involve impropriety by the police, it should not be defined restrictively. It is certainly arguable that the questioning here was oppressive. Even if this is not accepted, the combined effect of Shamila's vulnerable state and the form of questions used render the confession unreliable. The court may well exercise its discretion to exclude the interview in its entirety (rather than just the part containing the confession).[10] Section 78 of PACE allows any evidence to be excluded if, in all the circumstances, it would be unfair to admit it. It is clear that the courts approach the question of 'fairness' in this context as an assessment of the reliability of the evidence rather than an opportunity to punish police misconduct (*R v Khan* [1996] 3 All ER 289). It seems that this is a case in which exclusion of evidence would be appropriate.

[11] There is no need for a lengthy conclusion to the answer, as a clear decision has been set out at each point.

Although the initial arrest was lawful, police misconduct during detention will assist Shamila in defending the charge she faces. She may also have grounds to lodge a formal complaint.[11]

 Make your answer stand out

- By discussing the applicability of Article 6 to this case, and addressing some of the case law concerning the impact of sections 34–37 of the Criminal Justice and Public Order Act 1994 on procedural fairness. Consider, for example, *Condron* v *UK* (2001) 31 EHRR 1. This would show the examiner that you can set the facts of the scenario in the broader context of human rights law.
- By explaining the available remedies in more detail and highlighting the fact that breaches of the Codes of Practice cannot, in and of themselves, give rise to an action in tort (s. 67(10) PACE), as this will demonstrate that you have detailed knowledge of the relevant statutory provisions. Remedies are an aspect of police powers that are often overlooked.
- By incorporating a discussion of the efficacy of the Independent Police Complaints Commission. You could note that Liberty (2009) has raised concerns regarding complainants who lack mental capacity, which is clearly relevant to this scenario.

! Don't be tempted to . . .

- Speculate whether or not the confession would have been made if an appropriate adult had been present. The facts give no indication of this, and therefore you should only consider whether or not there are grounds to exclude it. Often, students are diverted into discussing hypothetical situations that are not highlighted in the scenario. It is important to focus on the information that has been provided.
- Confuse the provisions of the Codes with those in the statute. A common mistake is to say that the police have the power to arrest under Code G. This is incorrect: the statute gives the power, and the Code stipulates the manner in which it should be exercised.

Question 8

The regulation of surveillance in the United Kingdom contains sufficient safeguards to ensure that the privacy of citizens is respected.

Discuss.

Answer plan

→ Outline the development of RIPA and subsequent legislation.

→ Identify key cases concerning the regulation of surveillance.

→ Explain some of the criticisms of the regulation of surveillance.

→ Consider the effect of the Investigatory Powers Act and the extent to which it will address concerns.

Diagram plan

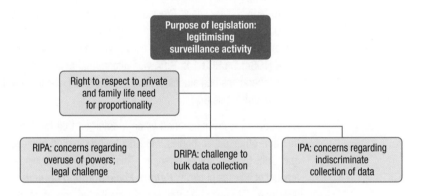

A printable version of this diagram plan is available from **www.pearsoned.co.uk/lawexpressqa**

Answer

It is clear that the police and other investigating bodies need to conduct covert surveillance to gather intelligence in order to detect and prevent crime. The Regulation of Investigatory Powers Act 2000 (RIPA) attempted to provide a legislative framework to control the authorisation of surveillance and to ensure compliance with the European Convention on Human Rights. The Act proved controversial due to the misuse of powers by local authorities. Litigation in the domestic courts and the European Court of Justice exposed a failure of the Act to regulate the collection, storage and sharing of bulk communication data that has led to further legislation. In 2016, the Investigatory Powers Act was enacted aiming to ensure that all surveillance activity is now subject to statutory control.[1] Although the government has argued that the new Act provides comprehensive mechanisms to ensure that

[1] It is clear that this question will require an understanding of the objectives of the recent legislation, so it is imperative to set out the aim of the Act at the outset.

[2] Using the language of the Convention here reassures the examiner that you have understood the requirement to consider compatibility of surveillance law with the treaty.

[3] This is a good point to make, as it makes clear that the purpose of the legislation was never intended to protect privacy. This directly addresses the statement set out in the title.

powers are used appropriately, opponents have argued that it will lead to a greater degree of intrusive surveillance and has the potential to [2]undermine the right to respect for private and family life.

RIPA was not enacted as a measure to increase privacy protection, but rather as a necessary measure to protect intelligence agencies from challenges under the Human Rights Act 1998, which incorporated the European Convention on Human Rights into domestic law.[3] Article 8 guarantees the right to respect for private and family life, however, this is a qualified right. The qualification permits interference with that right where necessary for a specified purpose and, crucially, where 'prescribed by law'. Previous case law in the European Court of Human Rights had led to findings against the UK government as surveillance had lacked a basis in legislation (see for example *Malone v UK* [1984] 7 EHRR 14). RIPA was intended to ensure that intelligence operations had sufficient legal specificity to bring them within the ambit of Article 8(2).

RIPA powers were questioned when it emerged that local authorities and other public bodies were deploying directed surveillance and CHIS for very minor offences. This resulted in a considerable amount of adverse publicity. *Paton v Poole Borough Council* (2010) (IPT/09/01/C) concerned the use of surveillance powers to investigate whether or not a family lived within a school catchment area. The Investigatory Powers Tribunal (IPT) found that insufficient regard had been given as to whether the operation had been a necessary and proportionate measure in the investigation of crime. It is doubtful whether this kind of activity was envisaged by those drafting the Bill as a weapon in the fight against terrorism and organised crime. As a response to such concerns, the Protection of Freedoms Act 2012 imposed a seriousness threshold, and a requirement for magistrates' approval of authorisations made by local authorities. This change has increased the protection of privacy.[4] It should be noted that the Protection of Freedoms Act did not introduce additional safeguards to regulate the use of surveillance by the police.[5]

[4] It is crucial to note the amendments made by this legislation, and to note the impact upon the central issue.

[5] This is a useful point to make, as it demonstrates the piecemeal way in which safeguards have been dealt with in the developing legislation.

The revelations made by the American intelligence whistleblower, Edward Snowden, showed that GCHQ had routinely collected bulk communication data in the United Kingdom and shared this with

American intelligence agencies. The disclosures focused attention on the regulation of surveillance and a series of court actions in both the domestic courts and international courts challenging the legality of government actions, particularly in respect of the collection, storage and sharing of mass communications data. In 2014, the Data Retention and Investigatory Powers Act was enacted with relatively little Parliamentary scrutiny in part as a response to the decision in ***Digital Rights Ireland Ltd*** v ***Minister for Communications, Marine and Natural Resources*** (C-293/12) EU:C:2014:238; [2015] Q.B. 127 (ECJ (Grand Chamber)). [6]This Act too, was subject to challenges by Conservative MP David Davis and Labour Deputy Tom Watson, and the group Privacy Rights International.

The Investigatory Powers Act 2016 can be seen as a response to developing technologies necessitating methods of surveillance not envisaged in 2000, and also to the numerous legal challenges to the methods and extent of state surveillance. [7]Just as with RIPA, the IPA should be understood not as an instrument designed to limit surveillance, but rather to ensure that the legality of surveillance activity is protected. The Act sets out detailed provisions allowing a number of agencies to apply for warrants authorising the collection of communications data (Part 3), bulk interception (Part 6) and a framework to govern the subsequent retention and sharing of information (Part 4). There are provisions outlining procedures to be followed in respect of material that could be subject to legal or judicial privilege, and judicial approval for certain warrants issued by the secretary of state is required. Part 8 outlines the roles of the Investigatory Powers Commissioner, the Investigatory Powers Tribunal and the Information Commissioner in ensuring that there is proper oversight. Given the number of agencies now able to collect, retain, and scrutinise data, it is perhaps arguable that comprehensive oversight will be difficult to achieve.[8] [9]Litigation by the campaign group Privacy Rights International showed that there had been 47 instances of non-compliance with regulations in a two-year period within MI5, and an internal memorandum had been sent by the Secret Intelligence Service warning staff against the practice of using the system to check addresses, birthdays and other information for personal reasons.

[6] While it is not necessary to provide a great deal of detail regarding the cases referred to here, it is a good idea to include a brief summary, as it highlights the fact that the regulation of surveillance has been a contentious issue.

[7] This is a point worth making, as the central argument is that the legislation is not primarily concerned with safeguarding privacy.

[8] This is an important point to make and returns the focus of the answer to the central issue of rights protection.

[9] It is helpful to include this information, as it lends support to the point made about the problems of oversight.

David Anderson QC, the Independent Reviewer of Terrorism Legislation has given a cautious welcome to the Act arguing that it gives 'legal sanction to a range of powers which have already proved their worth' and provides unprecedented transparency (David Anderson, The Investigatory Powers Act 2016 – an exercise in democracy, available at https://terrorismlegislationreviewer.independent.gov .uk/the-investigatory-powers-act-2016-an-exercise-in-democracy/). Critics, on the other hand, argue that the degree of oversight is insufficient in light of the wide and intrusive powers permitted. Liberty have argued the provisions will make 'us all less safe, and less free' (Liberty, No #snoopers charter https://www.liberty-human-rights.org.uk/ campaigning/no-snooperscharter).

Article 8 of the European Convention on Human Rights allows a member state to take steps that interfere with respect for private and family life, provided that the activity is prescribed by law for a specified purpose, and is limited to the extent that is necessary to achieve that purpose. [10]It is clear that much of the surveillance regulated by the various statutory provisions is unlikely to breach the Convention provided that the various bodies who have oversight of the system have sufficient resources and are robust. Targeted surveillance of individuals suspected of involvement in criminal or terrorist activity is unlikely to be problematic. Arguably, bulk interception warrants permitted under the Investigatory Powers Act could be challenged on the basis that collection of communications data is indiscriminate and therefore disproportionate. [11]In the case of *Zakharov* v *Russia* (2015) (47141/06) the European Court of Human Rights held that, in order to be permitted under Article 8, surveillance should be aimed at a clearly identified person or premises, and it appears the new Act will be susceptible to similar challenges.

[10] Here, the answer develops the point made earlier regarding the difficulty of ensuring oversight.

[11] It is advisable to include cases concerning other jurisdictions only if you are able to explain the relevance to potential litigation concerning domestic law.

Taken together, the legislation governing surveillance in the UK creates a complex and comprehensive framework that does provide clarity regarding the extent of permitted activity and mechanisms to ensure that privacy is protected. The concern must be, however, that the extent of surveillance by a wide range of authorities for numerous purposes may prove impossible to regulate effectively.

Make your answer stand out

■ By ensuring that you remain up to date with a rapidly developing area of law. At the time of writing, the decision in the European Court of Justice in the case of *Watson, Brice and Lewis* v *Secretary of State for the Home Department* (2016, C-698/15) has thrown the legality of the new legislative provisions for bulk data collection into doubt.

■ By commenting on the scandal concerning the leaked information by the American, Edward Snowden, regarding surveillance carried out by US authorities with the co-operation of the UK. It is important not to lose focus on the question. The relevance would be that reports suggested that GCHQ felt that the regulatory framework of RIPA allowed for greater intrusion with less supervision than would be possible in the US (see for example Hopkins, N. and Ackerman, S. (2013), Flexible Laws and weak oversight gave GCHQ room for manouevre, *The Guardian*, 2 August).

! Don't be tempted to . . .

■ Spend too long outlining case law concerning general issues of privacy under Article 8. Students can fall into the trap of discussing irrelevant matters that do not deal with surveillance.

■ Spend time explaining the concept of a qualified right, or the precise provisions in Article 8(2). This is not a question about the ECHR. It is important to show that you understand that the Convention is a likely reason to challenge the regulation of surveillance, but ensure that you focus on the legislation itself.

 Try it yourself

Now take a look at the question below and attempt to answer it. You can check your response against the answer guidance available on the companion website (**www.pearsoned.co.uk/lawexpressqa**).

Gina and nine friends are dismayed to hear that the local community centre has been hired for a meeting of a group campaigning to legalise hunting with hounds. They decide to hold a protest outside the centre. On the evening in question, they arrive and stand outside, with placards saying 'Hunting is murder'.

After a short while, the police arrive and an officer asks who the organiser of the protest is. Gina steps forward and the officer tells her she could be arrested as no notice has been given of the protest.

At this point, some of the hunt supporters come out of the building and start threatening Gina and her friends. The police officer tells Gina that the protest better stop or he will have to arrest them for breach of the peace.

Just then, one of the hunt supporters punches a protestor and things get out of hand. Several of the protesters start throwing their placards at the police and the hunt supporters. When more police arrive, Gina and her friends are arrested on suspicion of riot.

Advise Gina of the legalities of the police actions.

www.pearsoned.co.uk/lawexpressqa

 Go online to access more revision support including additional essay and problem questions with diagram plans, and You be the marker questions, and to download all diagrams from the book.

Information: access and protection

How this topic may come up in exams

This topic lends itself to either essay questions, or problem scenarios. Questions will tend to focus either on the ability of the individual to protect personal information from scrutiny, or on the access to information held by the state, so you will need to be able to identify the subject matter of the particular question. In either case, you will need to be familiar with the relevant statutory provisions and a considerable amount of case law. The topic overlaps with the study of the European Convention on Human Rights, as questions typically demand analysis of how the Human Rights Act has affected domestic law.

■ Before you begin

It's a good idea to consider the following key themes of information (access and protection) before tackling a question on this topic.

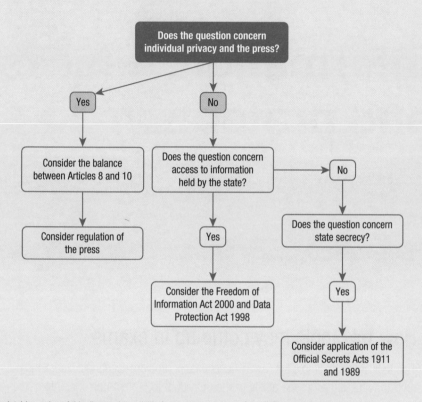

A printable version of this diagram is available from **www.pearsoned.co.uk/lawexpressqa**

❓ Question 1

Simone Jenkins is a celebrity who presents a children's television programme. She has a lucrative career which includes advertising campaigns aimed at children. She has been interviewed for magazines and other media outlets, and has made statements condemning infidelity and drug use. For a number of months, rumours have been circulating that Simone has been unfaithful to her partner. Simone has been advised by a relative employed by a newspaper that, next Sunday, there will be a tabloid story including an interview with an individual claiming to have had a long-running affair with her, and photographs of her seemingly taking drugs at a party.

Simone fears that, if any details about these allegations are made public, her reputation and consequently her career will be damaged. She would like to know what she can do to prevent the story being published, and whether or not she should have been contacted by the paper to advise her of their plans.

Her relative does not know which newspaper intends to publish the story, or who the individual is that has supplied the photographs.

Advise Simone of any action she can take.

Answer plan

→ Briefly explain the nature of the competing rights under Articles 8 and 10.

→ Discuss the requirements of a breach of confidence claim.

→ Explore the issues concerning prior restraint with reference to recent cases.

→ Discuss the effect of a failure to give prior notification.

Diagram plan

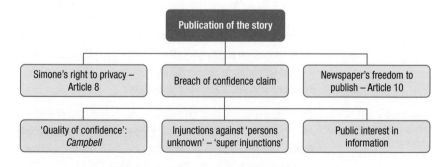

A printable version of this diagram plan is available from **www.pearsoned.co.uk/lawexpressqa**

Answer

Article 8 of the European Convention on Human Rights provides that an individual is entitled to respect for their private and family life. Article 10 protects freedom of expression. When a newspaper seeks to expose facts about an individual that the individual would rather keep private, a conflict between these Convention rights arises.[1] Simone's potential claim for injunctive relief will be considered in the light of recent decisions concerning the appropriate way to resolve the conflict of competing rights.

[1] You will be rewarded for recognising that the discussion must take place in the context of conflicting rights, so it is worth highlighting this in the introduction.

When untrue information is published about an individual, then that individual can seek redress through an action in defamation.[2] This may not provide a satisfactory remedy for Simone. First, it will not assist if either allegation can be shown to be true, and secondly, it could be argued that any remedy given after publication is ineffective as the information is, by then, in the public domain. Therefore, Simone may wish to consider a claim for breach of confidence, and seek an injunction to prevent publication of the information.[3]

[2] This is not a question about defamation, so there is no need to demonstrate any knowledge of this topic.

[3] This is the key issue, as it addresses the specific concern of the person seeking advice: how to stop publication.

Prior to the Human Rights Act, it was clear that there was no substantive right to privacy in English law. An individual could, however, protect information through the doctrine of confidence. In order to be successful, it would need to be shown that the confidential information had been disclosed in circumstances giving rise to a duty of confidence, and that further disclosure would be detrimental to the applicant.[4] An action could restrain disclosure by third parties under the 'Spycatcher' principle (*A-G v Guardian Newspapers (No. 2)* [1990] 1 AC 109).[5] Simone would have no difficulty in arguing that information from a partner, or ex-partner, fell within circumstances creating the duty. It is well established that intimate personal relationships imply such a duty (*Argyll v Argyll* [1967] Ch 302). However, it would be harder to demonstrate a confidential relationship with the individual who had taken the photographs.

[4] Make sure that you do not spend long on outlining the previous law. Summarise the test as succinctly as possible.

[5] There is no need to give the facts of the 'Spycatcher' case; all that is required is a demonstration that you understand that it establishes a test for restraint of third parties.

The Human Rights Act has led to developments of the law of confidence which would assist. The House of Lords confirmed in *Wainwright v Home Office* [2004] 2 AC 406 that the HRA did not introduce a right to privacy.[6] However, *Campbell v MGN Ltd* [2004] 2 AC 457 significantly reformed the law on breach of confidence, to the extent that it now incorporates the tort of misuse of private information. This

[6] It is worth making this point, as some students confuse the incorporation of the right to respect for private life with a right to privacy. Mention of this authority will show confidence in the subject matter.

[7] The explanation of what is meant by 'expectation of privacy' allows the examiner to see that you can relate the law to the specific issues raised in the problem scenario.

[8] Although this is not a case about 'human rights law' per se, the balance of rights should be mentioned, as all authorities since the HRA are concerned with how this balance should be struck.

[9] This case received a great deal of media attention and, in the main, it was concerned with whether or not publication of the story in newspapers overseas meant that the injunction in the United Kingdom should be lifted. It is important to ensure that you focus on the aspect of the case that has direct relevance to the scenario.

[10] This may seem like a fairly minor point, but marks will be awarded for dealing with this issue. The scenario clearly states that Simone cannot locate the source of the information, and therefore a comprehensive response should cover the issue.

may assist in restraining publication of all the material here. Following **Campbell**, it is clear that the courts will first ask whether or not the information concerned has a 'reasonable expectation of privacy'. This test is less restrictive, as there is no need to establish the pre-existing relationship. The law is less concerned with the context in which the information was obtained than with the nature of the content. There is some authority to support the suggestion that covert photographs may attract special protection, as arguably a picture has the potential to be more intrusive and damaging than the written word[7] (**Douglas v Hello! (No. 3)** [2006] QB 125). If the information can be said to be private, then the court must ask whether this is outweighed by arguments in favour of publication, either because the material is in the public domain; or that publication is in the public interest. Here, the courts must balance the Article 8 rights of the applicant against the Article 10 rights which protect free expression in the press.[8] It appears that this will be done on a case-by-case basis and therefore the court will seek to balance the threat posed to Simone's interests against the right of the public to be informed about activities of individuals who are in the public eye. Recently, the Supreme Court has confirmed the need to address the question of public interest, with Baroness Hale questioning whether publication of details of a celebrity's sex life in order to criticise them could ever be justified using Article 10 (**PJS v News Group Newspapers Ltd** [2016] UKSC 26[9]).

Simone will seek an injunction to restrain publication pending resolution of a claim for misuse of private information and/or breach of confidence. There is a need for the careful scrutiny of such applications, as it is accepted that the value of news may diminish if delayed (**Observer and the Guardian v United Kingdom** (1992) 14 EHRR 153). Here, however, the particular issues for consideration are whom the application should be made against, and how far any prohibition on publication should extend.

It is possible to seek an injunction against 'persons unknown'.[10] It is not uncommon for a celebrity to become aware that an unidentified individual possesses private information that they intend to disclose. By obtaining an injunction against an unspecified respondent, newspaper groups can be restrained from publication as third party recipients of the information under the 'Spycatcher' principle. (See, for example, **TUV v Person or Persons Unknown** [2010] EWHC 853 or **Middleton & Anor v Person or Persons Unknown** [2016]

EWHC 2354 (QB).) Thus, Simone can seek to restrain publication of the photographs from an unknown source.

A similar situation arose in the case concerning the footballer, John Terry, who sought to prevent publication of a story concerning his affair with a team mate's partner (*John Terry (previously referred to as LNS)* v *Persons Unknown* [2010] EWHC 119 (QB)). Simone appears to want to suppress any mention of the story. If she were to apply for an injunction, a report of her success could arouse public speculation. Terry sought (and was initially granted) what has been referred to as a 'super-injunction', restraining publication not only of the information but of mention even of the proceedings themselves. The use of such broad injunctions has been the subject of considerable academic, media and political criticism but, in any event, following *Terry*, it appears that Simone will be unsuccessful. The judge refused to renew the injunction on the basis that on the facts, he did not feel there would be an actionable claim and further, that even if there was, damage to Terry's commercial interests could be addressed by compensation. In this situation, it seems possible that the courts would determine that the freedom of the press did indeed outweigh Simone's right to privacy, as an adequate remedy exists for any harm resulting from publication.[11] Simone is not entitled to prior notification from the press. This matter was considered by the European Court in *Mosley* v *United Kingdom* [2012] EMLR 1.[12] The applicant claimed that the failure of the state to impose an obligation for prior notification on the press breached his Article 8 and 13 rights, as if notification is not given, then an effective remedy is denied as restraint cannot be obtained. The European Court rejected the argument as to impose an obligation for prior notification in all cases would be a disproportionate restriction upon press freedom.

It seems that Simone would be best advised to bring an action for breach of confidence and misuse of private information, and to seek an interim injunction to restrain publication. She is unlikely to be able to obtain a so-called 'super-injunction', and is not able to obtain redress for the absence of prior notification.[13]

[11] Where there is a direct parallel between a reported case and the situation in a scenario, then it is worth explaining this. The aim is not to demonstrate that you know the facts, but rather, to draw some conclusions about how the precedent will be applied in the instant case.

[12] Credit will be given for reference to this matter, as it demonstrates that you have an awareness of the law as it is evolving, beyond the issues covered by the textbooks.

[13] As the issues have been discussed in the body of the answer, the conclusion can be a brief summation of the key points covered.

Make your answer stand out

- The *Mosley* case has been the subject of academic debate. You would be rewarded for examining the arguments regarding notification in more detail. Helpful comment and analysis can be found in Phillipson, G. (2009) Max Mosley goes to Strasbourg; Article 8, claimant notification and interim injunctions, *Journal of Media Law*, 1: 73, and a response by Scott, A. (2010) Prior notification in privacy case: a reply to Professor Phillipson, *Journal of Media Law*, 2(1): 49–65.

- The treatment of privacy by the press was a key issue which emerged during the Leveson Inquiry and led to the establishment of a new code of conduct for Editors in 2016. A good analysis of the potential impact of the code can be found in Keppel-Palmer, M. (2016) The Emperor's new clothes – IPSO's new version of the Editors' Code of Practice, *Entertainment Law Review* 27(3): 92–7.

- You should make sure you keep up to date with emerging case law. You may find links to recent cases, and some commentary, via the International Forum for Responsible Media (http://inform.wordpress.com/).

! Don't be tempted to . . .

- Discuss the facts of the cases. It can be particularly tempting here, as you will probably remember the details easily due to the publicity they received. Do remember that only the *ratio* is important!

- Lose sight of the facts of the scenario. Students sometimes set out the law clearly, but do not use the points made to draw conclusions about the particular facts provided.

Question 2

'It is well known that in English law there is no right to privacy' (Glidewell J in *Kaye* v *Robertson* [1991] FSR 62).

Assess this statement in the light of developments following the Human Rights Act 1998.

Answer plan

→ Briefly explain the traditional approach to privacy in English law.

→ Outline the effect of the HRA.

→ Assess the development of the law by focusing on major cases.

→ Consider the extension to the law of confidence.

→ Analyse how far this provides effective protection of personal privacy.

Diagram plan

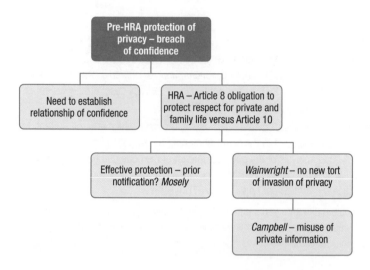

A printable version of this diagram plan is available from **www.pearsoned.co.uk/lawexpressqa**

Answer

[1] Setting out the conclusion at the start of the essay shows confidence and the ability to reach an informed view.

[2] This question asks you to evaluate how the law has changed since 2000, when the HRA came into effect. Therefore, it is essential to set out the position prior to that point.

[3] The parameters of the discussion need to be established. Here, you have stated clearly what the focus of the answer will be but, importantly, explained to your examiner why you have made that choice.

The case of **Kaye v Robertson** [1991] FSR 62 was decided prior to the HRA, which incorporated the European Convention on Human Rights into domestic law. Article 8 protects the right to respect for private and family life. Nonetheless, in 2004, the House of Lords emphatically denied that the HRA had created a new action for invasion of privacy (**Wainwright v Home Office** [2004] 2 AC 406). It will be argued that the HRA has allowed the judiciary to provide more robust protection for individual privacy.[1]

Prior to 1998, private information could be protected in a number of circumstances.[2] First, information regarding court proceedings could be protected by way of a court order, and in respect of juvenile proceedings, the order would be made unless a successful application was made to lift reporting restrictions in the public interest. Further, an individual was able to protect personal information from dissemination if it could be established that publication would amount to a breach of confidence. It is this issue that requires discussion, as this is the area where it can be said that the HRA has had the most impact.[3] Confidence arises from

[4] These two cases are critical as they each mark a significant development in the law. In any question dealing with actions for breach of confidence, you will need to show that you recognise why they were important.

a particular relationship. Often, this arises from contractual obligations. *Argyll v Argyll* [1967] Ch 302 established that marriage was an intimate relationship giving rise to a duty of confidence. The principle developed further in *A-G v Guardian Newspapers (No. 2)* [1990] 1 AC 109 (the '*Spycatcher*' case),[4] in which it was held that third parties who received information obtained in a confidential relationship were also subject to restraint. Hence, a measure of protection existed for celebrities, politicians, and others who wished to prevent details of their private lives being exposed in the press.

[5] You need to be able to highlight the limitations of an action for breach of confidence in order to evaluate whether the HRA has been effective in remedying any of these issues.

To establish an action for breach of confidence prior to the HRA, the applicant would need to demonstrate that the information had 'the quality of confidence', and was obtained in circumstances creating a duty of confidence. Further, it would need to be shown that the unauthorised use of the information would be detrimental. Thus, information already in the public domain could not be restrained.[5] It could be argued that it is in the public interest to reveal certain kinds of private information, if this exposes corruption, or hypocrisy.[6] In *Woodward v Hutchins* [1971] 1 WLR 760, the court declared there is 'no confidence in iniquity'. In that case, a celebrity who had sought publicity could not complain about coverage of his private life.

[6] This is a key point to make, as it will be suggested that the post-HRA balance between Articles 8 and 10 is, to an extent, dealing with the same issue.

[7] The answer highlighted the potential for 'public interest' that existed in pre-HRA actions for breach of confidence earlier, so there is no need to repeat the points here.

Even in cases where it was clear that a gross intrusion of privacy had occurred, in the absence of a confidential relationship, there was little effective protection. This was the situation in *Kaye v Robertson* which prompted Glidewell LJ to suggest that Parliament should review the issue. Following the inception of the HRA, the courts, as a public body (s. 6) have a responsibility to provide a remedy for an individual who can demonstrate that their Article 8 rights have been infringed. It should be noted, however, that there is a concurrent duty to uphold the protection of freedom of expression guaranteed by Article 10. In dealing with cases where restraint of publication of private information is sought, the judiciary is required to conduct a balancing exercise between the competing rights. Therefore, it cannot be said that an individual is always entitled to privacy, and indeed it could be argued that the matters that will fall to be considered are scarcely different from those which were relevant before 1998.[7] Sebastian Coe was unable to prevent publication of details of an extra-marital affair on the grounds that, on balance, the freedom of the press and public interest outweighed his desire to keep the matter private (*Lord Coe v MGN* (2004, QBD, unreported)).

[8] It is absolutely critical to include this point as the extension to the law of confidence is, without doubt, the most significant development in this area resulting from the HRA.

[9] *Campbell* is the most important case in this area and must be included.

[10] Marks will be awarded here, as the answer doesn't just give the *ratio* of the case; it also explains clearly how this represents a change in the law. This shows real understanding.

There is, as emphasised in ***Wainwright***, no new tort of invasion of privacy. What is clear, however, is that the judiciary has felt enabled to develop the doctrine of confidence, so that it can now be said to incorporate an action for the misuse of private information.[8] The critical case is that of ***Campbell v MGN Ltd*** [2004] 2 AC 457,[9] concerning an action in respect of publication of photographs of the model Naomi Campbell entering a drug rehabilitation unit, having previously denied taking drugs. The key distinction is that there is no longer a requirement to demonstrate a pre-existing relationship of confidence provided that it can be shown that the information carries with it a reasonable expectation of privacy.[10] This allowed Campbell to seek redress for the publication of photographs taken by a stranger. Once the threshold of reasonable expectation is passed, the courts will then consider whether or not the information is already in the public domain and, finally, whether there is a public interest in publication. It can be seen, then, that the case represents a significant extension to the legal protection for individual privacy, as it enables an action to be brought in a broader range of circumstances. The judiciary, however, has emphasised that Article 8 rights do not have primacy over those contained in Article 10 and, therefore, there will always be a careful balance to be struck.

[11] The question asked for consideration of the individual's right to privacy, so, having shown how the law has developed, there should be an evaluation of the limitations of the protection now provided.

Even where an action can be brought in confidence, on the basis that private information has been misused, this will not always provide the protection that an individual may hope for.[11] Many cases contain an application for injunctive relief to prevent publication pending the resolution of the matter. However, where the individual does not have notice of the impending publication, any action after the event will be unable to prevent the material entering the public domain. Redress is only available through complaint to the Press Complaints Commission, or by obtaining damages for breach of confidence. The matter was considered by the European Court of Human Rights in ***Mosley v United Kingdom*** [2012] EMLR 1 where the applicant argued that, without an enforceable right to prior notice of publication, he was denied an effective remedy. His application failed as it was held that a blanket requirement for prior notification would be a disproportionate limitation on press freedom.

It is fair to say that, even before the advent of the HRA, the courts were mindful of the need to balance the rights of the individual against the importance of the freedom of the press. The incorporation of the right to respect for privacy has undoubtedly obliged the court to provide a measure of protection in a broader range of circumstances. It seems that, had **Kaye v Robertson** been decided today, the action for breach of confidence would have been successful, as the information carried the reasonable expectation of confidence outlined in **Campbell**. It cannot be said that this creates an automatic right to privacy in every case, as the courts must still balance the individual's wishes against the freedom of the press.

 Make your answer stand out

- You could expand the discussion about limits on the protection of privacy that still exist by exploring the developing case law, and what this suggests about the appropriate balance between Articles 8 and 10. Ensure that you keep up to date with new authorities as they emerge. The UK Human Rights Blog is run by Crown Office Chambers, and provides a free updating service that should alert you to new cases: http://ukhumanrightsblog.com.

- By considering the extent to which there is now a body of case law which appears to accept that there is a right to privacy (see, for example, *Hannon and Dufour v News Group Newspapers Ltd* [2014] EWHC 1580 (Ch) in which the judge referred to the 'newly emerging wrong of breach of privacy').

- By incorporating additional academic opinion on the law of privacy. A good starting point would be the *Journal of Media Law*, which often contains relevant material for this topic. Although the law has developed since publication, the textbook by Feldman, D. (2002) *Civil Liberties and Human Rights in England and Wales*, Oxford: Oxford University Press, remains an authoritative resource.

! Don't be tempted to . . .

- Engage in a lengthy explanation of Convention law. You should explain the need to balance Articles 8 and 10 but your focus should be on application of the law in the domestic courts.

- Spend too much time outlining the law prior to the Human Rights Act. When you are asked to evaluate an area of law in light of the HRA, your examiner does require you to consider how far the Act has signalled a change; therefore you have got to outline the 'old' law but try to ensure the bulk of the answer considers the current position.

- Ignore the issue of effective remedies. Even if it is accepted that the law now does seem to protect more kinds of private information, we can see that there is debate about whether prior restraint is effective.

❓ Question 3

Jenna obtains a part-time job as an administrative assistant with the Home Office. On commencing her employment, she was asked to sign the Official Secrets Act. She did this, but paid it little attention.

While filing some documents, Jenna comes across a memorandum marked 'classified', which warns that a large number of persons who entered the United Kingdom are no longer traceable. The memorandum further states that many of these individuals originate from countries characterised by high levels of terrorist activity. Later that day, Jenna hears on the news that the minister responsible for immigration answered a question in Parliament about security, and claimed that the tracking procedures for asylum seekers are excellent.

Jenna feels that this is highly misleading. She discusses this matter with her brother, Karl. Karl is a freelance journalist and he writes an article for the *Sunday Record*. In the week prior to publication, the paper begins to show television adverts claiming that 'insider information' from the Home Office will expose ministerial lies.

All employees in Jenna's department are told there will be an investigation into the leak. Advise Jenna of any possible consequences for her, and her brother.

Diagram plan

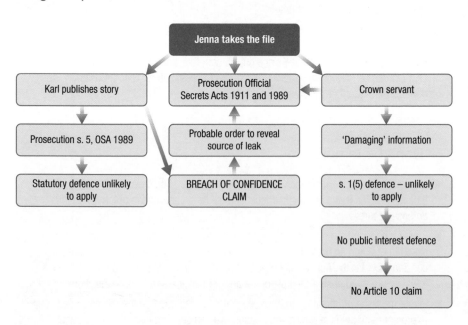

A printable version of this diagram plan is available from **www.pearsoned.co.uk/lawexpressqa**

Answer plan

→ Outline the main provisions of the Official Secrets Acts.

→ Specify the nature of the information protected.

→ Distinguish between the obligations of (and consequences for) Jenna and Karl.

→ Consider any possible defences.

→ Briefly consider additional measures that could be taken for breach of contract, or breach of confidence.

Answer

[1] A brief introduction can show that you have been able to see all the key issues highlighted by the scenario.

Jenna and Karl may be subject to prosecution for offences contrary to the Official Secrets Acts 1911 and 1989. In addition, Jenna could face an action for breach of confidence and breach of contract. The Official Secrets Act 1989 does provide some defences, and the efficacy of these will be considered.[1] The liability of the parties will be considered separately, as there is variance between their positions.

[2] You should aim to summarise the purpose of the law as succinctly as you can, so that you can begin to focus on the issues relevant to the parties as soon as possible.

[3] As you have decided that this is unlikely to be relevant, you should avoid spending time discussing the Official Secrets Act 1911.

[4] There is no need to give any detail about those categories that are not going to be relevant to Jenna.

The Official Secrets Acts aim to protect the interests of the state by preventing the unauthorised disclosure of information held by various government departments.[2] Section 1 of the 1911 Act remains in force, and prohibits the disclosure of information that could assist an enemy for a purpose prejudicial to the state. This is a serious offence, and is generally concerned with activities that could be classified as espionage. It is unlikely that Jenna will be prosecuted under the 1911 Act.[3] The 1989 Act categorises types of information that are protected, from security and intelligence (s. 1), defence (s. 2), interests abroad (s. 3) or criminal investigations (s. 4). It seems likely that the information regarding asylum seekers could be categorised as information concerning security and intelligence.[4]

As Jenna is a Crown servant, she may face prosecution for an offence under section 1(3). In order to be liable, it will be necessary for the Crown to prove that the information meets the 'harm' test; it must be shown that it is, or is likely to be, 'damaging'. Damage is not further defined in the Act; however, it appears likely that this will be straightforward for the Crown. The case of ***Chandler* v *DPP*** [1964] AC 763 was concerned with section 1 of the 1911 Act but, in that case, it was held that it was for the government to determine what constitutes the 'interests of the state'. This appears to suggest that the

[5] As you are asked to advise Jenna and explore possible defences, you need to spend time setting out the relevant legal principles and applying them to the facts, even if it might seem obvious that they will not apply. A diligent lawyer will carefully examine all the options to ensure that the client is properly advised.

[6] You will be rewarded for being able to reach a clear conclusion about the likely application of the law to these facts.

[7] The question explicitly states that Jenna feels the information is misleading, which is an invitation to discuss whether or not there is a 'public interest' defence.

[8] Here, the answer demonstrates an awareness that proceedings in this area are concerned with matters that are not strictly legal, as there is a broader, political, implication.

judiciary is likely to defer to executive determinations of harm. The statute does afford Jenna with a defence under section 1(5) if she is able to prove that she did not know or have reason to believe that the disclosure was damaging.[5] On a literal interpretation, this imposes a reverse burden of proof upon the defendant. This has been held to be contrary to the provisions of Article 6(2) of the European Convention on Human Rights, as it infringes the right to a fair trial (*R v Keogh* [2007] 1 WLR 1500). Section 3 of the Human Rights Act will be utilised to read the provision as conferring only an evidential burden. If Jenna is able to raise some evidence that she did not know the information was damaging, then it will be for the Crown to disprove that assertion. Given that the memorandum was marked as 'classified', and she has confirmed awareness of her obligations by signing the Act, it is probable that the defence will fail.[6]

Jenna may wish to argue that she disclosed the information because it was in the public interest.[7] It may seem desirable that a public servant who uncovers evidence that Parliament has been misled should be entitled to act as a 'whistleblower'. Under the 1911 Act, Sarah Tisdall was prosecuted and imprisoned for disclosing information to journalists. She had done so as she believed that a minister had made false statements to the Commons. The case, and that of *R v Ponting* [1985] Crim LR 318, caused considerable disquiet and, arguably, led to the 1989 Act. The statute does not, however, provide any defence of public interest. This was confirmed in *R v Shayler* [2003] 1 AC 247, in which the House of Lords confirmed that the 1989 Act provides a mechanism for reporting concerns to a superior who may authorise disclosure (s. 7), and this would have been the correct procedure. Nor can Jenna argue that a prosecution would infringe her Article 10 right to freedom of expression, a point also dismissed in the *Shayler* litigation. Article 10 is a qualified right, and infringement is permitted if necessary for national security.

Jenna does not appear to have any defence available to her. Her best hope is that the Crown may feel that the adverse publicity that could accompany any trial outweighs the need for a prosecution.[8] Katharine Gun was prosecuted under the Official Secrets Act in 2003 after disclosing information obtained in the course of her employment to the *Observer* concerning an American request to the United Kingdom to assist in surveillance of foreign diplomats. She intended to argue that she had the defence of necessity, on the basis she acted to prevent an illegal war. It is clear, following **Shayler** (above), that there was no prospect of success. Nevertheless, the Crown offered no evidence, as it appeared that the airing of the matter in court would have been damaging.

The Crown will wish to prevent publication of the material. The most straightforward means will be to seek an injunction for breach of confidence as the material was obtained in circumstances imposing a duty of confidence. An action can be brought against the paper, and it is by this means that the Crown will be able to determine that Jenna is the source of the information. Although section 10 of the Contempt of Court Act allows journalists to protect their sources, this can be overridden in the interests of national security. It was through such an action that Tisdall was identified; **A-G v Guardian Newspapers (No. 2)** [1990] 1 AC 109.[9]

[9] A good answer will be able to show the connection between actions against the newspaper and investigation of the source of the leak.

Both Karl and the proprietors of the newspaper will be liable for an offence contrary to section 5 of the 1989 Act, which makes it an offence for a person who receives classified or confidential information to further disclose it.[10] There is a requirement to prove that the disclosure was made with relevant mens rea, that the defendant knew, or had reason to believe, the information would be damaging. Fenwick (2007) suggests that this may afford some degree of protection for journalistic freedom, as it could feasibly be argued that the journalist took the view that disclosure was in fact beneficial to the public interest (p. 603). There are as yet no authorities to confirm this view and nor does it seem that there is special protection afforded to the Article 10 rights of the press when issues of security are engaged. In **A-G v The Times** [2001] 1 WLR 885 an injunction was refused, with regard paid in the judgment to Article 10, but in that case, the primary reason to allow publication was that the information was already in the public domain. That is not the case here, and therefore the authority does not assist Karl.

[10] Although you are advising Jenna, you were asked to address the implications for her brother, so you must address the possible offences under section 5.

Jenna and Karl both face prosecution under the Official Secrets Act 1989 in respect of the disclosure of the information. Karl will be unable to protect Jenna's identification as the source of the information. The Human Rights Act does not offer any solace for either party and there do not appear to be any arguable defences.[11]

[11] The conclusion briefly summarises the advice given, demonstrating that you have applied your knowledge to answer the specific questions asked.

✓ Make your answer stand out

- By expanding the discussion of the relationship between the Contempt of Court Act and Convention rights. A good discussion of this topic can be found in: Stone, R. (2012) *Civil Liberties and Human Rights* (9th edn). Oxford: Oxford University Press.

- By engaging in a more critical analysis of the 'harm' test which is applicable to the section 1 offence. It has been argued that the test is potentially broad in scope and lacks definition. See the criticisms of the Act contained in: Fenwick, H. and Phillipson, G. (2006) *Media Law*. Oxford: Oxford University Press, pp. 923–48. This would demonstrate an awareness of the academic arguments raised by the facts in this scenario. You must make sure that you do not stray too far from the objective of advising the parties. So, for example, in this instance you may incorporate reference to the criticisms raised by Fenwick and Phillipson that 'damage' is so poorly defined that any disclosure Jenna makes could be interpreted as 'damaging'.

- By exploring the issues raised in the *Shayler* litigation regarding Article 10 in more detail. Similar issues were addressed in the case of *A-G* v *Blake* [2001] 1 AC 268, in which the House of Lords declined to determine whether section 1 was too widely drawn. Reference to additional cases, where relevant, shows familiarity with the subject material.

! Don't be tempted to . . .

- Discuss the historical development of the law. This question does not require you to consider the reasons why the 1989 Act came into existence. You need to be applying the law that is relevant and drawing conclusions about what is likely to happen to Jenna and Karl.

- Engage in a lengthy discussion of section 1 of the 1911 Act. It can be tempting to show the examiner that you have remembered everything about the topic, but you will get better marks for focusing on the law relevant to the parties here.

- Make statements about what is likely to happen to the parties without providing support from the authorities. While you would be given a mark for noting that there is no 'public interest' defence, more credit will be awarded for stating that this proposition of law is confirmed in the *Shayler* case.

Question 4

'Unnecessary secrecy in government leads to arrogance in governance and defective decision-making . . . People expect much greater openness and accountability from government than they used to.' (White Paper (1997) *Your Right to Know* (Cm. 3818). London: HMSO)

To what extent has the Freedom of Information Act 2000 succeeded in creating open government?

Answer plan

→ Outline the aims of the Act.

→ Identify the categories of information available and discuss the process of making a request.

→ Assess the impact of the Act with reference to particular examples.

→ Draw conclusions about the effectiveness of the legislation in meeting its aims.

Diagram plan

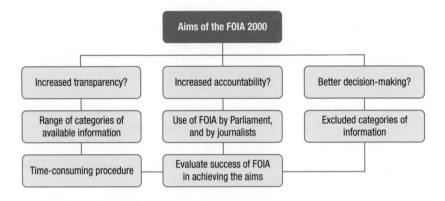

A printable version of this diagram plan is available from **www.pearsoned.co.uk/lawexpressqa**

Answer

The Labour party made a manifesto commitment to increase open government prior to election in 1997. In December of that year, the White Paper *Your Right to Know: White Paper on Freedom of Information* (Cm. 3818, London: HMSO) was published, and this led to the Freedom of Information Act 2000, fully implemented in 2005. The Act allows the public rights of access to information held by public bodies, subject to certain exceptions and limitations. Perhaps the most notorious use of the Act thus far has been in respect of requests made concerning expenses claims made by MPs, leading to the scandal in 2009. It will be argued that, while the Act may have led to greater transparency, the effect upon the process of government decision-making has been minimal.[1]

[1] Here, the answer suggests that a fairly complex argument is going to be developed, drawing a distinction between openness and better government.

The Data Protection Act 1998 granted individuals access to information held about them to ensure accuracy. The Freedom of Information Act, however, conferred a broader right of access to information held by a range of public bodies including local and central government, Parliament, the police, schools and colleges, and the NHS. The Act aimed to increase transparency and accountability, improve the decision-making process of government, and also to increase public trust and participation in government.[2] Worthy and Hazell (2010) have argued that the Act has succeeded in achieving the first of these aims, but has not increased participation or trust in government, or impacted upon the decision-making process.

[2] In order to evaluate the impact of the Act, it is necessary to show that you understand the purpose of the legislation.

Requests for information must be made in writing, and the recipient must respond within twenty days. Public authorities are not obliged to disclose all information that is requested.[3] Certain classes of information are subject to an absolute exemption (including, for example, information concerning the formulation of government policy (s. 35), or information relating to security matters (s. 23)). The Act also exempts other kinds of information if disclosure is likely to prejudice specified interests (this includes information which may prejudice the economy, law enforcement and criminal investigations). Further, a request may be refused on the grounds that the information is, or will be, available by other means (ss. 21–22), or if the cost of providing the information is excessive (s. 11).

[3] The question asks for discussion of the effect of the legislation. It is necessary to demonstrate understanding of how the law operates but this can be done in a brief paragraph.

The Act is overseen by the Information Commissioner, who will adjudicate any appeal against a decision to refuse a request for disclosure. The Information Commissioner can issue an enforcement notice, and decisions of the Information Commissioner are subject to appeal either by the person making the request, or the body which holds the information.

The Act has been utilised to a limited extent by Parliament as a mechanism for obtaining information held by government.[4] Worthy and Hazell have found that parliamentary questions remain the primary method for MPs to obtain information; with approximately five times more tabled questions than freedom of information requests in any session. Nevertheless, the Act has provided a means to obtain information where the answers to questions have been unsatisfactory or evasive. For example, the All Party Parliamentary Group on Extraordinary Rendition sought data regarding the movement of individuals

[4] Many answers will focus on the use of the Act by members of the public (and journalists), but a recognition of the potential use by Parliament recognises the constitutional position of the legislature in ensuring government accountability.

5 When dealing with an area
of legislation that has not
generated a great deal of
case law, it is important to
make sure that illustrative
examples of the law in
operation are included.

6 This is a key point in the
argument that is being
developed, suggesting that
the impact of the Act is, in
fact, fairly minimal.

7 This shows a fairly detailed
level of current awareness
and also suggests that the
Act is not as significant as is
sometimes suggested, which
helps to point towards the
eventual conclusion.

8 There is very little case law
in this area, so there will be
credit given to an answer that
demonstrates knowledge of
any available authorities.

9 At this point, having discussed
the effect of the Act on
transparency, it is appropriate
to draw a 'partial' conclusion
before moving on to a different
part of the argument.

10 The quote in the question
raises the issue of the
decision-making process,
so a good answer will
consider not only access to
information, but the effect
of the legislation on how
government operates.

across boundaries, following perceived reticence in response to parliamentary questions.[5]

The most extensive use of the Act has been by journalists, who represent the vast majority of requesters. It is well known that the MPs' expenses scandal of 2009 was triggered by freedom of information requests made by an investigative journalist, Heather Brooke. It should be noted, however, that the utility of the Act is undermined by the procedure attendant on making a request. The 20-day response time may well mean that by the time information is received, the currency of an issue has faded so that it is no longer newsworthy.[6] This is magnified when the initial response is a refusal to release the information, necessitating a lengthy appeal process. Heather Brooke made her first request for information regarding receipts in 2005. Her investigations certainly generated considerable publicity for the issue, and the release of limited information, but the scandal finally broke when the full details of the claims for additional costs allowance was leaked from a Whitehall source.[7] More recently, the Court of Appeal has overturned a refusal of a request made in 2005 (**BBC v Sugar** [2010] EWCA Civ 715).[8] This gives some support to an assertion made by a number of respondents in the study conducted by Hazell *et al* (2010). that the appeals process is utilised by public bodies to delay the release of information and, indeed, deter some from pursuing an action. A report by the Campaign for Freedom of Information (Frankel and Gunderson, 2009) states that the average request takes almost 20 months to be concluded. The cost of legal action is feasibly a real bar to members of the general public.

It can be seen, then, that the Act has allowed access to a broad range of information, and has led to a degree of increased transparency and accountability. The limitations on the types of available information and the lengthy nature of the process have meant that the impact is perhaps less than was anticipated.[9]

One of the aims of the Act was to increase public participation in the process of government. It is difficult to see how this has been achieved. Relatively few requests are made by members of the general public. It may be that the release of information obtained by the media has increased public awareness of government issues; however, the White Paper also indicated that the decision-making process would be improved.[10] Conversely, a concern expressed by ministers during the passage of the legislation was that the decision-making process would be impaired. It was suggested that the fear of having to disclose information would deter civil servants from providing information to ministers, thus hindering the process of full and frank debate. In the event, sections 35 and 36 restrict access to all information regarding the formulation of policy and other information is subject to the harm test. Thus, it seems clear that the Act has had no impact on the manner in which government decisions are made.

It was also hoped that public trust in the process of government would be improved. Given the scale of the public anger following the release of information regarding expenses, it is clear to see that this objective has not been achieved. Rather, the efforts made to obstruct access to the information led to a perception of secrecy; this was not assisted by the parliamentary time given to a Private Member's Bill proposing amendments to the Act which would have excluded much of the detail regarding individual MPs' expenses.

[11] The conclusion can be brief as it simply summarises points made throughout the answer as the argument developed.

The Freedom of Information Act has allowed details regarding the machinery of government to be obtained. It cannot be said, however, that the Act has led to open government, as a result of restricted access to much information and the unwieldy appeals process.[11]

 Make your answer stand out

- By referring to a broad range of illustrative examples. As the law is fairly recent, there is not a great deal of case law authority to draw on. A really good source of information (where much of the material referred to here can be found) is the work of the Constitution Unit at UCL, headed by Professor Robert Hazell. Publications can be found online at www.ucl.ac.uk/constitution-unit.

- By using what case law there is to support your arguments. A good starting point is the discussion of the topic in Bradley, A. and Ewing. K. (2010) *Constitutional and Administrative Law* (15th edn) London: Pearson, pp. 283–8, which outlines the key authorities to date. This will show your examiner that you have a good knowledge of this developing area of law.

! Don't be tempted to . . .

- Simply set out the legislative provisions in detail. The bulk of the marks here are awarded for analysing the impact of the law on the operation of government. You do need to show that you understand the key provisions of the Act, and, in particular, the existence of exemptions. Try to provide a brief summary or overview so that your answer can then address the central topic.

- Ignore the wording of the quotation provided. The question requires you to consider the impact of the Freedom of Information Act on the workings of government, but the quote also suggests that openness leads to better decision-making and you should address this aspect of the question. This can be a small point, as in this answer, which states quite briefly that the decision-making process is unaffected.

Question 5

'[A] decision of a judicial body should be final and binding and should not be capable of being overturned by a member of the executive.' (R (Evans) v Attorney General [2016] UKSC 21 per Lord Neuberger para 115)

Discuss the constitutional issues raised in the litigation concerning the 'black spider memos'.

Diagram plan

Briefly outline case	Identify Constitutional significance	Identify Constitutional significance
• Emphasis on the appeal process for FOI	• Rule of Law – no person is above the law • Separation of Powers - judicial function of preventing abuse of power	• Parliamentary supremacy • Judicial law making?

A printable version of this diagram plan is available from **www.pearsoned.co.uk/lawexpressqa**

Answer plan

→ Outline the history of the case.

→ Identify the key principles of rule of law, separation of powers and parliamentary supremacy.

➔ Explain the courts' approach to these.

➔ Consider the governmental response.

Answer

---

[1] It is important to show that you understand this point, and can place the decision in a constitutional context.

[2] The danger of trying to address the Supreme Court's approach to the European Union Directive is that you could easily lose focus on the central themes of the answer, which concern the relationship between the domestic Parliament, the executive and the judiciary. It is, though, a good idea to make the parameters of the discussion clear in your introduction.

[3] Although the case is important because of the implications it has for the separation of powers and the rule of law, it is impossible to explain this clearly without some understanding of how the freedom of information request process operates.

[4] Take care not to give too much detail regarding the exemptions contained in the Act, but it does make sense to choose one of those claimed by the Attorney General in the *Evans* case as an illustration.

In 2005, the Guardian newspaper journalist Rob Evans made a request under the Freedom of Information Act 2000 and the Environmental Information Regulations 2004 to various government departments. He was requesting the disclosure of correspondence between the Prince of Wales and government ministers. It was not until ten years later that, following a Supreme Court ruling, the Guardian was able to print a story giving details of the so-called 'black spider memos'. Disclosure was sought on the basis that, Evans argued, they may show a lack of political neutrality on the part of the heir to the throne. The case has constitutional significance not because of the content of the communications between Prince Charles and members of the government.[1] It raises issues regarding the operation of the separation of powers, the rule of law and parliamentary supremacy. The case dealt with issues relating both to domestic law and European law.[2] This discussion will focus only on the matters relating to the interpretation of the Freedom of Information Act.

In order to understand the constitutional significance of the Supreme Court decision, it is necessary to briefly outline the stages which followed the initial request.[3] The Freedom of Information Act was introduced as part of an extensive programme of constitutional reform undertaken in the first part of the Blair administration. The Act aimed to increase transparency in government with the stated intention of improving decision making and increasing public participation. It created an obligation for public bodies to disclose information on request unless an exemption could be applied. Section 35(1), for example, makes it possible for a government department to withhold information relating to matters including the development of policy.[4] If a request is refused, the maker is entitled to appeal the decision to the Information Commissioner (s. 50) and, if the Information Commissioner upholds the decision, to the Information Tribunal.

Evans followed this process and the case was transferred to the Upper Tribunal, which ultimately ordered disclosure of the letters in September 2012. One month later, the Attorney General issued a certificate of statutory veto pursuant to section 53 of the Freedom of Information Act, on the basis that he had determined 'on reasonable grounds' that the disclosure of the material was not in the public interest.

Evans sought judicial review of the Attorney General's decision and was ultimately successful in the Supreme Court. The Supreme Court held, by a five to two majority, that section 53 did not authorise the Attorney General to issue a veto on the basis that he reached a different conclusion from the Upper Tribunal. Lord Neuberger's leading judgment made it clear that he viewed the issue as one of constitutional significance, as it touched directly on the rule of law.[5]

[5] Here, by referring directly to the question, you will reassure your examiner that you have not lost sight of the purpose of the question.

Dicey stated that the rule of law requires that: 'Every man, whatever be his rank or condition, is subject to the ordinary law of the realm'.[6] It has long been established that government ministers are bound by judicial decisions. In *M v Home Office* [1994] 1 AC 377 the then Home Secretary, Kenneth Baker, was found to be in contempt of court for failing to obey a court injunction. Lord Templeman observed that failure to do so would 'establish the proposition that the executive obey the law as a matter of grace and not as a matter of necessity, a proposition which would reverse the result of the Civil War'. In this case, it appeared that the Attorney General wished to use a power of veto to avoid the effect of a judicial decision he did not agree with and Lord Neuberger held that a different interpretation of the public interest to that of the Upper Tribunal could not constitute a 'reasonable ground' under s53. He emphasised that it is fundamental to the constitution that judicial decisions should be binding on the parties, and therefore that executive decisions are subject to review. The judiciary has frequently noted that if Parliament intends to remove such a fundamental right then it would need to be done in the clearest possible terms (see, for example, *R (Jackson) v Attorney General* [2006] 1 AC 262).[7]

[6] You do not need to set out the whole of Dicey's explanation of the rule of law. Instead, it is appropriate to focus only on the point that is most directly relevant to the case.

[7] This is useful authority to cite as it shows that you are familiar with a broad range of relevant case law, and understand how this case relates to previous authorities.

Maintenance of the rule of law requires an independent judiciary able to review the actions of the executive and is, in this respect, intertwined with the constitutional principle of the separation of powers.[8] It is clear that Lord Neuberger felt that to interpret section 53 as allowing a Minister to set aside a decision he or she does not agree with would undermine the ability of court to fulfil their constitutional function of ensuring accountability. However, the dissenting judges argued that in reaching this conclusion, the Supreme Court had undermined

[8] Students often view each area of the syllabus as entirely discrete topics, but here, the answer demonstrates an understanding of how the various constitutional doctrines are linked.

[9] As this was a majority decision, it is useful to note the dissenting view.

the Supremacy of Parliament.[9] Elliott (2015) has noted that while the rule of law does protect the judicial role as the final arbiter of disputes, it also 'views with suspicion judicial intransigence in the face of clear legal provisions enshrined in an Act of Parliament'. Lord Wilson felt that the majority, in refusing to uphold the veto, went far beyond the limits of statutory interpretation and instead, effectively, rewrote section 53 (para 118). Viewed from this perspective, then, the Supreme Court decision undermined the separation of powers set out by Lord Diplock in **Duport Steels Ltd v Sirs** [1980] 1 WLR 142: 'Parliament makes the laws, the judiciary interpret them'.[10]

[10] This is an important point to make, and links directly to the conclusion.

The case ultimately resulted in disclosure of the disputed letters, but did not resolve the constitutional tensions between the executive and the judiciary. In response to the decision the government created an Independent Commission to review the Freedom of Information Act which reported in March 2016. The Commission took the view that the Act was, on the whole, working well. They did, however, recommend that Parliament legislate to provide additional clarity regarding the exercise of the veto. The government has not followed the recommendation, and instead confirmed the veto would only be used following a decision by the Information Commissioner, which, it would seem, endorses Lord Neuberger's view that the judiciary should have 'the last word'.

[11] Here, the conclusion is supported by the preceding paragraphs setting out the differing views of the judges in the case.

The case can be seen as a confirmation of the judicial role in preserving both the separation of powers and the rule of law by asserting the right to control the executive. There is an argument, however, that the case can be viewed as evidence of an increasing willingness on the part of the judiciary to take decisions which diminish parliamentary supremacy.[11] Perhaps the key significance of the case is that it exposed some of the uncertainty that can arise from an uncodified constitution reliant on interlocking, and sometimes conflicting, principles.

✓ Make your answer stand out

■ By including a more detailed discussion of the dissenting judgment and the relevance of parliamentary supremacy. Although the article only touches briefly on the case, the views expressed by the Attorney General at the time of litigation are a good starting point. Dominic Grieve QC (2016), 'Can a Bill of Rights do better than the Human Rights Act?' *Public Law*. April: 223–34.

■ By exploring in more detail the government response to the ruling. A good place to start would be the evidence given to the Independent Commission considering the Freedom of Information Act https://www.gov.uk/government/publications/independent-commission-on-freedom-of-information-report

■ By exploring in more detail some of the case law mentioned in the answer, to develop the argument that there is an increase in judicial activism.

! Don't be tempted to . . .

■ Spend too long detailing the history of the case or outlining the content of the memorandum. This is not a question that is asking you about the conduct of the Prince of Wales: it is about the extent of the constitutional power of the judiciary and the executive.

■ Outline the provisions of the Freedom of Information Act in great detail. You should keep this to the minimum to demonstrate an understanding of the veto.

■ Ignore the alternative views expressed by the dissenting judges; this would result in an unbalanced answer.

📝 Question 6

'Free speech includes not only the inoffensive but the irritating, the contentious, the eccentric, the heretical, the unwelcome and the provocative provided it does not tend to provoke violence. Freedom only to speak inoffensively is not worth having' (Lord Justice Sedley, *Redmond-Bate* v *DPP*).

To what extent are the courts willing to protect individuals from offence?

Answer plan

→ Explain the qualifications upon Article 10.

→ Consider prosecutions of individuals engaged in protest.

→ Discuss social media prosecutions.

→ Analyse the relationship between public opinion and judicial decisions.

Diagram plan

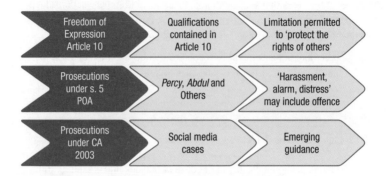

A printable version of this diagram plan is available from **www.pearsoned.co.uk/lawexpressqa**

Answer

Article 10 of the European Convention on Human Rights (ECHR) obliges signatory states to protect freedom of expression. Freedom of expression is, however, a qualified right, meaning that it can be restricted for one of the purposes specified in Article 10(2). In the United Kingdom, there are a number of statutory controls upon freedom of speech. Many of these are arguably uncontroversial, such as the criminalisation of the incitement to racial or religious hatred (Racial and Religious Hatred Act 2006) which is a limitation that can be justified under Article 10(2) as necessary for the prevention of crime. It is legitimate for the state to limit freedom of expression in order to protect the rights of others, which leads us to ask whether or not this incorporates a right to be protected from material that they find offensive.[1] This issue has been the focus of considerable media and judicial attention in a series of cases involving either public protest, or the use of social media.[2]

Section 5 of the Public Order Act 1986 (POA) criminalises behaviour likely to cause harassment, alarm or distress in a public place.[3] In **Percy v DPP** [2001] EWHC 1125 (Admin), the High Court overturned the appellant's conviction under section 5 where the behaviour in question was defacing an American flag during a protest at an American air base. In doing so, it was held that disrespectful or contemptuous conduct during an otherwise lawful protest is not prohibited; only

[1] This introduction is effective, because it succinctly explains that the key legal issue is the interpretation of 'rights of others' in the ECHR.

[2] Here, the answer indicates the particular area that will be the focus for the discussion. It is a good idea to set these parameters in the introduction.

[3] You must give the definition, because the decisions in the cases you are discussing turn on the word 'distress'.

behaviour that is intentionally or recklessly abusive, threatening or insulting. Although the conviction was quashed on the basis that the District Judge had approached the balancing exercise incorrectly, it should be noted that Mrs Justice Hallett accepted the lower court's finding that it was legitimate to claim the service personnel should be protected from actions denigrating their flag.[4]

[4] This is a really important point to make to develop your argument that the judiciary is now prepared to curtail actions that cause offence.

This somewhat tentative acceptance that 'harassment, alarm or distress' includes 'offence' has been reinforced by the more assertive judgment in *Abdul v DPP* [2011] EWHC 247 (Admin).[5] The defendants in that case staged a protest against military action in Afghanistan and Iraq during a parade of British soldiers, and shouted phrases such as 'British Soldiers Murderers' and 'Go to Hell'. In this case, the convictions under section 5 were upheld by the High Court, rejecting the appellants' claim that their Article 10 rights had been infringed. Khan (2012) has pointed out that the regiment submitted evidence confirming that they had not been offended by the protest, but the court nevertheless held that the 'citizens and public of Luton' could constitute a category of persons whose rights could legitimately be protected.

[5] Do not be afraid to offer your evaluation of a judgment: this shows that you have read the cases and are confident enough with the subject to draw inferences from the words used about the development of the law.

Whether or not this argument is accepted, there is a distinction to be made between speech or actions directed at an identifiable person or group during a public protest, and comments made on social media about a person or group which are not directed to, or even necessarily seen, by them.[6] The Communications Act 2003 prohibits the use of the 'public electronic communications' network for sending messages that are either 'grossly offensive' or of an 'indecent, obscene or menacing character' (s. 127(1)). In *Chambers v DPP* [2012] EWHC 2157 (Admin) the court stated that internet social media sites such as Twitter should be considered to be part of the public communications network for the purposes of the Act.[7] It is fair to say, however, that the growth of social media has created new challenges for the state in determining when to prosecute under an Act which (as was noted in *Chambers*) was drafted at a time when few could have predicted the impact of such sites. In the summer of 2012, the Director of Public Prosecutions decided not to prosecute an individual who posted an offensive message regarding the Olympic diver, Tom Daley.[8] In a statement about the decision, he stated that the message had been intended as a joke aimed at family and friends and was not part of any campaign against Daley (available at http://blog.cps.gov.uk/2012/09/dpp-statement-on-tom-daley-case-and-social-media-prosecutions.html).

[6] You need to make it clear why social media prosecutions are particularly contentious.

[7] There is no need to consider the facts of this case, as it focused on a message that was said to be 'menacing'. The question has clearly directed you to discuss the narrower issue of 'offensive' speech. No marks would be available for analysing the factual background of this case; it is only included to explain why social media prosecutions are brought under this Act.

[8] Reference to this statement demonstrates that the student has read around the set texts, and as a result, can draw on very current sources.

The statement acknowledged the need to consider Article 10, and conceded that the CPS is working in largely 'uncharted' territory, reaching decisions on a case-by-case basis.

[9] This part of the answer shows how a breadth of knowledge enables you to engage in critical analysis of the topic.

Such an ad hoc approach to the issue results in contradictory decisions, as there have been prosecutions in cases that cannot objectively be said to concern statements substantially different to those in the Daley case.[9] Matthew Woods pleaded guilty to an offence under section 127(1) and was sentenced to 12 weeks in custody in October 2012 in respect of offensive comments posted on Facebook concerning the highly publicised disappearance of a young child. Azar Ahmed was convicted at trial in respect of messages he posted on Facebook stating that soldiers should die and go to hell. This message contained no specific threat and was not directed at any particular individual, but two persons complained to the police. The decisions to prosecute Woods and Ahmed appears to fly in the face of both the DPP's recent statement and a line of judicial authorities reflecting the opinion expressed by Lord Justice Sedley that the courts should protect freedom of speech even where the speech in question is unpalatable to many. The announcement of the DPP in October 2012 that consultation meetings will be held with a view to issuing guidelines regarding social media prosecutions is welcome and it is to be hoped some clarity is provided.

[10] This is an important point to make because it shows how the 'right', if it exists, is a creation of interpretation.

The ECHR does not contain any specific protection for the 'right not to be offended'. What, then, could the basis be for judicial determinations that restrictions on offensive speech fall within the ambit of Article 10(2) protection of the 'rights of others'?[10] Khan (2012) dismisses the notion that such a right is incorporated into Article 8 as an aspect of individual autonomy, pointing out that even if that were to be accepted, the speaker would be equally entitled to protection (p. 197).

[11] At the outset, the answer acknowledged that speech can be restricted to prevent crime. It is a point worth reinforcing in conclusion, to make clear that you recognise the distinction between offensive and criminal forms of expression.

Despite this, the cases noted above do demonstrate a willingness by the judiciary to accept that freedom of expression can legitimately be restricted to prevent offence even where there is no other criminal activity.[11] This should be a matter of concern, as it does appear that prosecutors and members of the judiciary have been responsive to public opinion rather than the legal principles underpinning the Convention. No cases concerning the use of social media have reached the Court of Appeal or the Supreme Court so it may well be that in due course senior members of the judiciary will reassert the need for robust protection of Article 10 rights. At the present time, however, it seems that the courts are willing to take steps to protect citizens from offence.

✓ Make your answer stand out

- By showing an awareness of recent academic commentary. At the time of writing, the issue of social media prosecutions is still fairly new, but if you check journals regularly you will be able to find new articles when they are published. Criminal law journals are a useful source for comment on recent cases.

- By being prepared to engage with the discussion of Article 8 and autonomy alluded to in the answer. This is quite a complex area but the Khan (2012) article is a good starting point. Cited in that article is the work by Mead, D. (2010) *The New Law of Peaceful Protest: Rights and Regulations in the Human Rights Act Era*, Oxford: Hart Publishing. Mead sets out the argument that Article 8 may involve personal autonomy, and the book is itself a useful resource (although note that this is a rapidly changing area and the law has developed since publication).

- By considering the relationship between Strasbourg and the domestic courts. In particular, you could consider the fairly broad margin of appreciation generally afforded to signatory states to deal with these kinds of issues. This deference may result in a lack of robust protection for freedom of speech in the domestic arena.

! Don't be tempted to . . .

- Ignore the importance of the qualifications upon Article 10. A successful response to this question will depend upon recognising the need to assess the validity of restrictions designed to protect the rights of others. You will need to be able to give a clear explanation of the operation of qualified rights.

- Simply describe the key cases. You must use your knowledge of the facts of these cases to draw some conclusions about the direction that the developing law is taking. This is the kind of question which demands that you articulate an opinion.

❓ Question 7

Miranda works for a local newspaper – *The Daily Grind* – as a crime correspondent. She also maintains a Twitter account detailing her life as a reporter, and a blog.

The editor, who usually decides what stories to use, goes away for two weeks.

On the first day of the editor's holiday, Miranda is delighted to be assigned to cover a breaking story concerning the gruesome murder of a college lecturer. One of her police contacts tells her that one of the victim's colleagues, Sally, a criminal law lecturer, has been arrested. Miranda begins to research what she can about Sally. She speaks to some of Sally's ex-students, and gets detail about the kind of things that she taught. She writes her 'exclusive' which appears on the front page of *The Daily Grind* the next day. The headline reads: 'Ghoulish tutor obsessed with death and gore'. Within the article, Miranda notes that homicide took up about half of the lecture programme that Sally delivered.

Sally is released without charge the day after the story appears, and a second person, Tim, is arrested a few days later. He is charged with murder, and appears in the magistrates' court, where a trial date is set, and the matter is committed to the Crown Court for trial. That day, Miranda blogs:

'From my seat in the press gallery I am sure I was looking into the eyes of a cold-blooded killer. There is no doubt whatsoever, this man is a monster. The Crown referred to a DNA match found on the victim's clothing, so guilt looks like a foregone conclusion.'

She sends a Twitter message that states:

'The accused says nothing apart from his name.'

Miranda is surprised when she arrives at work the next day to see a furious email from the editor of the paper, as he says her actions may result in the paper facing court action.

Advise Miranda of the legal consequences that may arise from the newspaper article and the blog entry.

Answer plan

→ Explain the tension between various Convention rights.

→ Outline the elements of a contempt of court.

→ Assess whether or not the article and the blog could be contempt.

→ Consider whether or not the position is different regarding the tweet.

Diagram plan

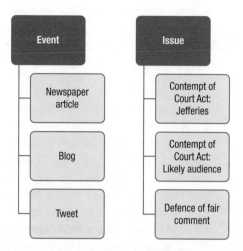

A printable version of this diagram plan is available from **www.pearsoned.co.uk/lawexpressqa**

Answer

[1] Surprisingly, the fact that reporting court proceedings engages Article 6 is one that is often missed, so inclusion of this point will be rewarded.

The freedom of the press to report upon court proceedings has long been recognised as a key component of open justice, and is now protected by Articles 6 and 10 of the European Convention on Human Rights.[1] Article 10 protects freedom of expression and the right to receive information, and Article 6 makes it clear that a public hearing is one of the requirements of a fair trial. Both of these rights, however, are qualified and permit restrictions to be made where necessary to protect the rights of others. Reporting of court proceedings can be viewed as a way of protecting Article 6 rights, but equally, coverage that is biased can make it impossible to secure a fair trial, particularly in criminal cases where a jury may be influenced by material seen in the media. Limitations can be placed upon the reporting of criminal proceedings to prevent prejudicing the defendant's right to a fair trial, and failure to respect these can be a contempt of court (now governed by the Contempt of Court Act 1981 (CCA)). Miranda (and the newspaper) faces the possibility of prosecution in respect of each part of the scenario.

[2] The answer will need to consider whether or not there has been contempt in three separate instances. You can avoid unnecessary repetition by setting out the elements of liability at the outset.

Contempt of court is a matter of strict liability (s. 1), and can apply to any publication aimed at the public at large (or a section of it) which creates a substantial risk of prejudice or impediment in live proceedings.[2] Contempt cases are brought by the Attorney General, and there has been a sharp increase in the number of such cases under the current incumbent, Dominic Grieve.

The publication of the story concerning Sally may well be an actionable contempt, and is analogous to the facts surrounding *A-G v MGN Ltd and another* [2011] EWHC 2074. That case concerned the publication of stories about Christopher Jefferies, who was arrested in connection with a high-profile murder case, but never charged with any offence. The court held that 'proceedings' do not begin at the point of charge, and in fact, are 'live' from the point of arrest.[3] In this case, proceedings would be brought against the newspaper, not the individual journalist. *A-G v MGN Limited and Others* [1997] 1 All ER 456 set out key principles for consideration in cases of contempt. When considering the 'substantial risk' of prejudice, it is not necessary to consider the actual effect of the article, only the position at the time it was published. It will not, then, be possible for the newspaper to claim that the course of justice was not impeded as Sally was never actually charged. The court would have to find that the material was likely to be seen by a potential juror, and, crucially, that it would be capable of prejudicing a juror by the time of the trial.[4] The newspaper could try to argue that, had Sally been charged, there would have been a significant delay before trial and that the risks would have been minimal by that point. Given the ruling in the Jefferies case, this is unlikely to be successful as the material here could be held to be similarly serious.[5]

[3] The facts of this case are fairly well known, but take care to set out the key legal issue that the court had to determine, rather than being sidetracked by describing the content of the stories published about Jefferies.

[4] Never forget that you are being asked to advise Miranda, so ensure that you relate all your legal points to the facts given in the scenario.

[5] Sometimes, students do not mention the legal arguments that they have considered and discounted. It is far better to show your examiner how and why you have reached your conclusions.

[6] As you have set out the matters that need to be proved at the outset, and dealt with the issue of 'live' proceedings earlier, you can deal with this aspect of liability regarding the blog in a single sentence.

Clearly, when Tim appears in court, there are live proceedings.[6] In dealing with the blog entry, at first glance, it seems that the comments clearly create a risk of prejudice as Miranda has made it clear that she believes him to be guilty. She may, however, wish to argue that the blog is not a publication that creates a substantial risk. Jurors are now customarily warned to refrain from looking at the internet, and therefore Miranda could argue that any juror reading the blog during the trial would be disobeying judicial instructions. The facts here could be distinguished from those in *A-G v Associated Newspapers Ltd and another* [2011] EWHC 418 (Admin).[7] In that instance the court felt that a warning against internet research may not have prevented

[7] Here, the answer demonstrates the ability to consider the application of authorities.

jurors seeing prejudicial material on newspapers' websites, as they were advised they could read daily news reports and this could be confusing for jurors who read news online. A blog, however, is not in that category. The difficulty with this is that, unlike the case cited above, no jurors have yet been selected, and a potential juror may come across the material in the mean time. Miranda could argue that, if the readership of the blog is modest, the risk of prejudice could not be said to be 'substantial' as the likelihood of a potential juror reading it would be slim. Alternatively, she could argue that the material is unlikely to be prejudicial as any jury would focus on the evidence presented to them, and would not be swayed by the obviously subjective view of the defendant's appearance in the blog.[8] These arguments may assist in respect of the first part of the statement, but reference to evidence presented is clearly prohibited. The Judicial Studies Board guidance of 2009 makes it clear that restrictions apply to the reporting of all preliminary hearings,[9] and only brief factual details about the defendant, the trial listing date and matters relating to bail can be published. The only other matter to consider is whether or not it would be Miranda or the newspaper who would be held liable here.[10] This would depend upon whether the blog was part of the newspaper's own online presence. If it is not linked to, or promoted by, the newspaper's own website, it is likely that she would be personally liable.[11]

The use of Twitter and other social media has created new challenges in seeking to prevent prejudice due to the difficulties in monitoring and policing usage. It is quite clear that a tweet can be a 'publication' as defined by section 2 of the CCA. The Attorney General suggested that contempt proceedings could be brought against users of Twitter who revealed the identity of a person protected by a so-called 'super-injunction'.[12] Individuals working in media or other public roles often make it clear in their profile that views expressed are theirs and not their employers. If Miranda has done this, the paper would not be liable. In any event, the content of the tweet is not prohibited and would be considered no more than a 'fair and accurate' account of proceedings, and therefore not actionable (s. 4).

In summary,[13] it appears that the newspaper would be liable for contempt in respect of the story published relating to Sally if proceedings were brought. If either the paper, or Miranda, faced action in respect of the blog, the statements may be found to be sufficiently prejudicial to amount to a contempt. There can be no action in respect of the tweet.

[8] There are a number of possible ways to view the risk of prejudice here, and you will be rewarded for recognising these.

[9] By recognising the specific considerations which apply to the particular hearing, this answer demonstrates a really detailed knowledge of the topic.

[10] The question specifically referred to the email from the editor fearing action against the paper. Although you are directed to consider all possible consequences, it would be useful to draw a distinction between two issues.

[11] It does not matter which conclusion is reached on this point, as long as you explain the thinking behind it.

[12] There is no need to give details about the injunction matter, the only relevance is the fact that use of social media can be a contempt.

[13] It can be difficult to conclude a problem scenario: a brief summary of the advice will suffice.

Make your answer stand out

■ By expanding the discussion about the decision in the Jefferies case. Comments made in the judgment indicated that it was a possibility that coverage could have prejudiced the trial of the person eventually tried for the murder, making his conviction less likely. This, it is suggested, points towards something of an extension of the principles governing contempt as the 'proceedings' prejudiced may be separate to those concerning the individual subject of reports.

■ By considering the issues raised by the use of social media in more detail, in particular, concerns surrounding the ability of jury members to conduct internet research.

■ By utilising some additional academic comment on the area. You could look at the research by Thomas, C. (2010) commissioned by the Ministry of Justice: *Are Juries Fair?* and Murdoch, C. (2012) The Oath and the Internet, *Criminal Law and Justice Weekly*, vol 176, March, which contains more recent comment on the issue of jury use of the internet.

 Don't be tempted to . . .

■ Spend time speculating about whether or not prejudice was caused by these events. This is unnecessary and misunderstands the aim and purpose of the CCA.

■ Make unsupported statements of opinion about Miranda's conduct. You must take care to find authorities that help you to see what conclusions are likely to be drawn by the courts dealing with these events.

@ **Try it yourself**

Now take a look at the question below and attempt to answer it. You can check your response against the answer guidance available on the companion website (**www.pearsoned.co.uk/lawexpressqa**).

> The state's power to collect and share personal and private information about individuals calls into question the commitment to protecting Article 8 rights. Discuss.

www.pearsoned.co.uk/lawexpressqa

 Go online to access more revision support including additional essay and problem questions with diagram plans, and You be the marker questions, and to download all diagrams from the book.

Bibliography

Abrahams, A. (2008) The Ombudsman as part of the UK constitution: A contested role? *Parliamentary Affairs*, 61(1): 206–215.
Allan, T.R.S. (2001) *Constitutional Justice: A Liberal Theory of the Rule of Law*. Oxford: Oxford University Press.

Bagehot, W. (1963) *The English Constitution*. London: Fontana.
Bamforth, N. (2001) The true 'horizontal effect' of the Human Rights Act 1998. 117 *LQR*, 34.
Barber, N. (2009) Laws and constitutional conventions. *LQR*, 125.
Bingham Centre for the Rule of Law, JUSTICE and the Public Law Project (2015) *Judicial Review and the Rule of Law: An Introduction to the Criminal Justice and Courts Act 2015, Part 4*, BICRL, London.
Bingham Centre for the Rule of law (2015) *A Constitutional Crossroads: Ways forward for the United Kingdom* (London).
Blackburn, R. (2004) Monarchy and the personal prerogatives. *Public Law*, 546.
Blackstone, W. (1787) *Commentaries on the Laws of England* (10th edn).
Bondy, V. and Sunkin, M. (2009) *The Dynamics of Judicial Review Litigation: The Resolution of Public Law Challenges before Final Hearing*. London: Public Law Project, www.publiclawproject.org.uk/documents/TheDynamicsofJudicialReviewLitigation.pdf.
Bradley, A. (2011) The sovereignty of parliament – form or substance? in J. Jowell and D. Oliver (eds), *The Changing Constitution* (7th edn). Oxford: Oxford University Press.
Bradley, A. (2012) The Damian Green affair – all's well that ends well? *Public Law*, Jul 396–407.
Bradley, A. and Ewing, K. (2010) *Constitutional and Administrative Law* (15th edn). London: Pearson.
Brazier, R. (1999) *Constitutional Practice* (3rd edn). Oxford: Oxford University Press.
Brazier, R. (2008) *Constitutional and Administrative Law* (8th edn). London: Penguin.
Brazier, R. and Fox, R. (2011) Reviewing select committee tasks and modes of operation. *Parliamentary Affairs*, 64(2): 354–369.
Brighton Declaration (2012) High Level Conference on the Future of the European Court of Human Rights, http://hub.coe.int/20120419-brighton-declaration.
Brown, J. (2013) Carwyn Jones: The UK must continue down the road to becoming a federal nation, The Independent, 26 December 2013.

Cabinet Office (2010) *Cabinet Manual*, www.cabinetoffice.gov.uk/sites/default/files/resources/cabinet-manual.pdf.

Cameron, D. and Clegg, N. (2011) Foreword to the Draft House of Lords Reform Bill, www.official-documents.gov.uk/document/cm80/8077/8077.pdf.

Campbell, D. (2009) The threat of terror and the plausibility of positivism. *Public Law*, 501.

Campbell, D. and Young, J. (2002) The metric martyrs and the entrenchment jurisprudence of Lord Justice Laws. *Public Law*, 399.

Campbell, M. (2010) *Police Searches on the Parliamentary Estate*. HC 62, www.publications.parliament.uk/pa/cm200910/cmselect/cmisspriv/62/62.pdf.

Cane, P. (1995) Standing up for the public. *Public Law*, 276.

Carlile, Lord (2011) Sixth Report of the Independent Reviewer pursuant to section 14(3) of the Prevention of Terrorism Act 2005. London: Home Office, www.homeoffice.gov.uk/publications/counter-terrorism/independent-reviews/lord-carlile-sixth-report?view=Binary.

Carney, D. (2013) Covert surveillance of suspects in police vehicle. *Policing Journal*, 86(4): 340–45.

Chamberlain, N. (2009a) Special advocates and procedural fairness in closed proceedings. 28 *CJQ*, 314.

Chamberlain, N. (2009b) Update on special advocates and procedural fairness in closed proceedings. *CJQ*, 28: 448.

Chapman, J. (2012) Leveson Report: Defiant PM refuses to accept Leveson's call for laws to control the press, The Daily Mail, 30 November 2012.

Cowley, P. and Stuart, M. (2005) Parliament: Hunting for votes. *Parliamentary Affairs*, 58(2): 258–71.

Craig, P. (1992) Legitimate expectations: a conceptual analysis. *LQR*, 108: 79.

Craig, P. (1997) Formal and substantive conceptions of the Rule of Law: an analytical framework. *Public Law*, 467.

Craig, P. (2007) The Rule of Law, Appendix to the Sixth Report of the House of Lords Constitution Committee, http://www.publications.parliament.uk/pa/ld200607/ldselect/ldconst/151/15102.htm.

Culture Media and Sport Committee (2010) Press Standards, Privacy and Libel. HC 361–62.

Culture, Media and Sport Committee (2012) News International and Phone-Hacking. HC 903.

de Smith, S. and Brazier, R. (2008) *Constitutional and Administrative Law* (8th edn). London: Penguin.

Delegated Powers and Regulatory Reform Committee (2015) 2nd Report HL 12.

Dewan, T. and Dowding, K. (2005) The corrective effect of ministerial resignations on government popularity. *American Journal of Political Science*, 49: 46–56.

Dicey, A. (1885) *The Law of the Constitution*. London: Macmillan.

Edwards, D. (2017) *Miller, Law and Revisionism*, U.K. Const. L. Blog (available at https://ukconstitutionallaw.org/)

Elliot, M. (2007) Bicameralism, sovereignty and the unwritten constitution. *Int'l J Const L*, 5: 370.

Elliott, M. (2013) *Law, Rights and Constitutional Politics*. Research Paper 55/2013, Cambridge Faculty of Law http://www.law.cam.ac.uk/ssrn/.

Elliott, M. (2013) A Damp Squib in the Long Grass: the report of the Commission on a Bill of Rights. *European Human Rights Law Review*, 2: 137–51.

Elliot, M. Devolution, Federalism and a New Constitution for the UK, LSE Constitution UK, 2014, http://blogs.lse.ac.uk/constitutionuk/2014/01/08/devolution-federalism-and-a-new-constitution-for-the-uk/

Elliott, M. (2015) *A Tangled Constitutional Web – The Black-Spider Memo's and the British Constitution's Relational Architecture. Public Law*, Oct: 339–50.

Elliott, M. (2015) *Declarations, Quashing Orders and Declaratory Judgments: The Hawke Case and s 84 of The Criminal Justice and Courts Act 2015*, www.publiclawforeveryone.com

Elliott, M. (2017) *Analysis of the Supreme Court's judgment in Miller*, www.publiclawforeveryone.com

Elliot, M. and Thomas, R. (2014) *Public Law* (2nd edn). Oxford: Oxford University Press.

Evans, J. G. (2008) Devolution in Wales: claims and responses, 1937–1979, Parliamentary Affairs, 61(2): 414–28.

Ewing, K.D. and Tham, J. (2008) The continuing futility of the Human Rights Act. *Public Law,* 668.

Feldman, D. (2002) *Civil Liberties and Human Rights in England and Wales*. Oxford: Oxford University Press.

Fenwick, H. (2007) *Civil Liberties and Human Rights* (4th edn). London: Routledge-Cavendish.

Fenwick, H. (2009) Marginalising Human Rights: Breach of the peace, 'kettling', the Human Rights Act and public protest. *Public Law*, 737.

Fenwick, H. (2013) Prisoners' voting rights, subsidiarity, and Protocols 15 and 16: Re-creating dialogue with the Strasbourg Court? *UK Const. L. Blog* (27 November 2014), http://ukconstitutionallaw.org/tag/brighton-declaration/.

Fenwick, H. and Phillipson, G. (2006) *Media Law*. Oxford: Oxford University Press.

Forsyth, J. (2013) *Chris Grayling: I want to see our Supreme Court supreme again*, The Spectator, 28 September.

Foster, S. (2013) Going 'where angels fear to tread': How effective was the Backbench Business Committee in the 2010–2012 Parliamentary Session? *Parliamentary Affairs*, 66(3).

Fox, R. (2009) Engagement and participation: What the public want and how our politicians need to respond. *Parliamentary Affairs*, 62(4): 673.

Fox, R. and Blackwell, J. (2014) The Devil is In the Detail: Parliament and Delegated Legislation, The Hansard Society, London.

Frankel, M. and Gunderson, K. (2009) Delays in investigating Freedom of Information Complaints, www.cfoi.org.uk/pdf/foidelaysreport.pdf.

Gay, O. and Powell, T. (2004) *Individual Ministerial Responsibility – Issues and Examples.* Research Paper 04/31, House of Commons Library, www.parliament.uk/documents/commons/lib/research/rp2004/rp04-082.pdf.

Gearty, C. (2014) On Fantasy Island: British politics, English judges and the European Convention on Human Rights. *UK Const. L. Blog* (13 November 2014), http://ukconstitutionallaw.org.

Geddis, A. (2004) Free speech martyrs or unreasonable threats to social peace – Insulting expression and section 5 of the Public Order Act 1986. *Public Law*, 853.

Genn, H. (2013) Do-it-yourself law: Access to justice and the challenge of self-representation. *Civil Justice Quarterly*, 32(4): 411–44.

Grayling, C. (2014) Protecting Human Rights in the UK: The Conservative's proposals for changing Britain's human rights laws, https://www.conservatives.com/~/media/Files/Downloadable%20Files/HUMAN_RIGHTS.pdf.

Greenberg, D. (2015a) Dangerous Trends in Modern Legislation. *Public Law*, Jan: 96–110.

Greenberg, D. (2016) *Dangerous Trends in Modern Legislation, and How to Reverse Them*, Centre for Policy Studies, London.

Grieve, D. (2016) Can a Bill of Rights do better than the Human Rights Act? *Public Law*, Apr: 223–34.

Guide for witnesses giving oral evidence to a House of Commons Select Committee (2016) HC123 available at https://www.parliament.uk/documents/commons-committees/witnessguide.pdf.

Hadfield, B. (2005) Devolution, Westminster and the English Question. *Public Law*, 286–305.

Hale, Baroness (2011) Equal access to justice in the big society: The Sir Henry Hodge Memorial Lecture, http://www.supremecourt.uk/docs/speech_110627.pdf.

Hale, Baroness (2013) Who guards the guardians? Speech to Public Law Project Conference, http://www.supremecourt.uk/docs/speech-131014.pdf.

Harlow, C. (1978) Ombudsmen in search of a role. 41 *MLR*, 446.

Hart, H.L.A. (1994) *The Concept of Law* (2nd edn). Oxford: Oxford University Press.

Hawkes, S. (2013) Whiplash drives false insurance claims to 1 billion, Daily Telegraph, 24 July 2013.

Hazell, R., Worthy, B., Glover, M. (2010) The Impact of the Freedom of Information Act on Central Government in the UK: Does FOI work?. Palgrave.

Hickman, T. (2008) The courts and politics after the Human Rights Act: A comment. *Public Law*, 84.

HMIC (2012) *A review of national police units which provide intelligence on criminality associated with protest*. London: HMSO.

HMIC (2013) *A review of progress made against the recommendations of HMIC's 2012 report on the national police units which provide intelligence on criminality associated with protest*. London: HMSO.

Home Office (1997) *Your Right to Know: White Paper on Freedom of Information* (Cm 3818). London: HMSO.

Home Office (2010) Rapid review of counter-terrorism powers. Press release 13 July, www.homeoffice.gov.uk/media-centre/press-releases/counter-powers.

Home Office (2011) *CONTEST: The United Kingdom's Strategy for Countering Terrorism*, www.homeoffice.gov.uk/publications/counter-terrorism/counter-terrorism-strategy/contest-summary?view=Binary.

Home Office (2015) *Prevent* Duty Guidance: For Further Education Institutions in England and Wales 2015 available at https://www.gov.uk/government/uploads/system/uploads/attachment_data/file/445915/Prevent_Duty_Guidance_For_Further_Education__England__Wales_-Interactive.pdf.

Home Office (2015) Revised *Prevent* Duty Guidance for England and Wales. https://www.gov.uk/government/uploads/system/uploads/attachment_data/file/445977/3799_Revised_Prevent_Duty_Guidance__England_Wales_V2-Interactive.pdf.

Hopkins, N. and Ackerman, S. (2013) Flexible laws and weak oversight give GCHQ room for manoeuvre. *The Guardian* (2 August).

House of Lords Constitution Committee (2006) *Waging War: Parliament's Role and Responsibility*. 15th Report Session 2005–2006, www.publications.parliament.uk/pa/ld200506/ldselect/ldconst/236/23602.htm.

House of Lords Constitution Committee (2007) *Waging War: Parliament's Role and Responsibility*. 3rd Report Session 2006–2007, www.publications.parliament.uk/pa/ld200607/ldselect/ldconst/51/5102.htm.

House of Lords Constitution Committee (2011) *9th Report of Session 2010–2011* HL 89.

House of Lords Select Committee on the Constitution (2015) *Sixth Report of 2015–16, The Scotland Bill* HL 59.

House of Lords Select Committee on the Constitution (2016) *Sixth Report of 2016–17, English Votes for English Laws* HL 61.

Human Rights Joint Committee (2010) *Counter-Terrorism Policy and Human Rights (16th Report): Annual Review of Control Orders Legislation*.

Hyland, K. and Walker, C. (2014) Undercover policing and underwhelming laws. *The Criminal Law Review*, 8: 555–74.

Independent Commission on Freedom of Information Report, March 2016 available at https://www.gov.uk/government/publications/independent-commission-on-freedom-of-information-report.

Irvine of Lairg, Lord (2011) *A British Interpretation of Convention Rights*. www.ucl.ac.uk/laws/judicial-institute/docs/Lord_Irvine_Convention_Rights_dec2012.pdf further education institutions in England and Wales.

Jaconelli, J. (2005) Do constitutional conventions bind? *CLJ*, 64(1): 149.

Jennings, I. (1959a) *The Law and the Constitution* (5th edn). London: Hodder and Stoughton.

Jennings, I. (1959b) *Cabinet Government* (3rd edn). Cambridge: Cambridge University Press.

Joint Committee on the Draft Enhanced Terrorism Prevention and Investigation Measures Bill (2012) *Report*, www.parliament.uk/business/committees/committees-a-z/joint-select/terrorism-prevention-and-investigation-measures-bill/publications/.

Joint Committee on Human Rights (2005) Sixth Report, www.publications.parliament.uk/pa/jt200506/jtselect/jtrights/96/9602.htm.

Joint Committee on Human Rights (2006) 23rd Report, www.publications.parliament.uk/pa/jt200506/jtselect/jtrights/239/23902.htm.

Joint Committee on Parliamentary Privilege (2013) *Parliamentary Privilege* HL 30, HC 100.

Jowell, J. (2000) Beyond the rule of law: towards constitutional judicial review. *Public Law*, 671.

Jowell, J. and Oliver, D. (eds) (2000) *The Changing Constitution* (4th edn). Oxford: Oxford University Press.

Judge, Lord (2016) *Ceding Power to the Executive* Kings College Lecture, available at https://www.kcl.ac.uk/law/newsevents/newsrecords/2015-16/Ceding-Power-to-the-Executive---Lord-Judge---130416.pdf.

Kaufman, P. and Owen, T. (2013) The price of dignity and liberty: Legal aid for prisoners. *EHRLR*, 482.

Keppel-Palmer, M. (2016) *The Emperor's new clothes – IPSO's new version of the Editors' Code of Practice. Entertainment Law Review*, 27(3): 92–7.

Khan, A. (2012) A 'right not to be offended' under Article 10(2) ECHR? Concerns in the construction of the 'rights of others'. *EHRLR*, 191–204.

Knight, C.J.S. (2009) Expectations in transition: recent developments in legitimate expectations. *Public Law*, 15.

Lakin, S. (2013) Parliamentary privilege, Parliamentary sovereignty, and Constitutional Principle. *UK Const. L. Blog* (11 February 2013), http://ukconstitutionallaw.org

Law Commission (2010) Report, *Administrative Redress: Public Bodies and the Citizen* (No. 322), www.lawcom.gov.uk/docsAc322.pdf.

Leopold, P.M. (1999) Report of the Joint Committee on Parliamentary Privilege. *Public Law*, 604.

Leopold, P.M. (2011) Standards of conduct in public life, in J. Jowell and D. Oliver (eds) *The Changing Constitution* (7th edn). Oxford: Oxford University Press.

Lever, A. (2007) Is judicial review undemocratic? *Public Law*, 280.

Liberty (2009) *Liberty's response to the Independent Police Complaints Commission Consultation on the IPCC's proposed Statutory Guidance for the Police Service 2009*, www.liberty-human-rights.org.uk/pdfs/policy09/liberty-s-response-to-the-consultation-on-the-ipcc-s-proposed-statutory-guid.pdf.

Liberty (2011) *Progress on stop and search but control orders by any other name*, http://liberty-human-rights.org.uk/media/press/2011/progress-on-stop-and-search-but-control-orders-by-any-ot.php.

Lisvane KCB DL, Lord (2016) *The courts and Parliament. Public Law*, Apr: 272–84.

Loveland, I. (2012) *Constitutional Law, Administrative Law, and Human Rights: A Critical Introduction* (6th edn). Oxford: Oxford University Press.

Low, S. (1904) *The Governance of England.*

Macdonald, Lord (2011) *Review of Counter-Terrorism and Security Powers* (Cm 8003). www.homeoffice.gov.uk/publications/counter-terrorism/review-of-ct-security-powers/report-by-lord-mcdonald?view=Binary.

Mackie, J. (2009) Being Unreasonable *SJ*, 153/12.

Maer, L. (2010) *Hung Parliaments* SN/PC/04951, www.parliament.uk/documents/commons/lib/research/briefings/snpc-04951.pdf.

Malloch, T. (2014), Closing the gap: should damages be available for judicial review? *New Law Journal*, 4 July.

Marks, S. (2014) Backlash: the undeclared war against human rights. *European Human Rights Law Review*, 4: 319–327.

Marshall, G. (1971) *Constitutional Theory*. Oxford: Cavendish Press.

Marshall, G. (2002) The Crown and Bagehot's dubious death warrant. *Public Law*, Spring 4–8.

McKeever, D. (2010) The HRA and anti-terrorism in the UK: one great leap forward by Parliament but are the courts able to slow the steady retreat that has followed? *Public Law*, 100.

McKeown, M. and Thomson, S. (2010) The role of the House of Lords in a hung parliament. *Scots Law Times*, 19: 99.

McNamara, L. and Lock, D. (2014) Closed material proceedings under the Justice and Security Act 2013: A review of the first report by the Secretary of State (*Bingham Centre Working Paper 2014/03*), Bingham Centre for the Rule of Law, BIICL, London.

Mead, D. (2009) Of kettles, cordon and crowd control – Austin, Commissioner of Police for the Metropolis and the meaning of 'deprivation of liberty'. *EHRLR*, 376.

Mead, D. (2010) *The New Law of Peaceful Protest: Rights and Regulations in the Human Rights Act Era*. Oxford: Hart Publishing.

Mead, D. (2013) A chill through the back door? The privatised regulation of peaceful protest. *Public Law*, 1: 100–18.

Middleton, B. (2009) Sections 57 and 58 of the Terrorism Act 2000: Interpretation update. *Journal of Criminal Law*, 73: 203.

Millar, D. (2011) *Erskine May's Parliamentary Practice* (23rd edn). London: Lexis-Nexis Butterworth.

Ministerial Code of Conduct (2010) www.cabinetoffice.gov.uk/sites/default/files/resources/ministerial-code-may-2010.pdf.

Ministry of Justice (2013) *Responses to Human Rights Judgments*. Cmnd 8727.

Montesquieu, C. (1989) *The Spirit of the Laws*. Cambridge: Cambridge University Press.

Murdoch, C. (2012) The oath and the Internet. *Criminal Law and Justice Weekly* 176, March.

Murkens, J. (2017) *Miller in the Supreme Court: a welcome reminder of the function of a constitution and the rule of law* LSE Brexit Blog available at http://blogs.lse.ac.uk/brexit/2017/01/24/miller-in-the-supreme-court-a-welcome-reminder-of-the-function-of-a-constitution-and-the-rule-of-law/

Neuberger, Lord (2011a) Open Justice Unbound? Judicial Studies Board Annual Lecture 2011, www.judiciary.gov.uk/Resources/JCO/Documents/Speeches/mr-speech-jsb-lecture-march-2011.pdf.

Neuberger, Lord (2011b) *Report of the Committee on Superinjunctions: Superinjunctions, Anonymised Injunctions and Open Justice*, www.judiciary.gov.uk/Resources/JCO/Documents/Reports/super-injunction-report-20052011.pdf.

Otty, T. (2012) The slow creep of complacency and the soul of justice: Observations on the proposal for English courts to adopt 'closed material procedures' for the trial of civil damages claims. *EHRLR* 3: 267.

Parpworth, N. (2010) The Parliamentary Standards Act 2009: A constitutional dangerous dogs measure? *MLR*, 73(2): 262.

Phillipson, G. (2004) 'The greatest quango of them all', 'a rival chamber' or 'a hybrid nonsense'? Solving the second chamber paradox. *Public Law*, 352.

Phillipson, G. (2009) Max Mosley goes to Strasbourg; Article 8, claimant notification and interim injunctions. *Journal of Media Law*, 1: 73.

Public Administration Select Committee (2002) *The Second Chamber: Continuing the Reform, Fifth Report of Session 2001–02*, HC 494-I, www.publications.parliament.uk/pa/cm200102/cmselect/cmpubadm/494/49402.htm.

Public Administration Select Committee (2004) 4th Report Session 2003–2004, www.publications.parliament.uk/pa/cm200304/cmselect/cmpubadm/422/42202.htm.

Qvortrup, M. (ed.) (2013) *The British Constitution: Continuity and Change, A Festchrift for Vernon Bognardor*. London: Hart.

Raz, J. (1979) *The Authority of Law*. Oxford: Oxford University Press.

Renwick, A. (2016) *What happens if we vote for Brexit?* UCL Constitution Unit Blog available at https://constitution-unit.com/2016/01/19/what-happens-if-we-vote-for-brexit/

Roberts, A. (2013) Case comment: R v Plunkett (Daniel). *Criminal Law Review* 9, 765–769.

Royal Commission on the Constitution 1969–1973, Vol. 1, 1973, Cmnd 5460.

Russell, M. (2011) 'Never allow a crisis to go to waste': The Wright Committee Reforms to strengthen the House of Commons. *Parliamentary Affairs*, 64(4): 612.

Russell, M. and Benton, M. (2011) *Selective Influence: The Policy Impact of House of Commons Select Committees*, http://www.ucl.ac.uk/constitution-unit/publications/tabs/unit-publications/153.pdf.

Schaeffer, A. (2004) Reasons and rationalisations: Late reasons in judicial review. *JR*, 151.

Scott, A. (2010) Prior notification in privacy case: a reply to Professor Phillipson. *Journal of Media Law*, 2(1): 49.

Secondary Legislation Scrutiny Committee (2016) *Response to the Strathclyde Review: Effective parliamentary scrutiny of secondary legislation* HL 128.

Smarrt, U. (2016) *The Black Spider Memos: How a Guardian Journalist Succeeded in his 10-Year Quest Under The Freedom Of Information Act 2000*, European Intellectual Property Review, 37(8): 529–38.

Spano, R. (2014) Universality of diversity of Human Rights? Strasbourg in the age of subsidiarity? *Human Rights Law Review*, 14(3): 487–502.

Stone, R. (2001) Breach of the peace: the case for abolition. 2 *Web J CLI*.

Stone, R. (2005) *The Law of Entry, Search and Seizure* (5th edn). Oxford: Oxford University Press.

Stone, R. (2012) *Textbook on Civil Liberties and Human Rights* (9th edn). Oxford: Oxford University Press.

Straw, J. (1994) Abolish the Royal Prerogative, in A. Barnett (ed.), *Power and the Throne: The Monarchy Debate*. London: Vintage.

Sumption, J. (2011) Judicial and Political Decision-making: The Uncertain Boundary, The F.A. Mann Lecture, www.legalweek.com/digital_assets/3704/MANNLECTURE_final.pdf.

Sunkin, M. (2010) Remedies available in judicial review proceedings, in D. Feldman (ed.), *English Public Law* (2nd edn). Oxford: Oxford University Press.

Thomas, C. (2010) *Are Juries Fair?* London: Ministry of Justice, www.justice.gov.uk/downloads/publications/research-and-analysis/moj-research/are-juries-fair-research.pdf.

Varuhas, J. (2009) Governmental rejection of Ombudsman's findings: What role for the Courts? *Modern Law Review*, 71(1): 102–15.

Vile, L. (1998) *Constitutionalism and the Separation of Powers* (2nd edn). Indianapolis: Liberty Fund Inc.

Wade, H.W.R. (1955) The basis of legal sovereignty. *Cambridge LJ*, 172.

Wade, H.W.R. (1996) Sovereignty – Revolution or Evolution? *LQR*, 112: 568.

Wagner, A. (2014) The Monstering of Human Rights https://adam1cor.files.wordpress.com/2014/09/the-monstering-of-human-rights-adam-wagner-2014.pdf

Wakeham, Lord (2000) *A House for the Future* (Cm 4534), www.archive.official-documents.co.uk/document/cm45/4534/4534.htm.

Waldron, J. (1990) *The Law*. London: Routledge.

Waldron, J. (2006) The core of the case against judicial review. *Yale Law Journal*, 115: 1346.

Walker, C. (2010) The threat of terrorism and the fate of control orders. *Public Law*, 4.

Walker, C. and Horne, A. (2012) The Terrorism Prevention and Investigations Measures Act 2011: One thing but not much the other? *Crim LR*, 6: 421–38.

Wheare, K.C. (1966) *Modern Constitutions* (2nd edn). Oxford: Oxford University Press.

White Paper (1997) *Your Right to Know* (Cm. 3818). London: HMSO, www.official-documents.gov.uk/document/cm38/3818/3818.pdf.

Woolf, Lord (1996) *Access to Justice*, webarchive.nationalarchives.gov.uk/+www.dca.gov.uk/civil/final/index.htm.

BIBLIOGRAPHY

Woolf, Rt Hon Lord, Jowell, Sir J. and Le Sueur, A. (eds) (2013), *De Smith's Judicial Review*, 7th edn, London: Sweet & Maxwell.

Worthy, B. and Hazell, R. (2010) Assessing the performance of freedom of information. *Government Information Quarterly*, 27(4): 352.

Wortley, N. and Stockdale, M. (2014) The admissibility of footwear impressions obtained in breach of PACE. *Journal of Criminal Law*, 78(1): 6–11.

Zander, M. (1995) *The Police and Criminal Evidence Act 1984* (3rd edn). London: Sweet & Maxwell.

Index